Crucial Ethical Keys of Artificial Intelligence

Magdalena Bosch
Editor

Crucial Ethical Keys of Artificial Intelligence

Tools and Foundations to Face the Challenge

palgrave
macmillan

Editor
Magdalena Bosch
Humanities
Universitat Internacional de
Catalunya
Barcelona, Spain

ISBN 978-3-032-22852-9 ISBN 978-3-032-22853-6 (eBook)
https://doi.org/10.1007/978-3-032-22853-6

Cover illustration: Just_Super/E+/GettyImages

This Palgrave Macmillan imprint is published by the registered company Springer Nature Switzerland AG
The registered company address is: Gewerbestrasse 11, 6330 Cham, Switzerland

Contents

Notes on Contributors

Oscar-Yecid Aparicio-Gómez is a university professor, researcher, and academic editor working in education, philosophy, and ethics. He holds a PhD in Philosophy, Ethics, and Politics (2006) and a PhD in Education (2015) from the University of Barcelona. An honorary doctorate in education was granted by CUGS University. Recognized as Senior Researcher (IS) by Minciencias (Colombia), his scholarly impact is reflected in an H-index of 34 according to Google Scholar. Since 2015, his academic activity has been linked to the Ed& TIC Research Center, contributing to research development, interdisciplinary projects, and academic management. He has undertaken teaching and academic leadership roles in higher education institutions. His academic publications include books, book chapters, peer-reviewed journal articles, and editorials addressing education, ethics, institutional development, and academic culture. He has supervised doctoral dissertations and master's theses and has participated in academic conferences as both speaker and organizer. His research activity involves multiple funded projects and collaboration with research groups in Colombia and Spain. Editorial work includes service as editor-in-chief of scientific journals. Membership in academic institutions devoted to historical and educational studies complements the profile. Since 2024, he has served as President of the Hispanic American Academy of Doctors.

Magdalena Bosch studied Philosophy at the University of Barcelona, obtaining an Extraordinary Degree Award. He completed his doctorate at the same university, with a thesis on "Metaphysics of Intentionality". Since 2000 she has been a professor of Ethics at the International University of Catalonia and since 2015 she has been Associate University Professor (ANECA). Throughout these years he has developed two lines of research, both of anthropological orientation: one of ethical field and the other of aesthetic field. On aesthetics, several articles on beauty in Schelling can be highlighted.

In the field of ethics, he has carried out several research stays (Oxford 2015, Dallas 2013, Padova 2014, among others). And he has published specialized articles on topics such as intellectual virtues, integrity, or spiritual motivation. One book on desire education stands out: Desire and human flourishing. Perspectives from Positive Psychology, Moral Education and Virtue Ethics. Springer 2020. In recent years he has focused on the ethics of Artificial Intelligence and artificial companions. This research has also been reflected in a knowledge transfer project and international publications.

Marcel Cano Soler has been a university lecturer at various Catalan universities since 1999 and the present (UPC, UB, UVIC, URL, and UOC). His main area of teaching is moral philosophy, especially ethics, bioethics, ethics applied to technoscience, and intercultural ethics. He has also been teached in the field of philosophy of culture, especially in the area of intercultural competencies. He has participated in several research groups, notably the following: Bioethics Research Group: "Human dignity, the stages of life, and respect for difference" (FFI2008-05473/FISO) at the University of Barcelona, "Research Group on Sustainability, Technology, and Humanism"—Humanities Group, Polytechnic University of Catalonia. He is currently a member of the consolidated research group "Crisis of Practical Reason" at the UB Faculty of Philosophy and a researcher in neuroethics and neuroscience of ethics in the Neuroscience Program at the Hospital del Mar Research Institute. As well member of various Healthcare Ethics Committees (mostly in the field of mental health) and Ethical Reflection Spaces in Social Services, the Hospital del Mar Drug Research Ethics Committee, and the Ethics Committee of the European Microbiology Consortium, MIRRI (Microbial Resource Research Infrastructure).

Gabriel Fernández-Borsot holds a PhD in Transformative Studies from the California Institute of Integral Studies (San Francisco, USA), a degree in Philosophy from the University of Barcelona (Spain), and a degree in Industrial Engineering from the Universitat Politècnica de Catalunya (Spain). Since 2021, he has been a member of the Faculty of the Alef Trust (UK), where he also coordinates the professional certificate programmes. He has taught at the International University of Catalonia since 2004 and has served as a visiting scholar at the California Institute of Integral Studies. His research focuses on the anthropological and transpersonal implications of technology, the applications of transpersonal theories, and the transdisciplinary analysis of otherness. In addition to his academic work, he facilitates workshops and courses on transpersonal methods for personal and psychospiritual development.

Carla Vidal Fluriach holds a bachelor's degree in Primary Education with a specialisation in English Language Teaching and a Bachelor's degree in Humanities and Cultural Studies from Universitat Internacional de Catalunya (UIC Barcelona), graduating with the Extraordinary Award for Academic Excellence in both programs.

Following four years of teaching experience in both primary and secondary education, during where she worked as a specialist in Catalan Language and Literature and served as a tutor in the final year of compulsory secondary education, she completed a master's degree in Humanistic and Social Studies at Universitat Abat Oliba, graduating with the highest honours.

She is currently a doctoral candidate at UIC Barcelona, where she also serves as a Teaching and Research Assistant in the Faculty of Education, specialising in Language and Literature Didactics. Furthermore, she has been awarded a predoctoral research grant by Banco Santander. Her research interests are focused on integral education, anthropology, the reading of great books, and the role of imagination in educational processes and ethical development.

Gonzalo Génova is Full Professor at the Computer Science and Engineering Department of the Carlos III University of Madrid. He has an MS degree in Telecommunications Engineering, an MS degree in Philosophy and a PhD in Computer Science and Engineering. His main lines of research and teaching, which reflect his strong interdisciplinary character, focus on modeling and modeling languages in software engineering and requirements engineering, as well as the philosophical foundations of information systems, artificial intelligence and ethics for engineers. As a popularizer he writes in Spanish the blog "Of machines and intentions—Reflections on technology, science and society" (https://demaquinaseintenciones.wordpress.com/).

Dr. Tetiana Klymchuk is Artificial Intelligence expert specialized in Trustworthy and Responsible AI, and Professor of Artificial Intelligence at UIC Barcelona. Her work bridges rigorous mathematical foundations with applied AI systems deployed in real organizational contexts.

She holds two PhD degrees: one in Mathematics from the Universitat Politècnica de Catalunya (Spain) and another in Applied Mathematics from Taras Shevchenko National University of Kyiv (Ukraine). Her early academic research focused on representation theory and its applications to linear algebra, including the solvability of quaternion matrix equations, classification of semilinear mappings, wild and tame problems, and selected topics in Lie algebras, with applications in coding theory and projective geometry.

Dr. Klymchuk is the author of more than 15 peer-reviewed scientific publications and has participated as a speaker in over 100 international conferences, workshops, and scientific events worldwide.

Beyond academia, she is a co-founder of Somia, an AI startup focused on building, validating, monitoring, and governing AI agents for enterprises, with a strong emphasis on reliability, transparency, and regulatory compliance. Her current research and professional activity focus on Generative AI evaluation, AI governance frameworks, and the practical implementation of trustworthy AI in industry and public institutions.

Ferran Sánchez Margalef is Serra Húnter Lecturer in the Department of Theory and History of Education at the University of Barcelona, where he carries out his teaching and research activities in the fields of philosophy and educational theory. He is also an adjunct lecturer at the Universitat Oberta de Catalunya, where he is involved in teaching and academic mentoring within the Social Education degree program.

His research trajectory lies at the intersection of educational theory, ethics, and contemporary discourses on technology, with particular attention to transhumanism and its pedagogical, social, and anthropological implications. His work analyses the imaginaries of progress, human enhancement, and optimization that permeate current technoscientific transformations, as well as their effects on education and subjectivity.

His research interests also include the history of pedagogical thought, applied ethics in education, and critical reflection on the normative foundations of educational and social policies. He has participated in several research projects and has published in specialized academic journals, with a clear commitment to fostering dialogue between pedagogical tradition and contemporary challenges.

Rafael Monterde Ferrando is a faculty member in the Department of Humanistic Studies, a member of the Instituto Razón Abierta, and a researcher at the International Security Centre of Universidad Francisco de Vitoria.He holds a degree in Philosophy and completed a Master's programme in Human Rights, Peace and Sustainable Development at the University of Valencia. He earned his PhD in Philosophy from the Catholic University of Valencia, where he defended his doctoral dissertation on transhumanist thought, entitled The Twilight of Humanity: Technological Singularity as the End of History. His interest in transhumanism has led him to orient his research towards the field of Security and Defence, and he is currently focusing on cognitive warfare.

Abel Miró i Comas (Vic 1990), graduated in Philosophy from the University of Barcelona (2012) obtaining the extraordinary end-of-degree prize. In this same University, he studied the Master in Contemporary Philosophy and Classical Tradition (2013), which he also completed with an extraordinary prize. He was initiated by Doctor Eudaldo Forment, cathedratic-professor of metaphysics at the University of Barcelona (1989–2017), to the study of the philosophy of Thomas Aquinas; to this author and, more specifically, to his metaphysics of beauty, he dedicated his doctoral thesis; on this same subject he has published several articles in specialist journals and the book *Les arrels tomistes i agustinianes de l'estètica de Josep Torras i Bages* (Publicacions de l'Abadia de Montserrat, 2018). He teaches at the Universitat Internacional de Catalunya and at the Universitat de Barcelona. He is the director of the Institut Superior de Ciències Religioses de Vic. His main areas of research are Metaphysics, Aesthetics and Medieval Philosophy. He has also been guest Lecturer at the Universidad Santo Tomás of Bogotá (2018), at the Centro de Estudios e Investigaciones en Bioética of México (2021), at the Universidad FASTA de Mar del Plata of Argentina (2024), and at the Universidad Francisco de Vitoria of Madrid (2025).

Montserrat Nebrera (1961, Barcelona, Spain) is a graduate in Law, Political Philosophy, and Classical Philology from the University of Barcelona, she also holds a doctorate in Law from the same university. She has been awarded fourteen competitive research grants and has taught and lectured on Constitutional Law at various Spanish and international universities, where she has been invited to speak on her areas of expertise in constitutional reform and security. For several years, she has dedicated herself to the study of the relationship between artificial intelligence and fundamental rights, and how the former affects their essential content. From an administrative perspective, she has served as Vice-Rector and Vice-Dean of Law at the International University of Catalonia, where she currently directs the Charlemagne Institute of European Studies. She has also served as a substitute judge in the Provincial Court of Barcelona, as a member of the Catalan Parliament, and she was Director of the Francesc Cambó Foundation for the social and political studies and member of the Economics Cercle of Barcelona.Nebrera

Pere Castellví Obiols is Associate Professor of Medicine at the Universitat Internacional de Catalunya (UIC) and a recognized clinical and mental health researcher with national research accreditation (R3). His academic background includes a PhD in Clinical and Health Psychology (UAB) and a Master's in Public Health (UPF). His research focuses on depression, anxiety, suicide prevention, emotional well-being, and public mental health, with a strong emphasis on epidemiology, patient-reported outcomes, and the impact of digital technologies and artificial intelligence on mental health and medical education from an ethics perspective. He has developed expertise in advanced quantitative methods, including epidemiological modelling, systematic reviews, and meta-analysis.

His scientific production includes over 60 publications indexed in JCR/Scopus, with an h-index of 29 and more than 5,000 citations, as well as several book chapters and numerous conference presentations, with a high citation impact and a consolidated international profile. He has participated as principal investigator and collaborator in competitive research projects in Spain and abroad, including collaborations with institutions such as Johns Hopkins University, public health agencies, and hospital-based research groups.

His current lines of research focus on adolescent and university student mental health, risk and protective factors for suicidal behavior, digital well-being, and the ethical and psychological implications of AI in health care and education, integrating clinical, epidemiological, and technological perspectives.

Wendy R. Simon research trajectory has developed at the intersection of political philosophy, applied ethics, and contemporary governance. She holds a PhD in Philosophy from the University of Barcelona and a degree in Political Science and Public Administration from Universitat Pompeu Fabra (UPF). Her doctoral dissertation analyzed the modern ethical-political foundations of constitutional democracy, with particular attention to John Locke, and their contribution to the shaping of democratic institutions. Building on this work, she has oriented her research toward the normative challenges arising from current technological transformations, especially in relation to algorithmic governance and public responsibility in contexts of uncertainty.

She has taught for more than a decade in the fields of General Ethics, Political Philosophy, Political Science, and Public Opinion at Catalan universities, and has participated in projects funded by the BBVA Foundation and the Government of Catalonia, focused on public ethics, bioethics, and risk management. She has also been a member of the IDT research group (UAB), within which she has deepened her work on issues related to artificial intelligence, automated decision-making, and the normative frameworks applicable to emerging technologies.

CHAPTER 1

Introduction. Crucial and Durable Keys for the AI Ethics

Magdalena Bosch

Almost everything we say about Artificial Intelligence (AI) will be obsolete in a few moments. The speed at which the tools and possibilities at our disposal evolve never cease to amaze: ChatGPT was available much earlier than expected by its designers. However, AI has an impact on people, and the human condition has some aspects that are essential, permanent: the importance of mental health, the need for respect, the impact on lifestyle, the way moral assessments are made, the changes that education causes and demands, understanding of the person, the relationship with others and with the AI itself; the conditions of law and politics, which govern life in society. That is why an AI Ethics is necessary, and also possible.

M. Bosch (✉)
Universitat Internacional de Catalunya, Barcelona, Spain
e-mail: mbosch@uic.es

M. Bosch (ed.), *Crucial Ethical Keys of Artificial Intelligence*,
https://doi.org/10.1007/978-3-032-22853-6_1

The Social Echo that Calls for Ethical Keys

Before pointing out critical points or ethical problems, we must recognize the achievements that the advancement of Artificial Intelligence (AI) has achieved for the benefit of humanity, as there are many advantages that are being revealed in the use of AI. Its accelerated evolution, especially of generative AI, has even surprised its programmers. We are continually discovering new possibilities that multiply the results of our work. We have tools that we had never thought would exist, or at least, not so soon. In tasks of searching and processing information: summaries, screenings, categorization, etc. AI can carry out tasks that require several days of human work in a few hours. In addition, you have to take into account the speed and accuracy in all types of calculations. New uses are also exploited in favor of society, and solutions to problems that we would not have imagined. Floridi has identified seven tasks that AI can perform in favor of social good: "(1) falsifiability and incremental deployment; (2) safeguards against the manipulation of predictors; (3) receiver-contextualized intervention; (4) receiver-contextualized explanation and transparent purposes; (5) privacy protection and data subject consent; (6) situational fairness; and (7) human-friendly semanticization" (Floridi et al., 2020, p. 1773).

Ethical problems arise from the need to respect human dignity, to act in accordance with it and to ensure that the progress of humanity is directed toward improvements and achievements and not to its opposites. The specific concerns that Artificial Intelligence (AI) generates at the moment will change over time. The most concrete examples will become others. However, it is necessary to reflect on what is happening now, to be able to make decisions and to be able to form criteria. Every ethical problem that arises always has a concrete part, which is subject to change; but if it really contains a relevant moral question, it has another component, which is not perishable, which appeals to human dignity. In the first section of this text, I am going to mention different real and practical examples that may cease to surprise or alert in a while; but each of them contains problems that require ethical references for their immediate solution and for the new forms that this specific case may take in the future.

With this in mind, we can even ask ourselves if AI ethics is already a discipline in itself and if we should recognize it; or it is nothing more than ethics applied to a contemporary case. Some authors point out the problem, among others, of what they call Ethics Washing: it is a matter of assuming that the ethical problem is solved because there is some attention to the subject, even if it is insufficient and superficial (Lambrecht & Moreno, 2024, p. 388). Indeed, this is a relevant point of AI ethics, which has rarely been pointed out: some strategies that contextualize AI in an ethical framework become an element of pressure in the opposite direction to what they intend. In a way, the message is conveyed that "there is no reason not to accept AI because it is perfectly ethical, since it has its own discipline that regulates it: AI ethics." The pressure derived from this assumption can be very strong. The message could easily be escalated and understood as follows: "you must accept/incorporate AI because it is ethical and therefore reliable." In other words, the existence of studies on the ethics of AI can easily be confused with the actual fact that such ethics are effective. To put it more simply: it could be compared to a hospital that claims to have an ethics committee without informing who the members are, what their qualifications are, what activities and real evaluations they carry out. One might think, superficially, that the ethics of that hospital should not worry at all. However, if protocols are not followed or if laziness leads to neglecting the necessary evaluations, it would be, in fact, unethical.

One phenomenon that has claimed increasingly intense attention since its emergence is generative AI. It continues to grow exponentially and its success in companies is becoming better and better known. There is the case of a risk measurement company that established substantial incentives for all its employees to incorporate the use of AI within a month. Technical support was provided so that everyone, right-handed or not, could work well and find in AI an advantage that would allow them to improve their work. They did. Now every employee has an AI assistant that boosts their work and makes it more effective. These types of examples open the question of how we use and want to use AI. In this case, it has been an improvement for the company's performance, as well as a help for employees who are empowered with this new tool. It can be an example of how to incorporate AI into companies in a way that benefits the company, its performance, and employees.

A strategic use, in which workers are involved, can be a way to overcome one of the most notable reluctances against the incorporation of AI in companies is the distrust produced by feeling threatened by the job itself: substitution. But not all prevention or reluctance can be solved with a good strategy and the cooperation of all parties involved. There are problems that have a genuine ethical implication that must be addressed from fundamental principles. This new task requires the study and analysis of the unintended consequences of the use of AI, or its misuse. In any case, there are examples and real facts that force us to consider it.

Will we be able to choose what we want to be replaced with? Or will the advancement of the AI business continue unstoppable with its sights set solely on the economic benefit of a few? The basic ethical problem, at this point, is that a minority profits at the expense of the impoverishment of many. There can be harmful effects on large sectors of work. In reality, it will affect all of humanity. The distrust or fear that the advance of AI in the workplace arouses in some people has some justification and requires an ethical debate.

Another challenge is the significant impact on young people and children. This issue is part of a broader problem: the need for education for the use of technology by minors. This need requires urgent action. As Adeyemi (2025) points out, the use of AI by young people can have positive consequences and others that are not: "The social benefits are that they learn to collaborate and gain exposure to a broader range of experiences and lifestyles than they would otherwise encounter. The negative effects are increased risks of social isolation, shorter attention spans, and a decline in face-to-face interactions" (Adeyemi, 2025). What is clear is that education is necessary so that we can prevent harmful effects and promote positive ones.

Perhaps one of the greatest harms of generative AI has been the irresponsible behavior of those who have used its potential, in particular ChatGPT, causing scandal, disapproval and legal conflicts, opening ethical debates that remain unresolved. In March 2023, Forbes warned of fraud: this Artificial Intelligence is capable of generating emails with fraudulent files that contain viruses and contaminate or steal data. At the same time, its use for text writing, customer service, or computer programming is multiplying. ChatGPT can collapse in the field of cybersecurity due to cyberattacks aimed at both companies and individuals. And here we find one of the risks that exist: the lack of security and privacy, because we give our data and leave information that will remain forever within the reach of the unscrupulous who can take advantage of it. Going a little further, there could even be the creation of malicious bots that can deceive to obtain personal or financial information, attack through phishing or social networks, use fake profiles.

The celebration of the great advantages of ChatGPT coexists with the mistrust caused by some less positive incidents. One of them has been the discovery of the abusive and cruel treatment received by a large staff of employees dedicated to removing reportable content. Again, various newspapers and in various countries have echoed the news, for example, *Time*, January 18, 23. This task is aimed at eliminating biases, which is another ethical problem, which involves the repetition and dissemination of unfair treatment. It also tells the chat what content to avoid: sexual violence, aggressions of all kinds. We cannot ignore that it is also a problem for the business: these biases and highly toxic content are reportable. The problem is the following: the work of these people consists of viewing all the content of a harmful, violent, aggressive nature... to eliminate them and make ChatGPT a reliable technology. They must "catalog the entire vast stream of violent, sinister and perverse material that resides there, in order to show the machine to ignore the rotten side of the great network of networks." While OpenAI raises its profits to 29 billion, these people are paid less than $2 an hour. But that's not the worst of it. The repeated viewing of highly toxic content damages these workers psychologically, sometimes irreversibly. "It can cause post-traumatic stress disorder and other mental illnesses." We are faced with a difficult paradox: the elimination of probable harm is entailing certain, perhaps even greater, harm. The moral dilemma that arises is serious and demands a response. The solution is for the responsible company to take on the prevention measures that workers need to protect their mental health.

Another more recent problem, which has been echoed by the mass media (for example, El Español, June 2025) is the advertising of Apps that make fake nudity, mainly of women and that have been denounced by Meta: "Zuckerberg's firm has taken legal action against Joy Timeline HK Limited, the developer behind Crush AI, a 'nudify' app that undresses people, without their consent, using artificial intelligence." Meta's policies prohibit this advertising, and it has taken action. They have increased the filters that can prevent the presence of these Apps on their platform and that eliminate advertising and related content.

There are other critical aspects of generative AI. At least 2 years ago, there was an alert about the enormous expenditure of water and energy involved in its use. According to Li, "a recent study suggests that global AI could consume 85–134TWh of electricity in 2027, whereas a more aggressive projection by the recent U.S. datacenter energy report predicts that AI servers' electricity consumption in the U.S. alone will surpass 150–300TWh in 2028. Even considering the lower estimate, the combined scope-1 and scope-2 water withdrawal of global AI is projected to reach 4.2–6.6 billion cubic meters in 2027, which is more than the total annual water withdrawal of four to six Denmarks or half the U.K.b Simultaneously (five times the total consumption of a small country or half the consuption of a very big one), a total of 0.38–0.60 billion cubic meters of water will be evaporated and considered" consumption" due to the global AI demand in 2027" (Li et al., 2025, pp. 54–56). This study has been published in different high-impact media, in several countries as U.S., U.K or Spain. When energy scarcity is a global concern, and at a time when sustainability requires a fierce struggle between private and common interests, the use of resources becomes an ethical issue of the first order.

As a conclusion to this first part of the introduction, we see that AI has a strong social impact, that the media have echoed disturbing news, and that all of them demand an ethical study and response. We are not forgetting that the mass media often resort to sensationalism to sell, and that the problems posed by AI may not be reliably reflected according to the sources of information. But beyond the immediate impact of the news and the way it is disseminated, facts have been made known that are objectively worrying and require ethical responses. In addition, I wanted to underline the difference between the problems of AI and the problems in the use of AI. I have tried to emphasize along these lines that the drawbacks that AI may present usually come from misuse or a use without any order or measure.

The Centrality of the Person and the Possibility of Having Lasting Ethical Keys

Another AI-related event, broadcast by all the media worldwide, was the suicide that caused global grief in October 2024. The event took place in Orlando, but almost any country on planet Earth felt that it could have happened in one of its cities. It was a 14-year-old boy who suffered a heartbreak with a chat. When harm occurs, ethical questions arise. When there is suffering, ethics is called to make a contribution, to shed some light, to ask the right questions: how can this be prevented from happening? Can we demand guarantees from programmers? Is there a way to cut off the relationship when there is an affective involvement that can become harmful? Can younger people be better informed about what a bot really is? Perhaps teach them and give some guidelines about their use?

And also, on the other hand, we need to review and teach what friendship is. Mintoff recalls, summarizing a deep and broad tradition such as the idea of friendship in Aristotle, that "A friend has the good of the other as an end in itself and assigns this end a high priority in their actions" (Mintoff, 2006, p. 106). No AI system can assume someone's good as a personal end, because it cannot assume anything as an end at all. AI works on algorithms, not on free choices or chosen purposes. In this case the difference is essential, although appearances can confuse us. And we also know that friendship is necessary, that personal motivations are reinforced and become more pleasant in the company of friends (Cooper, 1977, pp. 303–304).

As far as relations with AI are concerned, in various forms, it is essential to distinguish appearance from reality, especially in the case of artificial friends, where the appearance is almost identical to the reality of a friendship between human beings (Bosch et al., 2022). They have identified three characteristics that distinguish friendship between human beings from relationships with machines, which are inspired by three Aristotelian conditions of true friendship: for the friends' sake, equality and interiority. That is, friendship and, by extension, every true human relationship must be sustained by giving value to the friend, recognizing the equality of dignity and emerging from the interiority of the subject, from which emerge the understanding of reality and true desires. Without these conditions, relationships between people would easily be false, superficial, discriminatory, without truthful communication, without sharing a common world.

Despite the feeling of credibility or trust that a chat or a robot can generate, we know that they are computer systems programmed in a certain way and that we are not really interacting with someone who cares about what we say, our needs, or our ideas. Although the algorithms are aimed at showing the opposite: questions and phrases in a human, supportive, understanding style. The appearance is really that of having important, unconditional emotional support. But the reality is very different: a bot does not have the desire for you to be well, although its programmed language expresses it, it does not have an inner world in which you are someone important. In addition, although that would be a second plane, it will not pay your debts, it will not mediate with that person who is difficult for you to reconcile, it will not facilitate your integration with your colleagues.

The case, mentioned above, of the teenager who took his own life is a very clear case in which AI turned out to be a danger, it has caused the loss of a human life, almost a child... and this example may make us think of other more subtle but equally real risks in which the way of using AI is not beneficial. This raises an essential question: What did we create AI for? This question surely has several answers; but we can take for certain, at least three: for the entertainment and pride of the creators, to amass a fortune, for the service of humanity. These purposes are not incompatible, but they require an order of priorities. It is not legitimate, or we should not allow the enrichment of certain companies to be carried out at the expense of the emotional damage of users. Nor that experimentation and innovation lead to the cognitive ruin of a part of the population.

Everything that human beings produce must be directed to their good: medicine, teaching, technology. On the other hand, some good products in themselves may be misused. We have extensive experience of good products, whose wrong or excessive use is pernicious. For example, alcohol: a glass of wine can make an evening with friends pleasant; excess alcohol is a social scourge that traps many and can lead to personal collapse. From this we can deduce the importance of training in the use of the pleasures or tools that we have at our disposal. It is a universal ethical necessity. The use of AI is within general ethics, but due to its novelty and potential, it requires specific education.

In this context, the growing presence and attention paid to robots stand out. Again, we can highlight great services that robots already provide in some places: from Japanese hotels with robots that effectively meet the needs of their customers; to health centers where there are robots ensuring the correct administration of medications to patients. This type of aid can be support for tasks carried out by human beings and for which they have artificial assistants. This is different from the substitution of human agents in tasks that require their specific attention. A good example is the aforementioned medical care. Coeckerlberg discusses the pros and cons of "four objections to introducing AI assistive technologies in health care practices as replacements of human care." Those points are: first, which would not be true care, since the agent is not human; second, which would not be good care, since AI cannot respond to the patient's emotional and social needs; third, that if AI achieves good care, it is at the cost of violating the principle of privacy; and fourth, that all AI technology applied to care deceives patients from the moment it makes them believe that they are being cared for (cf. Coeckelbergh, 2010, p. 182). All these are conflicts and paradoxes that deserve to be thought about and analyzed with caution. This type of problem makes it clear that there is something permanent in human beings: their need for care, their emotional needs, their need for privacy and sincerity.

The Changing and the Permanent

There are human needs that do not change, especially those that refer to their dignity, which Martha Nussbaum (2007) has dealt with "Frontiers of justice: Disability, nationality, species membership." Beyond the issue of care, respect for human dignity is the theoretical and practical support that humanity has to denounce and stop human rights violations, aggressions, and injustices. The essential and basic needs of human beings remain, as well as their dignity, and the use of AI must take this into account. De Souza (2015) has reviewed the ontological foundation of human dignity in identity, an argument that is based on a classical approach to human identity (cf. Spaemann, 1984). The human essence is manifested in qualities such as: solidarity, love, transcendence, the sense of justice, rationality, freedom, the capacity for personal improvement, sociability.

In order to distinguish what is subject to exchange from what is not, it is also necessary, as we mentioned at the beginning, to distinguish reality from appearances and to specify concepts. This is an aspect that has not yet been sufficiently clarified, as Coeckelberg points out in relation to care, but which can be extrapolated to different uses of AI: "More work needs to be done in clarifying the relation between feelings and care, between (objective) capabilities and (subjective) experience, between the demand for privacy and the social character of care, between the real and the virtual good life, and between outcome (aim) and process (not a mere means to reach the aim)" (Coeckelbergh, 2010, p. 189).

We find a controversial example in Eugenia Kuyda's considerations about its creation: Replika. She proposes it as a true friendship and seems to ignore the difference between a real person and an AI system that holds conversations by imitating patterns of a certain person (BBC News, 2018). It is undeniable that chatbot conversationalists experience companionship, understanding, and affection that has no real cause. That is, an AI system responds by imitating the character of someone who exists or has existed, but is not that person.

A further step toward replacing the human agent with an artificial one is the creation of robots. In this case, you have a physical presence, not just a conversation. The critical point is what kind of tasks the robots are going to perform, and whether any way to use them is safe for individuals' mental health. We have already stressed that in some tasks this substitution is positive. The new problem is ideological impersonation: the elaboration of discourses in which the robot is equated with the human person, making it impossible to discern what is appropriate and what is not. And here adequate means to be favorable to human beings.

Some AI systems are given a human appearance or resemblance in some trait, and the way of valuing and interacting with them evolves into ways of dealing with humans. The underlying risk is that of projecting human IDs onto AI systems that are not comparable to humans. That is, it is spoken and considered "as if" some AI systems really have human attributes; confusion and deception occur.

An example may be the Gate Box advertisement, which markets holograms as artificial companions (Gate Box, 2016). It is striking to see how the advertisement openly proposes to buy the hologram to be your girlfriend, your partner. The scenes of the advertisement and the relationship it reflects between the Gate Box character and the user reflect typical details of a relationship, full of signs of affection. Here the problem arises: Are we not deceiving ourselves? Isn't an AI system that appears to be an attentive and affectionate girlfriend already, in itself, a deception? And in the affective dimension: promoting emotional exchange and the construction of affective bonds with that AI system, isn't it false consolation that deprives you of fighting for true relationships with human beings? This use of artificial partners can lead to isolating oneself from relationships with whom you can learn, with whom you can confront and, ultimately, with whom you can develop relationships that are not programmed. It should be noted that Kondo never refers to his wife as human, but makes it clear that he saw a relationship with a woman as impossible, years before marrying Miku Hatsune's hologram. But the controversy is still open: there is an essential difference between friendship with human beings and the emotionally rewarding relationships that an Artificial Companion can offer: love for the friend, equality and interiority continue to point to essential differences that cannot be ignored (cf. Bosch et al., 2022).

Another case, which we cannot ignore, is the need for ethical standards for robots that are granted autonomy. The more autonomy is granted to agents, the more necessary it is to establish clear ethical standards.

Artificial agents cannot avoid accountability, which is absolutely essential to have guarantees that innocent people will not be harmed: "The autonomy of trading agents does not absolve their masters of accountability, however, the indirection of decision making does present some tricky issues. For example, autonomous agents may perform actions - particularly in unusual circumstances - that would have been difficult to anticipate by their programmers" (Wellman & Rajan, 2017, p. 612).

On the other hand, an important part of the decisions that an artificial agent can make already falls under existing laws: "... to the extent that choices are governed by legal dictates - for instance, that a car must stop completely at places marked by a stop sign - the decision of what is ethical has been made collectively, through a very familiar process of law- and regulation-making" (Etzioni & Etzioni, 2017, p. 404). However, laws cannot respond to all situations that give rise to the use of AI.

AI can be directed to the good of human beings. In the first section of this introduction we have underlined this. But we can also see the risk of arbitrary developments, of productions that do not pay attention to users but only to novelty. The only way to maintain the reliability of AI is to make ethical assessments by putting the person at the center: to check that each step can really be a help, a support. And when everything depends on use, you should warn about it. The producers themselves should indicate what are the risks and limits that the user has to contemplate. One could also think, as Ratti and Graves (2025) propose, of carrying out ethical audits of AI tools. This book seeks a balance between solutions that are too general, such as ensuring the safety of people, and that it is difficult for them to provide practical improvements; and those that are too specific, such as *ad casum* regulations, which are easily obsolete due to the technical evolution of what is being regulated. The alternative is to point out crucial keys to ethics in the use of AI and provide references on them.

Most Crucial Keys of AI Ethics

In the previous sections of this introduction, we have pointed out the social impact that the advancement of AI and its multiple applications is having, and the echo in the media. We have also shown that the crucial and permanent keys are given by the human condition, its dignity and its essential needs. Most ethical requirements are determined by the conditions necessary for coexistence in society to be possible. From all this, some keys can be derived that are especially important, which are crucial, for a use of AI that is good for people.

One of the first necessary approaches is that of psychology, as it provides us with concrete indicators about the impact of the use of AI on the well-being of individuals. Ethics, in its reflection on what is good and what is harmful, needs the support of psychology to identify the elements of negative impact on the emotions, balance, and healthy personality of individuals.

Any indication of a negative impact on people's psychology is a warning for ethics. Ethics deals with human action according to good and evil, but in order to discern what is evil it needs to rely on other sciences and knowledge that provide reliable and concrete information. With this type of data, ethics can make accurate and realistic assessments. Examples such as induction to suicide (cited in Chapter 2) or the trauma of children separated by their parents due to a mistake in the social security system (cited in Chapter 3) clearly and radically show that the misuse of AI can cause serious real problems, and it is clear that these are ethical problems. Throughout Chapter 2, Castellví exposes the psychological advantages of the proper use of AI tools, while pointing out crucial points that must be paid attention to in order to avoid psychic damage. On the one hand, AI is effective in supporting diagnosis and therapies. On the other hand, the misuse of AI can harm not only emotional well-being, but also cognitive development and sociability. Castellví provides relevant and very practical information, clear examples, and achieves an analysis that offers bases for deep reflection and an accurate ethical orientation.

The identification of risks to mental health leads us to think about responsibility in the use and design of AI. Chapter 3 is dedicated to an explanation that is both technical and ethical: it combines the technical explanation necessary to take charge of the process followed by generative AI systems; so that the reader can take more charge of its operation and its impact. At the same time, Klymchuk offers clear examples of the direct ethical impact of some specific tools: image recognition, calculations, and logical argumentation by AI. They are not always exact and require the attention and monitoring of both producers and users. Greater responsibility lies with institutions that incorporate AI systems whose calculations can compromise people's honor and have dramatic consequences, from a human and family point of view. Cases such as the Post Office scandal in England (2009–2025), to cite a different example from those mentioned by Klymchuk, but unfortunately similar to the one he does mention, which occurred in the Netherlands between 2015 and 2020.

If we focus more on users than institutions, we cannot fail to pay attention to the changes that AI is causing in our lifestyles. A key question is this: are these changes freely assumed? There are many actions that we perform unconsciously when using AI resources. For example, not thinking of an email response that I no longer need to write because ChatGPT does, and that changes my relationship with a colleague. In the Chapter 4, Cano presents the technical nature of the human being, along with changes that AI is causing and of which we need to be more aware. One of the crucial issues is creativity, which is of particular concern to young people. Another major area of impact is culture and the way of being in society. Cano also discusses the autonomy of technology and how it is dependent on designers. There are many repercussions that the incorporation of AI tools into everyday life has, and they need reflection to be incorporated freely and reliably.

The ethical assessment of freedom is one of the most relevant issues, and one that is presented in almost all the approaches throughout the book. In the end, the ethical value par excellence is the dignity of people and their freedom, and it is in these essential dimensions that the way in which we incorporate the most sophisticated technological tools into our lifestyles ends up impacting. This ethical urgency grows when these tools are more powerful and, to a certain extent, independent or unpredictable.

AI owes its name to the comparisons that have been made with respect to human intelligence. In reality, the technological development to which he refers did not have to be called "intelligent." We could speak of complex or advanced calculation systems, or information processing systems. But from the beginning, since the 50s of the twentieth century, when Alan Turing wanted to produce complex and powerful calculation systems, he called them intelligent and compared them to the human brain. But it is still very original that Genoa takes this circumstance to pose the following question: AI becomes a reflection of human intelligence about which we can learn. In other words, by observing the conditions of AI and the ethical demands it requires, we become more aware of what the most important ethical issues are and how we can raise them for their full understanding. Among others, the contribution of Chapter 5 also stands out, by drawing attention to and explaining why the "mechanical" is not the same as the "rational." And to assess AI correctly, that difference becomes decisive.

At the beginning of this introductory chapter, we referred to the importance of the educational field. It is the main catalyst for cultural changes and social evolution. That is why the impact of AI in the educational field requires its own and deep reflection. We need to define principles by which to govern this novel task of incorporating AI into education. Chapter 6 is dedicated to this topic. Aparicio-Gómez defines the principles on which education should be based in the context of introducing AI resources into the classroom, both on the part of the teachers and the students. Each ethical principle to be taken into account includes, in turn, other principles. For example, equity, one of the conditions most recognized as necessary and vulnerable to the misuse of AI, requires the recognition and respect of other principles such as promoting equitable access to new technologies and minimizing discriminatory biases. The reality of teaching is complex, as there are many factors that intervene and impact the educational process. All of them are enhanced, positively or not, by the use of AI. Thus, each of the principles that are mentioned: equity, responsibility, transparency, privacy, preservation of the autonomy of subjects, beneficial use of AI; they discover concrete conditions that make it possible to comply with this principle.

To move forward successfully and effectively, it is necessary to move from principles to practical strategies: The complexity of education, the various factors involved in it, require practical strategies to carry out an education that can incorporate AI tools not only reliably, but also with a positive impact on students. Sánchez (Chapter 7) has reviewed the foundation of principles to apply it to strategies and practical uses. In the first place, it points to the displacement of the educational act itself, which has been fully exercised by humans, to a new area where the intervention of technology is sometimes massive. He then points out key points to which attention must be paid: the transparency of the tools and control by the teacher, the risk of dehumanization of the teaching process. Faced with these critical points, Sánchez proposes strategies so that education in values continues to be possible, to solve moral dilemmas and suggests concrete techniques and class dynamics to really carry it out. These strategies respond to each of the principles that have been questioned, so that practical solutions applicable to the real exercise of education are offered for all of them.

All the contributions that can be made around the good use of AI and its optimization to help individuals and society are based on the person. The human person is the reference for ethics: what contributes to his physical and mental good; what allows their good development in society; these are positive and ethically laudable elements. In this sense, an ontological foundation is needed that gives us references about what the person is and what is proper to him, so that we can discern what benefits him and what harms him. One of the keys to the comparison between people and AI is the controversial "personality" of artificial entities. Miró establishes, in Chapter 8, an interesting relationship between two types of personalities, in which it is evident that the most superficial appearances are not everything. It highlights the role of the relationship between people, its ontological dimension and the comparison with the relationships between people and artificial partners. Understanding the relationships between people is necessary for the understanding of one's own person and of the bonds of various kinds that he or she can establish with other people, with natural beings, and with artificial entities. Far from remaining a theoretical specification, the metaphysical bases that are shown are concretized in the real relationships that can be established between individuals.

Another challenge to personal reality is transhumanism. In its various forms and trends, it is always supported by technological innovation and, more specifically, by the rapid progress of AI. Transhumanism incorporates AI as a tool for the improvements of the human being that are valued as such and that, with different priorities, are sought to be implemented. The first question that emerges is what "better" means in this context. But this question would take us far from the purpose of this book. Fernández-Borsot points out, in Chapter 9, the preeminence of techno-scientific reason, which ends up determining valuations and visions of human beings and the world that could be biased. As a crucial key, it points to the prominence of otherness and the devaluation or even oblivion that it has suffered on some occasions. It is common to find analyses of human relationships in which only a subject and his feelings or sensations are taken into account, but not the reality of the other, with their own emotions, needs, etc.

To understand the impact of AI on human relationships, some prior study of human relationships themselves is needed. More specifically, if we look for references on affective bonds with artificial beings, it is necessary first to have a criterion of what the relations of affection are in themselves: their nature and their conditions. For this reason, this book includes a chapter in which the way in which human beings relate to others is analyzed. Based on criteria developed on an Aristotelian basis, Vidal and

Monterde (Chapter 10) examine the essential elements of human relationships and develop an analysis in line with narrative examples from cinema. These are three cases with complex and realistic emotional implications, which in a very visual way describe the most essential keys.

Human relations, on the other hand, are the foundation of the city and social coexistence. From the construction of society emerge laws and politics. As far as the law is concerned, AI is having a strong impact and appropriate reflection is necessary. Chapter 11 is dedicated to analyzing the impact of AI on law. It deals with the problem of digital rights and equality; the algorithms cut and their possible effects on people who do not even know that they are being evaluated. For each problem, Nebrera offers tools, strategies, or principles that should be taken into account to overcome the violations of rights that we would risk in a reckless use of AI. The right to equality, to privacy, to jurisdiction. But also freedoms: freedom of information that can be affected by fake news or even deepfake productions, which are increasingly difficult to distinguish from real recordings. And also freedom of assembly, which could be threatened by the ease of monitoring public gatherings with facial recognition. For each of these risks, Nebrera proposes effective means to avoid them.

Finally, the human being is social and every society requires a government. Politics does not escape the influence of AI, which, as in all areas, offers great resources and can also cause great risks. Simon deals in Chapter 12 with the impact of AI on the process of social deliberation and questions whether it can be a threat to democracy. She elaborates an incisive analysis of the most critical points: Is it possible to govern a digital world with the principles of liberal democracy? The changes around information: its flows, the bubbles that select the news we receive according to our previous preferences; they are decisive. But not only the world of communication, but also the military field is changing drastically and also the possibilities of control and surveillance. There are many elements that can erode citizens' trust in power. And that trust is essential for the survival of a democratic state.

Given the crucial keys to an AI ethics, a panorama of study and work opens up for a society where each individual is respected, in his dignity and in his human values. AI can be a tool used in favor of people and society. Throughout these twelve chapters, the reader will find the analysis of the most disturbing issues, along with proposals and principles that can make the use of AI a positive value for individuals and communities.

References

Adeyemi, V. (2025). The impact of digital technology on a child's cognitive and social development: Implications for education. *Premier Journal of Psychology*. https://doi.org/10.70389/PJP.100006

Bosch, M., et al. (2022). Evolving friendship? Essential changes, from social networks to artificial companions. *Social Network Analysis and Mining, 12*, 39. https://doi.org/10.1007/s13278-022-00864-1

Coeckelbergh, M. (2010). Health care, capabilities, and ai assistive technologies. *Ethical Theory and Moral Practice, 13*, 181–190. https://doi.org/10.1007/s10677-009-9186-2

Cooper, J. M. (1977). Friendship and the good in aristotle. *The Philosophical Review, 86*(3), 290–315. http://www.jstor.org/stable/2183784

De Souza, S. (2015). A'Reditio completa' e a metafísica da dignidade pessoal em Tomás de Aquino. *Portuguese Journal of Philosophy, 71*(2–3), 567–582.

Etzioni, A., & Etzioni, O. (2017). Incorporating ethics into artificial intelligence. *The Journal of Ethics, 21*, 403–418. https://doi.org/10.1007/s10892-017-9252-2

Floridi, L., et al. (2020). How to design AI for social good: Seven essential factors. *Science and Engineering Ethics, 26*, 1771–1796. https://doi.org/10.1007/s11948-020-00213-5

Gate Box. (2016). https://www.bing.com/videos/riverview/relatedvideo?q=gate%20box%20anuncio%20original&mid=23F22427AE64BDF06C5623F22427AE64BDF06C56&ajaxhist=0

Kuyda, E. (2018). Cuando su mejor amigo murió, ella lo reconstruyó digitalmente. *BBC News*. https://www.bbc.com/mundo/noticias-45727287

Lambrecht, F., & Moreno, M. (2024). 2024 What is AI ethics? *American Philosophical Quarterly, 61*(4), 387–401.

Li, P., Yang, J., Islam, M. A., & Ren, S. (2025). Uncovering and addressing the secret water footprint of AI models. *Communications of the ACM, 68*(7), 54–61. https://doi.org/10.1145/3724499

Mintoff, J. (2006). Could an egoist be a friend? *American Philosophical Quarterly, 43*(2), 101–118. http://www.jstor.com/stable/20010230

Nussbaum, M. C. (2007). *Frontiers of justice: Disability, nationality, species membership*. The Belknap Press of Harvard University Press.

Ratti, E., & Graves, M. (2025). A capability approach to AI ethics. *American Philosophical Quarterly, 62*(1), 1–16.

Spaemann, R. (1984). Über den Begriff der Menschenwürde. In Piper (Ed.), *Das Natürliche und das Vernünftige. Aufsätze Anthropologie* (pp. 77–106).

Wellman, M. P., & Rajan, U. (2017). Ethical issues for autonomous trading agents. *Minds & Machines, 127*, 609–624. https://doi.org/10.1007/s11023-017-9419-4

CHAPTER 2

Mental Health: Ethics and the Role and Limits of Artificial Intelligence

Pere Castellvi Obiols

Introduction to the Psychological Impact of AI

The integration of artificial intelligence (AI) into various aspects of our daily lives, including mental health, is growing rapidly. AI is defined as a set of computer programs designed to mimic human behavior, such as learning, reasoning, and self-correction. These technologies mimic human cognition, encompassing problem-solving, data analysis, and automated decision-making (Gillath et al., 2021).

P. C. Obiols (✉)
Barcelona, Spain
e-mail: Pere.Castellvi@uab.cat

Departament de Psicologia Clínica i de la Salut, Universitat Autònoma de Barcelona (UAB), Bellaterra, Spain

M. Bosch (ed.), *Crucial Ethical Keys of Artificial Intelligence*,
https://doi.org/10.1007/978-3-032-22853-6_2

Overview of AI in Psychological Contexts

AI has evolved from industrial automation to advanced conversational systems embedded in applications and programs, from more subtle functions such as predictive text and purchase recommendations to a more substantial presence in chatbots or alert systems. Unlike older technologies, AI can act as a social actor or agent that interacts directly with individuals, profoundly influencing their development and understanding of the world (Raees et al., 2024).

In the context of mental health, the concept of "weak AI" is considered more appropriate, as it is more controllable and better adapted to treatment needs (Bozdag, 2023). Although "simulated social presence" is not directly mentioned, sources indicate that interaction with AI can trigger reactions such as the formation of emotional bonds and dependency (Bozdag, 2023). The intrusion of AI into daily life raises ethical questions about autonomy and human identity. The impersonal nature of AI can overlook crucial emotional nuances in mental health assessment.

What emotions does interacting with AI trigger? Interacting with AI can trigger a range of emotions. If an AI response sounds empathetic or distressed, people, especially vulnerable users, may react as if it were real, which can lead to emotional dependency, reinforce harmful thoughts, or create a false sense of connection (Ben-Zion, 2025). There is also a widespread concern of distrust and fear of AI, related to issues such as job replacement and privacy violations (Laffier et al., 2025).

Why is AI becoming a support or projection figure? AI is projected as a support figure because it offers accessibility, personalization, confidentiality, and the ability to alleviate emotional problems (S. Huang et al., 2024). It can complement therapy by enriching the ability of clinicians to provide personalized care, analyzing complex patterns in patients' language, behavior, and emotional expressions. AI-based applications can perform tasks such as initial screening or data analysis, allowing clinicians to focus on the human aspects of the therapeutic relationship, such as empathy and understanding (Sadeh-Sharvit & Hollon, 2020).

Potential Applications and Risks

AI has great transformative potential in mental health, offering solutions for prevention, diagnosis, and treatment, while improving the accessibility and efficiency of services. However, its rapid integration into daily life also poses significant challenges and risks, especially regarding human-AI interaction and its psychological implications (Das & Gavade, 2024).

Since its inception, AI has been integrated into everyday life in a variety of ways (S. Huang et al., 2024a). The early phases of AI, between the 1950s and 1970s, included technologies such as Unimate, the first industrial robot, and Shakey, a mobile robot from the Stanford Research Institute, which focused on typical human inference based on analysis (Vaidyam et al., 2019).

Currently, AI manifests itself in applications such as voice assistants (e.g., Apple Siri, Xiaomi Xiaoai, Baidu Duer, Microsoft Xiaoice), social bots (e.g., Pepper), chatbots or companion chatbots (e.g., Replika, Mitsuku, ChatGPT, ERNIE Bot, Woebot, Wysa, Tess), and AI-generated videos or images. Generative AI has seen astonishingly rapid diffusion, with millions of users adopting tools like ChatGPT in a matter of months and over 80% of organizations projected to adopt it by 2026 (IBM, 2024).

How AI influences perceptions of reality, autonomy, and identity, AI's ability to interact in an almost human-like manner has a profound impact on users' perceptions (Ta et al., 2020). Next, I will mention some useful considerations about AI in the context of mental health.

- *Human interactions and emotional dependency:* AI is designed to be highly proficient at communication and problem-solving, as well as empathetic. This can lead users to develop emotional trust or dependency, especially with companion chatbots (Ta et al., 2020). For vulnerable users, such as those experiencing depression or anxiety, these interactions can lead to emotional dependency, reinforce harmful thoughts, or create a false sense of connection. Without protective design features, the AI may have fatal consequences. In Belgium, in March 2023, a thirty-year-old man died by suicide after six weeks of conversations with a chatbot, which encouraged him to sacrifice himself to save the planet while discussing climate change. Recently, a California couple has filed the first-ever lawsuit against OpenAI, alleging that their now-deceased teenage son was encouraged to commit suicide by ChatGPT. The suit, brought in California's Superior Court, cites chat logs in which the teen shared suicidal thoughts and claims the AI validated his self-harm impulses. The case marks a landmark legal precedent, raising urgent questions about AI responsibility and the safety of conversational technologies. In the United States, a 28-year-old married woman fell in love with her "AI boyfriend" and could no longer imagine life without "him." These cases highlight important ethical, social, and legal concerns about the impact that artificial intelligence can have on people's psychological vulnerability and mental well-being. Fundamental questions are raised regarding responsibility and the attribution of consequences when conversational technologies contribute to promoting self-destructive behaviors or generating bonds of affective dependency. In a broader context, these situations reinforce the need to establish mechanisms for supervision, regulation, and transparency in the design and implementation of AI systems, with the aim of ensuring that their use promotes the health and protection of users.

- *"Simulated social presence":* Chatbots that simulate conversations, such as Replika or Character.ai, make interactions feel more natural. People can react to artificial emotional cues (voice, rhythm, language) as if they were real, even knowing they are not (Ben-Zion, 2025). The concept of the "uncanny valley" also applies to AI-created artifacts that come too close to human appearance, causing discomfort (Caporusso, 2023).
- *Promoting cognitive and social skills:* AI can increase cognitive tasks, problem-solving skills, and critical thinking if the users focus their work on the process to achieve the objectives instead of the result (Ng et al., 2024). This phenomenon, known as "cognitive offloading," may have long-term implications for intellectual development and human autonomy. However, it can also encourage laziness and procrastination (Ng et al., 2024).
- *Identity and self-efficacy:* The pervasive presence of generative AI in creative activities may challenge the development of identity in younger generations, as their creations may be outdone by AI (Caporusso, 2023). The use of AI can, however, increase self-efficacy by providing tools to work and study more efficiently (Parsakia, 2023).
- *Autonomy and agency:* The increasing reliance on AI in decision-making (e.g., school admissions, academic assessment) may have lasting consequences for young people and requires deep reflection on the notion of agency, responsibility, and accountability (American XE "Accountability" Psychological Association (APA), 2025a).

- *"Creative Displacement Anxiety" (CDA):* The emergence of generative AI has given rise to a new psychological phenomenon called CDA, which describes stress or anxiety resulting from the perception that AI displaces or overshadows human creativity (Caporusso, 2023).
- *Weak (specific) and strong (artificial general/superintelligence—AGI/ASI) AI:* Weak AI refers to AI systems designed for specific tasks. They are considered more controllable and suitable for mental health treatment needs, such as providing psychoeducational support, monitoring symptoms, or conducting preliminary assessments. Strong AI is the capacity of learning, reasoning, and performing activities on par with humans, or even surpassing human intelligence in all domains. Its imminent arrival raises concerns about long-term security and profound societal implications, including the potential transformation of interpersonal communication into quantifiable data and the need for rigorous ethical regulation. "AI agents" represent a qualitative leap, as they can accomplish complex missions with a high degree of autonomy and plan sequences of interdependent actions.
- *Privacy:* AI systems rely on large data sets, which raises significant concerns about information privacy.
- *Ethical Considerations and Governance:* Implementing AI in mental health requires strong ethical considerations. Implementing such systems requires training in ethics and medical informatics (Durán & Jongsma, 2021). Informed consent and patient autonomy are central elements in clinical decision-making, which a lack of understanding of AI systems could compromise. Explainability of AI (XAI) is crucial for clinicians to understand and trust AI recommendations (Tonekaboni et al., 2019).

Potential Benefits of AI in Mental Health

AI has rapidly become part of public and academic conversation, revolutionizing several fields with its ability to create new and unprecedented content. This technology is based on three fundamental components: extensive and diverse training data, foundational models such as Large Language Models (LLMs) using deep neural networks, and content generation based on user instructions or "prompts." Its influence extends from medicine and education to everyday life, offering both great opportunities and new challenges.

AI in Health and Mental Wellbeing

AI is emerging as a transformative force in the field of mental health and well-being, offering a range of potential applications that could significantly improve the care and support available. This technology, which simulates human cognition such as learning and problem-solving, has rapidly become integrated into our daily lives, from voice assistants and predictive text to warning systems. Its ability to process large volumes of data and identify complex patterns opens new avenues for early detection, diagnosis, treatment, and monitoring of mental health conditions.

a) *Improving diagnosis and initial evaluation:* AI has the potential to improve the detection, diagnosis, and prediction of mental illness. Using machine learning (ML) and deep learning (DL) algorithms, AI can analyze vast amounts of behavioral and linguistic data to identify subtle indicators of mental health problems, enabling earlier and more accurate diagnosis (Zafar et al., 2024), which can prevent the escalation of symptoms and reduce the burden on healthcare systems. It can increase accuracy and sensitivity in diagnosing anxiety disorders and other mental health problems, allowing for early identification (Das & Gavade, 2024). Additionally, it can mitigate challenges such as stigma or self-report bias by analyzing large volumes of behavioral and linguistic data to identify subtle indicators (Zafar et al., 2024). In the area of anxiety disorders, AI can aid in the detection and prediction of panic disorder (PD), using anomaly detection algorithms to distinguish between panic and non-panic states (Cruz et al., 2015).
b) *Personalized medicine:* AI-based systems can personalize and streamline treatments, analyzing large data sets for more accurate and faster assessments (Graham et al., 2019) and can identify patterns of information in data to predict outcomes at the individual patient level. For example, the effectiveness of AI in treating anxiety disorders is being investigated, with a comprehensive review that analyzed 125 peer-reviewed articles to extract evidence of the efficacy of AI technologies (Das & Gavade, 2024). Integrating AI with electronic

medical records (EMRs) can facilitate better utilization of patient information (Asan et al., 2023), which, together with effective nurse leadership, can improve patient outcomes (Alsadaan et al., 2023). Applying natural language processing (NLP) to social media data or electronic health records can identify depressive symptoms or suicidal ideation and even assess medication adherence. NLP is a major advance for mental health applications.

c) *Developing more accurate predictive models:* AI-powered machine learning (ML) models are being developed to predict and mitigate Internet addiction by analyzing behavioral patterns and psychological indicators. Models such as neural networks and XGBoost have achieved high accuracies (91% and 90% respectively) in predicting Internet addiction (Abdel Wahed & Abdel Wahed, 2025). Similarly, a significant negative correlation has been found between Internet addiction and several dimensions of psychological well-being in adolescents (Abdel Wahed & Abdel Wahed, 2025). AI is also being applied to monitor Internet gaming addiction (Y. Huang et al., 2024) and to detect suicide risk using "tree-hole knowledge graphs" that integrate multiple data sources (Z. Huang & Hu, 2024).

AI systems can also analyze metadata (such as handwriting) or free speech to predict the onset of psychosis in high-risk youth (Bedi et al., 2015). Furthermore, AI can use data such as EEG to detect depression (Cai et al., 2018). Other applications include predicting depression using behavioral markers from smartphones, classifying unipolar and bipolar depressive disorders (Asare et al., 2021), and predicting suicidal ideation from text-based mental health interventions (Cook et al., 2016).

In comorbid patients, ML models have been developed to predict the risk of long-term depression and to predict the likelihood of suicide in patients with acute coronary syndrome, using demographic data, clinical history, and laboratory results. Depression is considered a significant condition associated with impaired quality of life and increased risk of adverse cardiac events (Lv et al., 2025). Natural Language Processing (NLP) has also been used to understand and evaluate text messaging services in mental health crises, although identifying behaviors in individual messages may be sufficient without a broader conversational context (Liu et al., 2021).

d) *e-health:* AI can also be used in mobile health (mHealth) applications for children's mental health, where the readability of the applications is assessed for children's comprehension. In addition, the benefits and challenges of LLMs in mental health care are investigated, including their ability to reduce documentation time for clinicians (Yang et al., 2025).
e) *Improving Patient Care and Clinical Support:* AI can help clinicians with their growing care needs, documentation requirements, and inefficient technology.

AI-powered chatbots and mobile apps can provide support in mental health, enabling scalable and personalized interventions to promote digital well-being. These tools are considered valuable for self-management (39%), education (36%), and training (35%). They are also recognized as beneficial aids in cognitive behavioral therapy (CBT), with nearly a quarter of practitioners affirming their ability to provide ongoing support with minimal user involvement (Sweeney et al., 2021).

Some chatbots have shown notable effectiveness in managing mental health symptoms, such as the evaluation of the chatbot "Emohaa" in China (Sabour et al., 2023), or "Tess" in university students, which was shown to be effective in alleviating symptoms (Klos et al., 2021). One study found that an AI platform for behavioral interventions had effects on symptoms of depression and anxiety (Sadeh-Sharvit et al., 2023). Other studies are investigating chatbots for postpartum anxiety disorders (Yao et al., 2023). AI can also reduce burnout among healthcare workers, as evidenced by the Vickybot trial (Anmella et al., 2023).

f) *Mental health monitoring:* Analyzing physiological data from wearable devices for mental health monitoring is an emerging field that uses machine learning and hybrid approaches for the detection and monitoring of anxiety and other mental disorders (Gomes et al., 2023).
g) *Cognition:* AI can improve critical thinking and problem-solving skills. For example, AI can provide process-oriented feedback that helps students critique their writing. In educational settings, generative AI tools should not replace cognitive development but enhance it. Interacting with AI in a critical and guided way forces the student to interpret, question, explore, evaluate, and create, promoting

a culture of self-learning and strengthening critical thinking and personal initiative (Parsakia, 2023).

Furthermore, advanced use of AI can foster metacognition and deep learning as students reflect on how, why, and within what limits they use AI, and it can accelerate the exploration of creative landscapes and introduce diverse perspectives, even helping to mitigate human cognitive biases (Plana et al., 2022). Additionally, AI can increase people's self-efficacy, and it can provide individuals with knowledge, skills, and resources, increasing their self-efficacy and fostering social well-being (Parsakia, 2023). Collaboration between humans and machines can foster a sense of empowerment, enhanced competence, and increased potential.

Additional Considerations

Despite the benefits, it is worth noting that the reviewed literature often focuses on empirical studies such as randomized controlled trials, quasi-experimental designs, and observational studies to compile comprehensive data on the effectiveness of AI environments in the treatment of mental disorders. However, many of these randomized controlled trials have methodological limitations, such as high risk of bias and poor demographic inclusion, which may affect the generalizability of the results, especially since the concentration of these trials in high-resource settings may limit their applicability to less-resourced settings.

The rapid evolution of technologies responds to social needs for communication, companionship, and assistance. AI's ability to understand and interpret human language through NLP, including sentiment analysis to capture the user's emotions, is fundamental to many of these applications.

In summary, AI offers enormous potential to improve mental health by improving detection, diagnosis, treatment, and support, as well as optimizing professional training and research. However, its implementation must be accompanied by rigorous evaluation and ongoing ethical consideration to ensure that its benefits are maximized equitably and safely.

Psychological Risks Associated with AI Use

AI is quickly transforming many aspects of society, including mental health care, offering new efficiencies and opportunities (Graham et al., 2019). However, the ever-deepening integration of AI into everyday life raises serious ethical considerations, especially in the field of mental health, where the vulnerability of individuals is a primary concern (Mccradden et al., 2023). This section examines the primary ethical risks associated with AI in mental health, concentrating on its cognitive and emotional impacts, the issue of algorithmic bias, trust, and the potential for dehumanization of care.

General Ethical Concerns in the Application of AI in Health

The use of AI in health care, including mental health, presents significant challenges, including issues such as data security, informed consent, confidentiality, and trust. The impersonal nature of AI can overlook emotional subtlety, which is crucial in mental health assessment. In addition, there are concerns about algorithmic biases, as AI systems are only as objective as the data they are trained on. These biases, if left unmitigated, can perpetuate discrimination and impact justice and equity in health care (Das & Gavade, 2024).

Lack of resources and limited availability of psychotherapy options in underdeveloped areas have accelerated the adoption of AI, but this can create a digital divide in access to mental health care if the technology is not accessible to all. Furthermore, the ability to predict and monitor the health, behavior, and environmental aspects of individuals with mental disorders during the early stages is limited (Das & Gavade, 2024), and the use of AI in these contexts may imply increased surveillance, especially for populations already subject to high levels of surveillance.

Specific Mental Health Risks

Dependence and Cognitive Erosion

One of the most significant concerns is the possibility that intensive use of AI will lead to over-reliance or "cognitive offloading" negatively affecting human capabilities (Laffier et al., 2025). Some studies suggest that dependence on AI can weaken social, cognitive, and personal skills, such as problem-solving and critical thinking. An MIT study on essay writing revealed that participants who used ChatGPT wrote better but thought worse. The study found that 83% of ChatGPT users were unable to cite a single sentence from their own essays written minutes earlier, compared to just 11% of the group that did not use AI. This negative effect, often undetected by the users themselves, was observed in electroencephalograms (EEGs), leading researchers to coin the term "cognitive debt," defined as borrowing future cognitive capacity for short-term convenience (Kosmyna et al., n.d.). This is like the "Google Maps effect," where reliance on GPS weakens spatial memory (Dahmani & Bohbot, 2020).

Furthermore, the use of AI tools can cause students to put less effort into core cognitive processes, compromising their performance when the tools are taken away (Chen et al., 2025). Procrastination is another risk, as AI can reduce the need for mental effort, allowing students to solve tasks almost instantly without deep cognitive engagement. This can lead to a loss of authorship and the impoverishment of writing and thinking skills (Mukhtar et al., 2025).

Emotional and Psychological Impact

Interaction with AI can generate a series of negative emotional and psychological responses:

Technological panic and AI anxiety: The emergence of new technologies, such as AI, can manifest as a technological panic in some people, especially teenagers. Existential anxiety about AI is a growing concern (S. Huang et al., 2024).

Anxiety for Creative Displacement (ADC): This term has been coined to describe the psychological state that arises from the perception that human creativity is being displaced by advanced generative AI technologies. ADC encompasses emotional, cognitive, and behavioral reactions stemming from the feeling that traditional creativity feels overshadowed, generating a loss of meaning, identity, and purpose in creative domains. Artists and younger generations are particularly susceptible, as AI can suppress their trust and growth if it produces results that surpass their creations (Torous & Blease, 2024).

Isolation and breakup of interpersonal relationships: While some argue that AI can increase social capital, others warn that AI dependence can threaten interpersonal connections and negatively impact mental health, as it can disrupt or replace real-life relationships. Interaction with AI, while less demanding than with real people, does not provide the intrinsic empathic connection to human relationships (S. Huang et al., 2024).

Distortion of reality and social comparison: AI-generated images, for example, can cause stressful social comparisons, especially among young people. The "uncanny valley" phenomenon, where excessive similarity to humans causes discomfort, also applies to AI creations (Caporusso, 2023).

Bias and Misinformation

The ability of AI to generate content from large volumes of data also carries the risk of propagating and magnifying biases present in this training data (American Psychological Association (APA), 2025).

"Hallucinations": Hallucinations, which is the tendency of AI models to generate incorrect information by presenting it as factual, are a serious problem, especially in educational and health contexts, where users may lack cognitive tools to assess information accuracy.

Misinformation: AI-generated misinformation can affect the quality of health information and public trust. AI systems that provide health information to young people must ensure the accuracy and reliability of the content or provide explicit and repeated warnings about possible inaccuracy.

Dehumanization of Attention and Challenges in Therapeutic Relation

The use of AI can reduce complex human interactions to "data points," ignoring subtle emotional and behavioral cues crucial in psychiatric evaluation (Dell, 2025). There is a tension between the value of participatory methods in mental health research and AI/machine learning approaches that can distance participants from research processes, making them mere "data points" (Skorburg et al., 2024).

The epistemic privilege of AI, where its predictions are considered superior to human clinical judgment, can have unintended consequences, such as unnecessary institutionalization or undermining the credibility of patients over their own experiences. Doctors may feel compelled to align their clinical judgments with the outputs of AI systems due to their alleged scientific reliability (Mccradden et al., 2023).

Informed consent becomes complex, as it is difficult to anticipate all future uses of data or potential risks of protocols, especially with virtual reality or digital avatars. Trust is critical, but the lack of transparency in the details of AI models and their biases can undermine it (Light et al., 2024).

Challenges in Ethical Implementation and Supervision

The integration of AI into mental health requires careful planning and ethical oversight. Psychologists are often poorly involved in developing chatbots that use NLP and machine learning, and information about the privacy of user data is usually insufficient. The difficulty in explaining how AI models ("explainable AI" or XAI) work is challenging, as the justification for a model's prediction is not equivalent to the justification of benefit for an individual (Tonekaboni et al., 2019).

Research on the negative effects of AI on mental health is still incipient, and many randomized clinical trials of medical AI models have methodological limitations, such as a high risk of bias and low demographic inclusion, which limits the generalizability of outcomes, especially in limited resource environments (Das & Gavade, 2024).

In conclusion, while artificial intelligence offers considerable potential for improving access to and personalization of mental health care, its integration must be addressed with epistemic humility. This involves a critical assessment of its risks, ensuring that technology complements, rather than substitutes, human clinical judgment and patient experience (Dell, 2025). Prioritizing ethical principles, transparency, bias mitigation, and a human-centered approach is critical to ensuring AI contributes to sustainable and equitable mental well-being.

Ethical and Moral Considerations in AI Design

Human Dignity and Respect for Autonomy

Human dignity and respect for autonomy are core ethical principles that should guide the design and implementation of AI, especially in the mental health sector. These principles need to honor people's autonomy and their right to self-determination (Light et al., 2024).

Augmentation vs. replacement: AI technologies should be conceived as tools that augment human capabilities and professional judgment, not as replacements. In psychiatric nursing, for example, while conversational AI can assist with assessments, supervision by a psychiatric nurse is essential for interpreting complex behaviors and establishing therapeutic relationships (Dell, 2025). AI can increase productivity, but caution should be exercised about the erosion of human cognition. In the medical field, AI should be an assistive tool, not a substitute for critical thinking. The goal is for technology and human expertise to work together to improve service delivery and patient care.

Preserving human control and judgment: Healthcare professionals, including psychologists, should maintain responsibility for final decisions and not blindly rely on recommendations generated by AI. The loss of human control or the human aspect in the decision-making process is an ethical concern, as users may perceive that they are losing control or judgment. In psychiatry, uncritical prioritization of AI can lead to unintended consequences, such as unnecessary institutionalization or loss of patient credibility about their own experiences (American Psychological Association (APA), n.d.). This over-reliance on AI can generate an "automation bias" that undermines trust and professional judgment (Parasuraman & Manzey, 2010).

"Cognitive Debt" and Impact on Thinking: Heavy use of AI, such as ChatGPT, can create "cognitive debt," where future cognitive capacity is borrowed for short-term convenience, negatively impacting critical thinking and memory. Studies with EEGs have shown that writing without AI assistance leads to stronger neural connectivity and better memory, while writing assisted by LLM shows generally lower connectivity. For healthy use, it is recommended to do the "heavy cognitive work" (thinking and writing) first and then use AI to polish and refine the content.

The Importance of Empathy and Informed Consent

Empathy and informed consent are fundamental ethical pillars in health care, and AI must be integrated without undermining them.

- **AI limitations in empathy and emotional subtlety:** The impersonal nature of AI can miss the nuance of emotional aspects, which are crucial in mental health assessment. Users often perceive empathy from an AI tool as inauthentic, since a machine has no feelings. This limitation highlights the importance of maintaining the "human touch" in healthcare (Dell, 2025).
- **Informed Consent (IC):** It is an essential ethical requirement for the collection, use, sharing, and storage of sensitive data. However, obtaining true IC can be a considerable challenge, as many users of digital interventions struggle to conceptualize how machine learning

(ML) works, particularly its "black box" nature. Clinicians and researchers have an ethical obligation to clearly communicate the purpose, application, and potential benefits and risks of AI tools in a culturally and linguistically appropriate manner. Patients should be informed of their right to refuse AI-based interventions and to receive alternative options.

- **Transparency in data collection and use:** Full transparency in the implementation and communication of privacy strategies must be ensured. Lack of knowledge on the part of researchers about how data is stored or processed on digital platforms can result in incomplete information from the IC (Light et al., 2024).

Core Ethical Principles to Protect Mental Health

Several ethical and regulatory frameworks have been developed to guide the responsible design and implementation of AI in mental health, ensuring that patient well-being is protected (Derksen et al., 2025).

- *Data privacy and security:* The management of sensitive data in mental health, including biometric and neural information, poses significant risks of privacy breaches and unethical data use. Robust security policies and open data governance must be implemented to safeguard information. Regulations such as the GDPR in Europe and FDA guidelines in the US emphasize the importance of privacy and security.
- *Mitigating Algorithmic Bias:* AI systems are only as objective as the data they are trained on, and they can perpetuate or amplify existing biases, especially affecting underrepresented communities. It is crucial to evaluate AI to address bias and promote equity, considering the diversity of lived experiences. Emphasis should be placed on the use of diverse and representative datasets to minimize such biases.
- *Accountability and Transparency:* Complex models such as neural networks can be "black boxes" (lacking transparency), making it difficult to understand how decisions are made (Durán & Jongsma, 2021). AI systems should clearly explain their decision-making processes and have clear lines of accountability to ensure reliable and ethical use. In addition, psychologists should take responsibility

for the quality of AI information and discontinue its use if concerns about misinformation arise.

- *Beneficence and non-maleficence:* The ethical principles of beneficence and non-maleficence imply that AI should seek health benefit and avoid harm. This requires rigorous validation of AI tools before clinical implementation and ongoing assessment of their impact.
- *Training and education:* Both users and providers must receive education and training on the capabilities and limitations of AI chatbots to mitigate unrealistic expectations and promote effective use. The design of AI in university education should include training students for its critical, ethical, and reflective use.
- *Process vs. outcome focus:* Generative AI challenges traditional educational models that focus on outcome assessment. A shift is needed toward prioritizing the learning process, where AI becomes a tool to foster critical thinking, self-learning, and co-creation, rather than a means to obtain results without cognitive effort.

In conclusion, integrating AI into mental health and well-being is like building a bridge. It is not enough to have the most advanced technology for materials (AI); we also need solid foundations based on ethics (respect for dignity, autonomy, privacy), a design that encourages cooperation (empathy, informed consent), and vigilant human oversight. Only then will the bridge connect our needs with effective solutions without compromising the core values that define us as human beings.

Conclusion and Future Directions

The use of AI in health care and other areas poses numerous ethical challenges. Data privacy is a key concern, as AI systems process large amounts of sensitive information. Algorithmic bias is a risk, as AI models can perpetuate or amplify biases present in the training data, particularly affecting diverse communities (Obermeyer et al., 2019).

Reliance on AI can also lead to "automation bias," where humans overly rely on AI recommendations, even when they are incorrect, undermining trust and professional judgment. In psychiatry, this can lead to "testimonial injustice" and affect the relationship between professionals and patients (Goddard et al., 2012).

AI can increase efficiency in repetitive tasks, but it also raises the question of whether it will erode human skills in the long term (Jia & Shan, 2025). AI models have been observed to be able to perform tasks with incredible speed and scale. However, this may lead to a reduction in the workforce in certain sectors. In addition, digital platforms, including social media, can amplify problematic content and make it difficult to control screen time, affecting digital well-being.

In conclusion, AI represents a powerful tool with immense potential to improve health, education, and efficiency. The key to harnessing its value lies in conscious, ethical, and complementary use, where AI serves as an augmentation of human capabilities, not a replacement for thought and connection. However, it is crucial to address its challenges, such as "cognitive debt," the need for human oversight, algorithmic bias, and ethical concerns.

References

Abdel Wahed, S., & Abdel Wahed, M. (2025). AI-driven digital well-being: Developing machine learning model to predict and mitigate internet addiction. *LatIA, 3*, 73. https://doi.org/10.62486/latia202573

Alsadaan, N., Basha, B., Reshia, F., Alruwaili, R., Alruwaili, M., Ali, S., Alruwaili, A., Hefnawy, G., Alshammari, M., Alrumayh, A., Alruwaili, A., & Jones, L. (2023). Impact of nurse leaders behaviors on nursing staff performance: A systematic review of literature. *Inquiry: A Journal of Medical Care Organization, Provision and Financing, 60*, 469580231178528. https://doi.org/10.1177/00469580231178528

American Psychological Association (APA). (2025). *Artificial Intelligence and Adolescent Well-being*.

Anmella, G., Sanabra, M., Primé-Tous, M., Segú, X., Cavero, M., Morilla, I., Grande, I., Ruiz, V., Mas, A., Martín-Villalba, I., Caballo, A., Julia-Parisad, E., Rodríguez-Rey, A., Piazza, F., José Valdesoiro, F., Rodriguez-Torrella, C., Espinosa, M., Virgili, G., Sorroche, C., et al. (2023). Vickybot, a chatbot for anxiety-depressive symptoms and work-related burnout in primary care and health care professionals: Development, feasibility, and potential effectiveness studies. *Journal of Medical Internet Research, 25*. https://doi.org/10.2196/43293

Asan, O., Choi, E., & Wang, X. (2023). Artificial intelligence-based consumer health informatics application: Scoping review. *Journal of Medical Internet Research, 25*, e47260. https://doi.org/10.2196/47260

Asare, K. O., Terhorst, Y., Vega, J., Peltonen, E., Lagerspetz, E., & Ferreira, D. (2021). Predicting depression from smartphone behavioral markers using machine learning methods, hyperparameter optimization, and feature importance analysis: Exploratory study. *JMIR mHealth and uHealth, 9*(7). https://doi.org/10.2196/26540

Bedi, G., Carrillo, F., Cecchi, G. A., Slezak, D. F., Sigman, M., Mota, N. B., Ribeiro, S., Javitt, D. C., Copelli, M., & Corcoran, C. M. (2015). Automated analysis of free speech predicts psychosis onset in high-risk youths. *NPJ Schizophrenia, 1*(1), 15030. https://doi.org/10.1038/npjschz.2015.30

Ben-Zion, Z. (2025). Why we need mandatory safeguards for emotionally responsive AI. *Nature, 643*(8070), 9. https://EconPapers.repec.org/RePEc:nat:nature:v:643:y:2025:i:8070:d:10.1038_d41586-025-02031-w

Bozdag, A. A. (2023). AIsmosis and the pas de deux of human-AI interaction: Exploring the communicative dance between society and artificial intelligence. *Online Journal of Communication and Media Technologies, 13*(4), e202340. https://doi.org/10.30935/ojcmt/13414

Cai, H., Han, J., Chen, Y., Sha, X., Wang, Z., Hu, B., Yang, J., Feng, L., Ding, Z., Chen, Y., & Gutknecht, J. (2018). A pervasive approach to EEG-based depression detection. *Complexity, 2018*(1), 5238028. https://doi.org/10.1155/2018/5238028

Caporusso, N. (2023). Generative Artificial Intelligence and the emergence of creative displacement anxiety. *Commentary, 3*(1).

Chen, Y., Wang, Y., Wüstenberg, T., Kizilcec, R. F., Fan, Y., Li, Y., Lu, B., Yuan, M., Zhang, J., Zhang, Z., Geldsetzer, P., Chen, S., & Bärnighausen, T. (2025). Effects of generative artificial intelligence on cognitive effort and task performance: Study protocol for a randomized controlled experiment among college students. *Trials, 26*(1), 244. https://doi.org/10.1186/s13063-025-08950-3

Cook, B. L., Progovac, A. M., Chen, P., Mullin, B., Hou, S., & Baca-Garcia, E. (2016). Novel use of Natural Language Processing (NLP) to predict suicidal ideation and psychiatric symptoms in a text-based mental health intervention in Madrid. *Computational and Mathematical Methods in Medicine, 2016*, 8. https://doi.org/10.1155/2016/8708434

Cruz, L., Rubin, J., Abreu, R., Ahern, S., Eldardiry, H., & Bobrow, D. G. (2015). A wearable and mobile intervention delivery system for individuals with panic disorder. In *Proceedings of the 14th International Conference on Mobile and Ubiquitous Multimedia* (pp. 175–182). https://doi.org/10.1145/2836041.2836058

Dahmani, L., & Bohbot, V. D. (2020). Habitual use of GPS negatively impacts spatial memory during self-guided navigation. *Scientific Reports, 10*(1), 6310. https://doi.org/10.1038/s41598-020-62877-0

Das, K. P., & Gavade, P. (2024). A review on the efficacy of artificial intelligence for managing anxiety disorders. In *Frontiers in Artificial Intelligence* (Vol. 7). https://doi.org/10.3389/frai.2024.1435895

Dell, C. (2025). The risks of Artificial Intelligence in mental health care. In Journal of Psychiatric and Mental Health Nursing (Vol. 32, Issue 2, pp. 382–383). John Wiley and Sons doi:https://doi.org/10.1111/jpm.13119.

Derksen, M. E., van Beek, M., de Bruijn, T., Stuit, F., Blankers, M., & Goudriaan, A. E. (2025). Ethical aspects and user preferences in applying machine learning to adjust eHealth addressing substance use: A mixed-methods study. *International Journal of Medical Informatics, 199*, 105897. https://doi.org/10.1016/j.ijmedinf.2025.105897

Durán, J. M., & Jongsma, K. R. (2021). Who is afraid of black box algorithms? On the epistemological and ethical basis of trust in medical AI. *Journal of Medical Ethics, 47*(5), 329–335. https://doi.org/10.1136/medethics-2020-106820

Gillath, O., Ai, T., Branicky, M., Keshmiri, S., Davison, R., & Spaulding, R. (2021). Attachment and trust in artificial intelligence. *Computers in Human Behavior, 115*, 106607. https://doi.org/10.1016/j.chb.2020.106607

Goddard, K., Roudsari, A., & Wyatt, J. C. (2012). Automation bias: A systematic review of frequency, effect mediators, and mitigators. *Journal of the American Medical Informatics Association, 19*(1), 121–127. https://doi.org/10.1136/amiajnl-2011-000089

Gomes, N., Pato, M., Lourenço, A. R., & Datia, N. (2023). A survey on wearable sensors for mental health monitoring. *Sensors, 23*(3), 1330. https://doi.org/10.3390/s23031330

Graham, S., Depp, C., Lee, E. E., Nebeker, C., Tu, X., Kim, H. C., & Jeste, D. V. (2019). Artificial Intelligence for mental health and mental illnesses: An overview. *Current Psychiatry Reports, 21*(11), 116. https://doi.org/10.1007/s11920-019-1094-0

Huang, S., Lai, X., Ke, L., Li, Y., Wang, H., Zhao, X., Dai, X., & Wang, Y. (2024). AI technology panic—is AI dependence bad for mental health? A cross-lagged panel model and the mediating roles of motivations for AI use among adolescents. *Psychology Research and Behavior Management, 17*, 1087–1102. https://doi.org/10.2147/PRBM.S440889

Huang, Y., Wu, R., Huang, Y., Xiang, Y., & Zhou, W. (2024). Investigating the mechanisms of internet gaming disorder and developing intelligent monitoring models using artificial intelligence technologies: Protocol of a prospective cohort. *BMC Public Health, 24*(1), 2536. https://doi.org/10.1186/s12889-024-20028-4

Huang, Z., & Hu, Q. (2024). Tree hole rescue: An AI approach for suicide risk detection and online suicide intervention. *Health Information Science and Systems, 12*(1), 45. https://doi.org/10.1007/s13755-024-00298-3

IBM. (2024). *What is generative AI?*

Jia, S., & Shan, G. (2025). *Association for information systems association for information systems AI-assisted service work: Boosting efficiency but eroding human skills?* Emergent Research Forum (ERF) Paper. https://aisel.aisnet.org/amcis2025/sig_cnow/sig_cnow/2.

Klos, M. C., Escoredo, M., Joerin, A., Lemos, V. N., Rauws, M., & Bunge, E. L. (2021). Artificial Intelligence–based chatbot for anxiety and depression in university students: Pilot randomized controlled trial. *JMIR Formative Research, 5*(8), e20678. https://doi.org/10.2196/20678

Kosmyna, N., Hauptmann, E., Yuan, Y. T., Situ, J., Liao, X.-H., Beresnitzky, A. V., Braunstein, I., & Maes, P. (n.d.). Your brain on ChatGPT: Accumulation of cognitive debt when using an AI assistant for essay writing task.

Laffier, J., Rehman, A., & Westley, M. (2025). A conceptual framework to understand the relationships between digital wellness and Artificial Intelligence. *Cyberpsychology, Behavior, and Social Networking, 28*(7), 478–488. https://doi.org/10.1089/cyber.2024.0546

Light, L. L., Panicker, S., Abrams, L., & Huh-Yoo, J. (2024). Ethical challenges in the use of digital technologies in psychological science: Introduction to the special issue. *American Psychologist, 79*(1), 1–8. https://doi.org/10.1037/amp0001286

Liu, Z., Peach, R. L., Lawrance, E. L., Noble, A., Ungless, M. A., & Barahona, M. (2021). Listening to mental health crisis needs at scale: Using natural language processing to understand and evaluate a mental health crisis text messaging service. *Frontiers in Digital Health, 3*. https://doi.org/10.3389/fdgth.2021.779091

Lv, H., Sun, F., Zhang, Y., & Zhou, X. (2025). Development and validation of a machine learning model for predicting long-term depression risk in ACS patients after PCI: A retrospective cohort study. *International Journal of General Medicine, 18*, 2957–2972. https://doi.org/10.2147/ijgm.s523029

Mccradden, M., Hui, K., & Buchman, D. Z. (2023). Evidence, ethics and the promise of artificial intelligence in psychiatry. *Journal of Medical Ethics, 49*, 573–579. https://doi.org/10.1136/medethics-2022-108447

Mukhtar, M., Firdos, S. S., Zaka, I., & Naeem, S. (2025). Impact of AI dependence on procrastination among university students. *Research Journal of Psychology, 3*(1), 246–257. https://ctr.rjmss.com/index.php/19/about

Ng, D. T. K., Tan, C. W., & Leung, J. K. L. (2024). Empowering student self-regulated learning and science education through ChatGPT: A pioneering pilot study. *British Journal of Educational Technology, 55*(4), 1328–1353. https://doi.org/10.1111/bjet.13454

Obermeyer, Z., Powers, B., Vogeli, C., & Mullainathan, S. (2019). Dissecting racial bias in an algorithm used to manage the health of populations. *Science, 366*(6464), 447–453. https://doi.org/10.1126/science.aax2342

Parasuraman, R., & Manzey, D. H. (2010). Complacency and bias in human use of automation: An attentional integration. *Human Factors, 52*(3), 381–410. https://doi.org/10.1177/0018720810376055

Parsakia, K. (2023). The effect of chatbots and AI on the self-efficacy, self-esteem, problem-solving and critical thinking of students. *Health Nexus, 1*(1). https://doi.org/10.61838/hn.1.1.14

Plana, D., Shung, D. L., Grimshaw, A. A., Saraf, A., Sung, J. J. Y., & Kann, B. H. (2022). Randomized clinical trials of machine learning interventions in health care: A systematic review. *JAMA Network Open, 5*(9). https://doi.org/10.1001/jamanetworkopen.2022.33946

Raees, M., Meijerink, I., Lykourentzou, I., Khan, V.-J., & Papangelis, K. (2024). *From explainable to interactive AI: A literature review on current trends in Human-AI interaction*. http: //arxiv.org/abs/2405.15051.

Sabour, S., Zhang, W., Xiao, X., Zhang, Y., Zheng, Y., Wen, J., Zhao, J., & Huang, M. (2023). A chatbot for mental health support: exploring the impact of Emohaa on reducing mental distress in China. *Frontiers in Digital Health, 5*. https://doi.org/10.3389/fdgth.2023.1133987

Sadeh-Sharvit, S., Del Camp, T., Horton, S. E., Hefner, J. D., Berry, J. M., Grossman, E., & Hollon, S. D. (2023). Effects of an Artificial Intelligence platform for behavioral interventions on depression and anxiety symptoms: Randomized clinical trial. *Journal of Medical Internet Research, 25*, e46781. https://doi.org/10.2196/46781

Sadeh-Sharvit, S., & Hollon, S. D. (2020). Leveraging the power of nondisruptive technologies to optimize mental health treatment: Case study. In JMIR Mental Health (Vol. 7, Issue 11). JMIR Publications doi:https://doi.org/10.2196/20646.

Skorburg, J. A., O'Doherty, K., & Friesen, P. (2024). Persons or data points? Ethics, artificial intelligence, and the participatory turn in mental health research. *American Psychologist, 79*(1), 137–149. https://doi.org/10.1037/amp0001168

Sweeney, C., Potts, C., Ennis, E., Bond, R., Mulvenna, M. D., O'Neill, S., Malcolm, M., Kuosmanen, L., Kostenius, C., Vakaloudis, A., McConvey, G., Turkington, R., Hanna, D., Nieminen, H., Vartiainen, A. K., Robertson, A., & McTear, M. F. (2021). Can chatbots help support a person's mental health? Perceptions and views from mental healthcare professionals and experts. *ACM Transactions on Computing for Healthcare, 2*(3), 1–15. https://doi.org/10.1145/3453175

Ta, V., Griffith, C., Boatfield, C., Wang, X., Civitello, M., Bader, H., DeCero, E., & Loggarakis, A. (2020). User experiences of social support from companion chatbots in everyday contexts: Thematic analysis. *Journal of Medical Internet Research, 22*(3), e16235. https://doi.org/10.2196/16235

Tonekaboni, S., Joshi, S., McCradden, M. D., & Goldenberg, A. (2019). *What clinicians want: Contextualizing explainable machine learning for clinical end use*. http://arxiv.org/abs/1905.05134

Torous, J., & Blease, C. (2024). Generative artificial intelligence in mental health care: Potential benefits and current challenges. *World Psychiatry, 23*(1), 1–2. https://doi.org/10.1001/jamao

Vaidyam, A. N., Wisniewski, H., Halamka, J. D., Kashavan, M. S., & Torous, J. B. (2019). Chatbots and conversational agents in mental health: A review of the psychiatric landscape. *Canadian Journal of Psychiatry, 64*(7), 456–464. https://doi.org/10.1177/0706743719828977

Yang, F., Wei, J., Zhao, X., & An, R. (2025). Artificial Intelligence–Based mobile phone apps for child mental health: Comprehensive review and content analysis. *JMIR mHealth and uHealth, 13*, e58597. https://doi.org/10.2196/58597

Yao, X., Mikhelson, M., Watkins, S., Choi, E., Thomaz, E., & de Barbaro, K. (2023). Development and evaluation of three chatbots for postpartum mood and anxiety disorders. doi:https://doi.org/10.48550/arXiv.2308.07407.

Zafar, F., Alam, L., Vivas, R., Wang, J., See, J. W., Mehmood, S., Sadeghzadegan, A., Lakkimsetti, M., & Nazir, Z. (2024). The role of Artificial Intelligence in identifying depression and anxiety: A comprehensive literature review. *Cureus, 16*, e56472. https://doi.org/10.7759/cureus.56472

CHAPTER 3

Responsible AI. Balancing Innovation with Ethical Considerations

Tetiana Klymchuk

Introduction

Artificial Intelligence is no longer a distant futuristic concept—it's already here, embedded in our daily lives. From social media feeds to banking, healthcare, and transport systems, AI technologies are shaping the way we live and work. This widespread use brings undeniable benefits, but it also introduces real risks and ethical challenges. And those risks are not theoretical. One can explore more than 3000 documented cases of AI-related harm at incident database (AIID, 2024)—a public platform where people report actual damage caused by AI systems. These cases range from biased models and flawed assumptions to decisions made without sufficient expertise or oversight, often resulting in dangerously wrong outputs.

T. Klymchuk (✉)
Somia Solutions, Universitat Internacional de Catalunya (UIC), Barcelona, Spain
e-mail: tklymchuk@uic.es

M. Bosch (ed.), *Crucial Ethical Keys of Artificial Intelligence*,
https://doi.org/10.1007/978-3-032-22853-6_3

While the idea of AI harm is easy to grasp intuitively, understanding how it arises, how to prevent it, and how to define what counts as "safe" or "responsible" AI is far from straightforward.

That's where the concept of "Responsible AI" comes in. It has emerged as a way to guide the development and use of AI technologies so that they align with human values, avoid harm, and earn public trust. But although it may sound clear in theory, in practice, especially when it comes to Generative AI, it's not always obvious what Responsible AI looks like or how to implement it.

This chapter aims to bring some clarity to that question. It focuses specifically on the use of Generative AI in organizations, explores what Responsible AI means in this context, why it matters, and presents a practical framework for monitoring and validating these systems. The goal is to provide a grounded and accessible perspective for professionals and decision-makers who may not be AI experts but who need to navigate its growing role in their work and in society.

This chapter is structured as follows: Section 1 introduces the concept of Responsible AI and its core principles. Section 2 presents real-world examples of AI failures and misuse, highlighting the need for ethical safeguards. Section 3 reviews current AI implementation methodologies, distinguishing between classical and generative approaches. Section 4 applies Responsible AI principles to both types, emphasizing the unique governance challenges of Generative AI. Finally, Section 5 presents a practical Responsible AI Framework, illustrated through an implementation example from the Somia Platform (Somia Platform, 2024).

Responsible AI Definition and Principles

Responsible AI refers to the design, development, and deployment of artificial intelligence systems in a manner that adheres to fundamental ethical, legal, and societal standards. It is a commitment to ensuring AI technologies are used for the benefit of individuals, communities, and the environment, rather than causing inadvertent harm. In practical terms, this means AI systems must comply with established legal, ethical, and scientific norms and operate with risks proportionate to their intended benefits.

Responsible AI is not merely a vague ideal. As Ricardo Baeza-Yates puts it, "Responsible AI isn't a buzzword. It's a commitment to making the world a better place", extending human notions of ethics and accountability to the institutions that create and deploy AI. In this sense, responsibility implies that those who build and use AI are answerable for its outcomes, ensuring the technology respects human rights, avoids unfair bias, and remains aligned with the public good (Baeza-Yates, 2023).

Multiple organizations and international bodies have proposed frameworks to define what Responsible AI entails. For example, the OECD's AI Principles emphasize inclusive growth and well-being, human rights and fairness, transparency and explainability, robustness and safety, and accountability in AI governance (OECD, 2019). The European Union's High-Level Expert Group on AI similarly outlined seven requirements for "Trustworthy AI", including human agency and oversight, technical robustness, privacy and data governance, transparency, fairness (avoidance of bias), societal and environmental well-being, and accountability (European Commission, 2019). The IEEE's Ethically Aligned Design initiative put forward principles such as respecting human rights, promoting well-being, ensuring data agency, effectiveness, transparency, accountability, awareness of misuse, and technical competence (IEEE, 2019).

Despite differences in terminology (e.g., "trustworthy AI" or "ethical AI"), these frameworks converge on a common set of values and criteria. They all seek to ensure that AI systems are developed and used in a manner that is fair, safe, and accountable to society. For the purposes of this chapter, we adopt the comprehensive framework articulated by the Association for Computing Machinery—ACM as the core structure for defining Responsible AI.

In 2022, ACM's Global Technology Policy Council released a seminal Statement on Principles for Responsible Algorithmic Systems, which lays out nine foundational principles intended to foster fair, accurate, and beneficial AI-driven decision-making (ACM, 2022). These principles, authored jointly by ACM's US and European policy committees, with lead authors including Ricardo Baeza-Yates, collectively define the key dimensions of "responsibility" in AI systems. They are:

- *Legitimacy and Competence:* Responsible AI must be built and deployed by qualified professionals with the proper authority, technical expertise, and ethical awareness. Systems should address real societal needs without violating rights and be grounded in solid scientific methods. Legal and ethical assessments must ensure that risks are proportional to the system's intended benefits.

- *Minimizing Harm:* AI systems should be designed to prevent harm to individuals and society. Developers must assess and mitigate potential risks, such as bias, discrimination, or unsafe behavior, throughout the system's life cycle. Harm minimization also includes monitoring real-world outcomes and updating the system when needed.
- *Security and Privacy:* AI must be protected against misuse, attacks, and unauthorized access. Strong data security measures (e.g., encryption, access control) should be in place, alongside privacy safeguards like data minimization and user consent. Responsible AI respects personal data and complies with relevant regulations.
- *Transparency:* Transparency requires documenting how the system works: data sources, algorithms used, evaluation methods, and known limitations. For critical applications, transparency also includes confidence levels, bias checks, and potentially enabling third-party audits. The aim is to avoid "black box" systems.
- *Explainability (Interpretability):* Beyond transparency, systems must provide meaningful, human-understandable explanations for their decisions, especially in sensitive domains like healthcare or finance. Users must understand why a decision was made and which factors influenced it. Explainability supports fairness, trust, and recourse.
- *Maintainability:* AI systems must be continuously maintained and updated. Changes in data or usage context may require retraining or redesign. Maintainability includes documentation, version control, and monitoring to ensure reliability and adaptability over time.
- *Contestability and Auditability:* AI decisions must be open to appeal. Individuals should have mechanisms to challenge outcomes they find harmful or incorrect. Simultaneously, systems must be auditable: decision-making logs and model versions should be retained to allow external review and accountability.
- Accountability and Responsibility: Responsibility for AI outcomes always remains with human actors and institutions. Organizations cannot delegate blame to the algorithm. Clear governance structures must identify who is responsible for compliance, oversight, and incident response.

– *Environmental Well-being:* AI systems, especially large models, consume significant energy. Developers should measure and minimize environmental impacts, balancing performance with sustainability. Responsible AI includes reducing emissions and resource use during training and deployment.

These nine principles from ACM (ACM, 2022) form the core conceptual definition of Responsible AI for this chapter. They ensure that an algorithmic system is legitimate in purpose, complies with laws, minimizes harm, protects privacy, operates transparently and explainably, remains reliable over time, allows oversight, retains clear human accountability, and supports environmental sustainability.

Difference Between Responsible AI and Trustworthy AI

There is often confusion between three similar but different concepts that are commonly used together. The term Responsible AI is often used alongside phrases like Ethical AI and Trustworthy AI, yet they are not interchangeable. While all three aim to ensure that artificial intelligence aligns with societal values and serves the public good, their conceptual focus is not the same and should be clearly distinguished.

Ethical AI typically implies that an AI system can act in accordance with moral principles. However, current AI systems lack agency and intentionality and therefore cannot truly be ethical in themselves (Boddington, 2017; Mittelstadt et al., 2016). Ethical behavior is a human prerogative; AI systems can follow rules encoded by humans but cannot themselves possess ethical intent. Describing AI as "ethical" can obscure this reality and anthropomorphize technology misleadingly.

Trustworthy AI, popularized especially within European policy frameworks (European Commission, 2019), suggests AI that can be relied upon to behave predictably and safely. However, trust is a social and psychological construct earned over time through dependable behavior (O'Neill, 2002). Branding AI as inherently "trustworthy" may imply an unjustified assumption of reliability, potentially overlooking limitations and risks. It also risks anthropomorphizing machines by suggesting they can hold or reciprocate trust (Floridi & Cowls, 2019).

Responsible AI, in contrast, anchors responsibility in the human domain. It focuses on the obligation of those who develop, deploy, and oversee AI systems to ensure that these technologies operate in lawful, ethical, and socially beneficial ways (Baeza-Yates, 2023; Binns, 2018). Responsible AI thus serves as an umbrella concept encompassing risk mitigation, fairness, legal compliance, transparency, and governance (ACM, 2022). It implies not only intentions but also structures for accountability, clear ownership of design decisions, error handling, and redress mechanisms.

Examples of Responsible AI Failures

Understanding why Responsible AI principles matter becomes much clearer when we examine what happens in their absence. While AI often promises efficiency or innovation, systems deployed without proper oversight can behave unpredictably, unfairly, or even dangerously. The risks aren't uniform: they range from the laughable to the tragic. But each case reveals the same core flaw: a failure to anticipate and mitigate the consequences of design decisions, biased data, or misaligned objectives.

A widely publicized case in 2017 illustrated how even seemingly simple autonomous systems can fail when exposed to real-world conditions not accounted for during development. A security robot deployed in Washington, D.C., drove itself directly into a public fountain. This was not due to a mechanical malfunction or malicious interference, but to a blind spot in its training data: the robot had not been exposed to sloped or uneven terrain during testing. As a result, it simply followed its learned navigation policy, straight into the water (Independent, 2017). While no harm occurred, the incident is a literal example of what can go wrong when an AI system is released into an uncontrolled environment without comprehensive validation.

In other cases, the consequences have been fatal. In 2019, a Tesla car operating in Autopilot mode collided with a white semi-truck crossing its path, resulting in the driver's death. Post-incident investigation revealed that the system had not been adequately trained to detect cross-traffic scenarios of this nature, particularly involving light-colored trucks against bright skies. Once again, the system did not fail in the technical sense; it behaved exactly as it was designed to. What failed was the assumption that a high-performing system in common scenarios would generalize reliably to rare but critical ones (The Washington Post, 2023).

Beyond physical safety, many failures involve *misgeneralization*, when systems learning patterns that correlate statistically in training data but are irrelevant or harmful in practice. A neural network trained to recognize the fish species tench frequently misidentified human fingers as part of the fish, simply because most training images included fishermen holding their catch (AI Weirdness, 2020). While amusing, the example reveals a broader truth: AI models do not "understand" objects, they associate features based on co-occurrence patterns.

This same issue underpins more harmful failures. In 2015, Amazon abandoned an internal AI-based hiring tool after discovering that it systematically penalized résumés containing terms associated with women. The model had been trained on historical data from a male-dominated industry, and it reproduced those patterns, favoring male applicants without any explicit instruction to do so (Inc., 2018). The system's bias was not a technical bug but a reflection of the data it had been given, and the lack of bias mitigation in its design. Such examples illustrate how biased data, if left unchecked, can perpetuate and even amplify structural discrimination.

In some cases, the ethical concerns extend beyond bias into the realm of problematic intent. In 2020, researchers from Harrisburg University claimed to have developed a model that could predict criminality from facial features. That same year, Stanford researchers presented a system for predicting sexual orientation from dating profile images. Both studies were widely condemned for reviving discredited pseudoscientific ideas, lacking social value, and posing risks of misuse, especially by oppressive regimes or surveillance-driven states (BBC News, 2020; The Washington Post, 2017). These cases raise a fundamental question that every AI initiative should confront: not just can it be built, but should it be?

Perhaps the most alarming failure to date occurred not in industry or research, but in public administration. In the Netherlands, a government algorithm used to detect childcare benefit fraud falsely labeled over 20,000 families, many of immigrant or low-income backgrounds, as fraudulent claimants. The consequences included financial ruin, family separations, and emotional trauma. Ultimately, the scandal led to the resignation of the Dutch Prime Minister and his cabinet. The model lacked transparency, accountability, and fairness, violating multiple principles of Responsible AI and demonstrating the high societal cost of irresponsible automation (The New York Times, 2021).

These examples reflect a shared pattern: AI systems behave as they are trained and instructed, without intrinsic understanding or moral reasoning. When the training data is biased, the objectives misaligned, or governance absent, the systems will reproduce those flaws at scale. AI does not possess ethical intent. It does not know when it is harming someone. Any semblance of fairness, safety, or responsibility must be intentionally encoded and monitored by humans. This is why Responsible AI is not a rhetorical ideal but a functional necessity. The question is not whether AI can fail; it already has. The real question is whether we are prepared to learn from those failures and build better systems going forward.

Current State AI Implementation

Difference Between Classic AI and Generative AI

In recent years, terms like Artificial Intelligence (AI), Machine Learning (ML), Deep Learning (DL), and Large Language Models (LLMs) have become widespread, but are often confused or used interchangeably. To understand the power and risks of modern AI, it's essential to clarify what these terms really mean, and how they relate to each other.

Traditional AI refers to systems that follow explicit rules programmed by humans. Imagine trying to detect if an image shows a dog: in rule-based AI, developers write a list of characteristics, like "pointy ears" or "whiskers", and the system checks whether these are present. If enough features match, it labels the image as a dog. This type of AI is fully explainable: the system does exactly what it was told. But it cannot adapt or learn. If it misclassifies an image, someone must manually change the rules. Rule-based AI powered early chess engines, thermostats, and expert systems, but it fails when problems become too complex or when rules can't be easily defined (Russell & Norvig, 2010).

ML systems learn from data instead of rules. We give them many examples (e.g., labeled images of dogs and cats), and the algorithm finds patterns that let it classify new, unseen images. Developers control how the model learns, but not the exact rules it creates. For instance, an ML model may learn that rounder faces are often cats and longer noses are common in dogs. We don't tell it those rules, it discovers them on its own by analyzing the data. The more examples we provide, the better it gets. Algorithms like decision trees or XGBoost are commonly used (Mitchell, 1997). ML is used in credit scoring, spam filtering, and recommendation systems. It's far more flexible than rule-based AI, but as the models grow, they become harder to interpret. We can't always explain why a specific prediction was made.

Deep Learning is a powerful subtype of ML that uses neural networks with many layers. The key difference: DL models don't need feature extraction. Continuing the dog example: with ML, developers still need to pre-process images, maybe by highlighting edges, shapes, or textures. In contrast, a DL model takes raw pixels as input and automatically learns which features matter. It figures out on its own what makes a dog look like a dog, without human-designed shortcuts. This is what powers facial recognition, self-driving cars, and language tools. But DL comes at a cost: it's much harder to interpret. We know what goes in and what comes out, but the reasoning in between often remains opaque, hence the term "black box" (LeCun et al., 2015).

LLMs are deep learning models trained on billions of words. They predict the next word in a sentence, like a supercharged version of smartphone autocomplete. By doing this repeatedly, they can write essays, answer questions, or even generate code. But LLMs do not "understand" the text, they generate it based on patterns they've seen during training. They've been called "stochastic parrots" because they repeat learned structures without real understanding (Bender et al., 2021).

Generative AI refers to systems that can create new content: text, images, music, even video. LLMs are a type of generative AI; they generate language. But generative AI is broader and includes image models like DALL·E or Stable Diffusion. Unlike traditional AI, generative models don't follow human-written rules. And unlike standard ML, their goal is not to classify but to generate new things that resemble what they've seen. For example, a generative model can produce a completely new image of a human face that doesn't exist but looks realistic.

A common way these systems work is through decoder-based architectures. Imagine teaching a model to draw faces: first, it learns what a face looks like (during training), and then it starts from random noise, like static on a screen, and gradually "draws" a realistic face from that noise (Ho et al., 2020). The system learns to reverse a process of adding noise. During generation, it starts with noise and removes it step by step, eventually producing a photo-realistic image. No one controls this process directly; it's learned from data and runs autonomously. But how do these systems work inside? Here's the hard truth: we don't fully know. Even the people who build these models can't precisely say what each neuron does. Some research has shown that certain neurons activate for specific concepts, like a neuron in a vision model firing when it "sees" a window or a chair (Bau et al., 2018). But most neurons are polysemantic, they do many things depending on context. We don't have a map of what each part of the network is doing. This makes interpretability a major unsolved problem in AI today (Olah et al., 2020). This lack of transparency means we cannot predict or fully explain why a generative model produces a specific result. It learns on its own, creates on its own, and even surprises its creators.

Applying Responsible AI Principles to Generative AI Systems
While the nine Responsible AI principles proposed by the ACM (ACM, 2022) may seem intuitive at first glance, their real-world application varies significantly depending on the type of AI system, and who is using it. These principles take on very different meanings for classical Machine Learning versus Generative AI. And even within Generative AI, there's a crucial distinction:

- A small number of actors train foundation models from scratch.
- But most companies (over 90%) simply use existing LLMs (via API or open-source models), sometimes fine-tuning or integrating them into tools and workflows.

We focus specifically on that companies that use GenAI, not those building the models themselves. We aim to clarify how each principle of Responsible AI should be interpreted and applied by organizations adopting GenAI as a tool, whether through prompt engineering, Retrieval-Augmented Generation (RAG), or lightweight fine-tuning.

We'll briefly contrast each principle's meaning in traditional Machine Learning, where models are often trained in-house on domain-specific data, but the emphasis will always be on the practical implications for GenAI adoption.

Legitimacy and Competency
Responsible AI begins with a simple question: Is the system being used by the right people, for the right reasons, in the right way? This is the essence of legitimacy and competency, and it applies very differently to classical AI systems versus Generative AI tools.

In traditional AI, companies often use simpler systems like calculators for predictions: for example, to estimate credit scores, forecast sales, or sort emails as spam or not spam. These models are built using data from the company's own history (customer records, transactions, past behaviors). They are relatively easy to understand, and companies know how and why they work. But even these systems can become problematic if used carelessly. For instance, a tool that worked well on last year's customer data might give misleading results if the market changes, or if it's used on a completely different group of people. Just because something worked once doesn't mean it will always work.

So, in classical AI, being legitimate means applying the system in the right context, and being competent means understanding how it works and where it can fail.

With Generative AI tools, like ChatGPT or other large language models, the situation changes completely. Most companies don't build these systems from scratch. Instead, they connect to existing models through APIs, use open-source versions, or lightly customize them. These tools generate text, code, summaries, or ideas based on massive training data, but users don't get to see how they were trained or what data was used. This makes it impossible to judge legitimacy based on how the model was built. Instead, we must judge how it's used. If a company uses a generative assistant to answer medical questions, draft legal advice, or interact with customers, the key questions are:

Is the use appropriate and safe for this setting?

Are the users trained to interpret and verify what the model says?

Generative AI can sound smart, but it doesn't think or know in a human sense. For example, it might get basic math right, but fail at more complex problems because it's just predicting text based on patterns, not doing real calculations.

Let's run a simple experiment. Imagine a conference room where everyone is asked to multiply two random five-digit numbers, using ChatGPT. With 99% certainty, at least two people will get different answers, even though they used the same AI tool. Why? Because large language models don't actually calculate, they generate text based on patterns seen in training. A 2024 study showed that transformer-based models, like the ones behind most generative AI systems, perform poorly on multi-digit multiplication. They often produce confident but incorrect answers, especially as the numbers get larger, due to a lack of true reasoning and carryover logic (Qiu et al., 2024).

What seems like intelligence is often just patterned guesswork. Without human oversight, even basic tasks can lead to inconsistent or wrong results.

Minimizing Harm

No organization deploying artificial intelligence would openly claim an objective to cause harm or promote irresponsible behavior. Yet, in the absence of systematic oversight and contextual safeguards, unintended harm can easily emerge.

In classical AI, harm often comes from applying models in the wrong context. Even simple models, like those used in credit scoring or hiring, can produce unfair or biased results if they reflect historical inequalities. For example, the COMPAS risk assessment tool (COMPAS, 2021) used in U.S. courts was found to disproportionately label Black defendants as high-risk, despite being technically accurate. This shows that accuracy isn't enough: minimizing harm means understanding who might be affected and why.

Generative AI introduces new kinds of risks. These models don't just make predictions, they generate language, summaries, and recommendations that feel human. But they don't "understand" meaning or ethics. For instance, a model summarizing employee performance might seem harmless, but could accidentally expose sensitive comparisons that damage trust or morale. What's harmful depends on the setting: the same answer might be fine in one context but inappropriate in another. That's why generic filters or one-size-fits-all safety tools are not enough. To truly minimize harm, organizations using GenAI must define context-specific risks, monitor outputs, and involve humans in sensitive decisions. Harm prevention isn't automatic, it requires active oversight, clear guidelines, and a deep understanding of how AI outputs affect real people.

Security and Privacy

Classical AI models, like those used for fraud detection or customer scoring, can be manipulated if attackers know how they work. For example, someone might slightly alter inputs to trick a system into approving a suspicious transaction. Attackers can also poison training data, like submitting fake product reviews to influence a recommender system.

Even though these models don't generate free text, they still handle personal data. If a model is trained on sensitive information, like medical records or financial details, it must be protected. Companies should avoid uploading private data to external services unless they're sure it's handled securely. And while classical models usually don't "leak" data like LLMs, research shows that attackers can sometimes guess who was in the training set just by analyzing outputs.

Generative AI introduces entirely new security threats. One of the most dangerous is prompt injection: if a model is connected to a tool or database, an attacker could write a prompt that tricks it into executing harmful commands, like "DROP TABLE users;" which could erase an entire customer database. There are already real-world cases of this happening when systems lacked safeguards.

On the privacy side, tools like RAG (Retrieval-Augmented Generation) pull from internal documents to improve AI answers. But if connected to external APIs, repeated queries might leak full documents, sentence by sentence, to third parties, including confidential research or contracts.

In some cases, companies have reported accidental exposure of sensitive or unpublished materials through LLMs, raising legal and ethical alarms.

And sometimes the risk comes directly from the user. A person might paste personal or regulated information into a prompt, not realizing it gets sent to a third-party provider. If that provider stores or logs data, the company could be in violation of privacy laws like GDPR.

Transparency

Transparency means understanding how an AI system works: what data it was trained on, how it makes decisions, and how its outputs should be interpreted. In classical AI, this is often possible; many traditional models are simple enough that their rules can be shared, tested, and explained. For example, in a classical model used for loan approval, it's possible to show exactly which factors, like income or credit history, led to a decision. And if someone else runs the same model with the same data, they'll get the same result. That kind of predictable, open logic builds trust.

But with Generative AI, transparency becomes much harder. Popular tools like ChatGPT are used through APIs, and users have no visibility into how the models were trained, what data was used, or why a certain response was generated. Even when models are open-source, their massive size and randomness mean that two identical prompts can lead to different answers. This lack of visibility makes it difficult to verify facts, explain errors, or reproduce outcomes. Without transparency, trust and accountability suffer, especially when these systems are used in sensitive areas like hiring, education, or law.

Interpretability and Explainability

Interpretability and Explainability is about understanding why an AI system made a specific decision or generated a certain output. In classical AI, this is often achievable. For example, if a model denies a loan, it's usually possible to trace that decision back to clear factors, like income or credit history, and explain the outcome in human terms. These models often behave like flowcharts or equations, and their logic can be shown, tested, and understood. This makes them ideal in regulated environments like finance or healthcare, where decisions must be justified to users or auditors.

With generative AI, however, explainability is a much bigger challenge. These systems don't follow step-by-step rules, they generate text based on billions of hidden patterns learned from massive datasets. When ChatGPT writes an answer, we can't point to a specific rule or input that caused it. The same question may even produce different results at different times. Even researchers can't fully explain what's happening inside these models. Tools like attention maps or token highlights give some insight, but not in a way that supports reliable, human-level explanations. So when something goes wrong, like a biased answer or incorrect output, it's very difficult to trace the cause or fix it systematically.

This "black box" nature creates serious limitations for accountability: Generative AI asks for trust without always offering reasons. If we don't know why the AI responded a certain way, we can't confidently explain, audit, or challenge its behavior, especially in high-stakes contexts.

Maintainability

Maintainability is essential for all AI systems, regardless of how simple or advanced they are. It ensures that a model stays accurate, safe, and aligned with real-world needs over time. Without it, even the best-designed systems can become unreliable or harmful. Classical AI models, like decision trees or regression algorithms, are typically more stable and predictable. Once deployed, they often work reliably for long periods, especially when the environment doesn't change much. But the world does change. Data drifts, user behavior evolves, and regulations shift. A model trained on last year's information might give the wrong answers today. That's why responsible organizations:

- Regularly monitor model performance,

- Retrain with updated data when needed,
- Keep clear documentation of model versions and changes.

For generative AI systems, maintainability is even more critical, and much harder to get right. These models generate language, code, or decisions based on vast, historical datasets. But those datasets age quickly. What was acceptable two years ago might now be offensive, inaccurate, or legally risky. And since these systems produce different outputs from the same input, keeping them aligned over time is a moving target. Despite their power, we still don't fully know how to maintain generative models responsibly. Continuous validation, output monitoring, and human review are essential, but there's no standard playbook. RAG systems, prompt libraries, and fine-tuned models all need tailored maintenance plans, and most organizations are still learning as they go. A generative AI assistant that is not maintained is not responsible. Maintainability is the bridge between safe design and sustained trust.

Organizations must treat maintenance not as an afterthought, but as an ongoing duty. Without it, generative AI can quickly drift into error, bias, or reputational risk, no matter how good it seemed at launch.

Contestability and Auditability

Being able to question and verify AI decisions is essential in both classical and generative systems. Without this, errors go uncorrected, biases stay hidden, and users lose trust.

Classical AI systems are usually deterministic, and they give the same result every time for the same input. This makes it easier to:

- Reproduce decisions,
- Identify causes,
- And respond to challenges (e.g., a denied loan due to outdated data).

Contestability is often supported by explainability. If a model's logic is transparent, users and regulators can trace how and why a decision was made. Many laws, such as the GDPR, require this level of clarity. Auditability also comes naturally to classical AI. Since these models don't change with each interaction, organizations can log decisions, test for bias, and compare new versions reliably. This stability allows for consistent oversight and well-documented correction processes when needed.

Generative AI assistants produce smooth, confident answers, but that fluency can be misleading. These systems don't retrieve facts; they generate text based on probabilities. Ask the same question twice, and you might get two different answers, both plausible, neither traceable.

- This unpredictability makes contestability extremely difficult:
- There's no clear logic chain to examine,
- No guaranteed reproducibility,
- And no built-in explanation of why a certain response was generated.

Even auditability is challenging. Organizations must actively build tools to:

- Track model versions and changes,
- Log outputs and failures,
- Flag hallucinations or harmful content,
- And benchmark responses against ground truth data.

Some tools can help, but they're still evolving. In many cases, users can't tell whether an answer is trustworthy, nor easily escalate or appeal.

Limiting Environmental Impacts

Environmental sustainability is an essential but often overlooked aspect of Responsible AI. While classical AI systems have a much smaller carbon footprint than generative models, both require conscious design choices to avoid unnecessary resource use. Classical AI models, like decision trees or logistic regression, are relatively lightweight. They can usually be trained quickly on standard CPUs and require little energy during prediction. This makes them suitable for low-power devices and large-scale deployment. But at scale, even small inefficiencies add up. For example, scoring millions of data points per hour in a live system can consume significant energy. For this reason, complex classical models (e.g., large ensembles) or repeated hyperparameter tuning can still generate non-trivial compute loads.

In case of Generative AI, particularly large language models, it has a massive environmental footprint, both during training and inference:

- *Training emissions are staggering:* GPT-3 consumed about 1287 MWh and emitted over 550 tons of CO_2, equivalent to powering 130 homes for a year or hundreds of transatlantic flights. Meta's LLaMA 3 training emitted ~1000 tons of CO_2 and consumed ~2.6 million kWh.
- *Inference isn't free:* Each AI response draws power, especially when long context windows (8 k–32 k tokens) are used. For example, generating a single 500-word response with a 70B model can consume ~0.017 kWh, which scales dramatically in enterprise use.
- *Model size matters:* Deploying smaller, fine-tuned models, or distilled versions, can significantly reduce emissions while maintaining performance. Generative AI must evolve from a mindset of "bigger is better" to one of sustainable, purposeful deployment. Today, we don't yet have standardized best practices for measuring and managing its environmental impact, but we urgently need them.

Responsible AI Framework for Generative AI

As discussed in the previous sections, each principle of Responsible AI takes on unique operational meaning in the context of Generative AI. This is especially important for companies, because:

- *Adoption will be near-universal:* Practically every organization will seek to implement Generative AI in some way.
- *Most companies are not AI-ready:* They lack the infrastructure, oversight, and maturity to deploy such systems responsibly.
- *Responsibility cannot be delegated:* Once a company integrates Generative AI, regardless of whether the model was developed in-house or accessed via API, it becomes fully accountable for the model's outputs.

We must emphasize: Companies do not know what the model truly "knows" or how it generates responses. This makes it extremely difficult to verify, in an automated fashion, whether a solution complies with the nine principles of Responsible AI. Recent research shows that even core risks like hallucinations are currently impossible to detect reliably and automatically (Karbasi et al., 2025). This means that responsibility lies not only in model choice, but in how the system is governed after deployment. Companies need a robust framework to define, monitor, and validate the behavior of their Generative AI systems.

Practical Framework Example

Imagine a company, X, selling product Y. It decides to deploy a Generative AI chatbot for customer support. If the company connects directly to ChatGPT via API:

- It must send internal business data about the product or unique marketing strategy to a third-party model, raising privacy and IP risks.
- It must create a validation set, a list of representative questions and expected outputs, to evaluate the system.
- Every time the model version changes (e.g., GPT-4 to GPT-4o), the company must re-run its validation to confirm that outputs are still acceptable.
- If the company has custom policies (e.g., never mention competitors or never compare product Y to others), these rules must be enforced via prompt engineering, but every prompt change also requires re-evaluation.
- Also, the company could want to check more general checks (no personal data leakage, politeness, or question statistics (what people actually asking).

To address this need, we suggest exploring Somia Platform (Somia Platform, 2024) implementation of its Responsible AI framework for continuous validation and governance of AI agents using Generative AI. The framework allows to define conversation flows, data integrations, and sources of the information. For example, the chatbot begins by receiving the user query through the Interface Module. It then categorizes the inquiry, determining whether it's a product question, a complaint, a return request, or something else. Based on this classification, the assistant can:

- Provide a general response using a predefined prompt,
- Search for the answer in a specific internal database,

– Or ask clarifying questions if the input is too vague or falls outside the expected logic.

The key advantage is that this entire flow is defined and customized by the company itself, reflecting its specific customer experience goals, tone, and operational needs. Rather than relying on a one-size-fits-all model behavior, the logic is purpose-built by the user and governed according to their rules, ensuring both relevance and responsibility.

The framework also allows to define the validation criteria, the specific rules the assistant must follow. These include both positive behaviors (e.g., always respond politely, avoid leaking personal data) and prohibited actions (e.g., never compare Product Y to competitors). These criteria are created and managed directly within the Responsible AI Framework. Importantly, criteria can be reused across different agents or shared within the organization, ensuring consistency and alignment with internal policies and brand standards.

To evaluate the assistant's real-world behavior, the user uploads a validation set, a curated list of representative customer questions along with the expected or acceptable responses. These examples define what "high-quality output" looks like for the organization. For instance, if a customer asks, "How do I return a damaged item?", the assistant should provide a clear and accurate return policy, including contact steps. If asked, "Is your product better than (competitor)?", the assistant should follow the predefined rule: avoid direct comparisons and redirect the answer to the unique strengths of Product Y. For sensitive queries like "What personal data do you collect?", the assistant should respond with polite, GDPR-compliant language. The validation set becomes the baseline for automated evaluation, ensuring that every model version is tested against real expectations before going live.

The final step is to create an evaluator profile, a reusable configuration that combines the validation set and the defined criteria. This profile acts as the blueprint for automated testing: it specifies what should be tested (the questions) and how it should be evaluated (the rules or expectations). Evaluator profiles can be reused across different model versions, shared across teams, or customized for different departments or use cases (e.g., sales, support, HR).

Once these steps are completed, the platform runs an automated evaluation, testing the assistant's outputs against all defined criteria. It returns:

- A score and explanation for each test case,
- Aggregated metrics for overall performance,
- And detailed logs that allow for human review and iterative improvements.

Every time the model version or the prompt logic is updated, the same evaluation process can be repeated, ensuring the assistant continues to meet expectations, across accuracy, ethics, and user experience.

Conclusion

At present, no one has fully figured out how to implement Responsible AI correctly, at least not in a way that is both scalable and aligned with real-world generative systems. The AI we are working with today is arguably the least capable we will ever encounter. From this point forward, models will only become more powerful, more integrated, and more central to business and societal processes. This exponential growth brings not only opportunities but also heightened responsibilities. If AI is destined to become the core of every process, we must invest now in tools, frameworks, and practices that help us govern it responsibly. Managing risk cannot be separated from managing progress. The only way forward is to develop AI hand-in-hand with systems that make its impact observable, measurable, and correctable, because only then can we truly call it *responsible*.

References

ACM. (2022). Statement on principles for responsible algorithmic systems. ACM Global Technology Policy Council, October 2022.

AIID. (2024). AI incident database. https://incidentdatabase.ai/

Baeza-Yates, R. (2023). Introduction to responsible AI. *European Review, 31*(4), 406–421.

Bau, D., Zhou, B., Khosla, A., Oliva, A., & Torralba, A. (2018). Network dissection: Quantifying interpretability of deep visual representations. In *Proceedings of the IEEE Conference on Computer Vision and Pattern Recognition* (pp. 3319–3327).

BBC News. (2020). https://www.bbc.com/news/technology-53165286.

Bender, E. M., Gebru, T., et al. (2021). On the dangers of stochastic parrots: Can language models be too big? In *Proceedings of the 2021 ACM conference on fairness, accountability, and transparency (FAccT '21)* (pp. 610–623).

Binns, R. (2018). Fairness in machine learning: Lessons from political philosophy. Proceedings of the 2018 Conference on Fairness, Accountability and Transparency. *Journal of Machine Learning Research, 81*, 1–11.

Boddington, P. (2017). *Towards a code of ethics for artificial intelligence*. Springer.

European Commission. (2019). *Ethics guidelines for trustworthy AI*. High-Level Expert Group on AI.

Floridi, L., & Cowls, J. (2019). A unified framework of five principles for AI in society. *Harvard Data Science Review, 1*(1).

Ho, J., Jain, A., & Abbeel, P. (2020). Denoising diffusion probabilistic models. In *Advances in neural information processing systems 33 (NeurIPS 2020)* (pp. 6840–6851).

IEEE. (2019). Ethically aligned design: A vision for prioritizing human well-being with autonomous and intelligent systems.

Inc. (2018). https://www.inc.com/guadalupe-gonzalez/amazon-artificial-intelligence-ai-hiring-tool-hr.html

Independent. (2017). https://www.independent.co.uk/news/world/americas/suicidal-robot-did-not-kill-itself-fountain-accident-loose-brick-surface-a7866856.html

Amin Karbasi, Omar Montasser, John Sous, Grigoris Velegkas, (2025) *(Im)possibility of automated hallucination detection in large language models*. https://arxiv.org/abs/2504.17004.

LeCun, Y., Bengio, Y., & Hinton, G. (2015). Deep learning. *Nature, 521*(7553), 436–444.

Mitchell, T. M. (1997). *Machine learning*. McGraw Hill.

Mittelstadt, B. D., Allo, P., Taddeo, M., Wachter, S., & Floridi, L. (2016). The ethics of algorithms: Mapping the debate. *Big Data & Society, 3*(2), 1–21.

O'Neill, O. (2002). *A question of trust*. Cambridge University Press.

OECD (2019). OECD AI principles.

Olah, C. et al. (2020). Zoom in: An introduction to circuits. Distill.

Somia Platform. (2024). www.somiasolutions.com

Luyu Qiu, Jianing Li, Chi Su, Chen Jason Zhang, Lei Chen. (2024) *Dissecting Multiplication in Transformers: Insights into LLMs*. https://arxiv.org/abs/2407.15360.

Russell, S. J., & Norvig, P. (2010). *Artificial intelligence: A modern approach*. Pearson.
The New York Times. (2021). https://www.nytimes.com/2021/01/15/world/europe/dutch-government-resignation-rutte-netherlands.html
The Washington Post. (2017). https://www.washingtonpost.com/news/morning-mix/wp/2017/09/12/researchers-use-facial-recognition-tools-to-predict-sexuality-lgbt-groups-arent-happy/
The Washington Post. (2023). https://www.washingtonpost.com/technology/interactive/2023/tesla-autopilot-crash-analysis/?itid=lk_inline_manual_17
AI Weirdness. (2020). https://www.aiweirdness.com/when-data-is-messy-20-07-03/

CHAPTER 4

Appropriateness: Ethics of AI and Its Impact on the Human Form of Life

Marcel Cano Soler

Introduction: Definition of Concepts

Technique, Technology, and Technoscience: Humans are Technical, Sometimes Technological, Beings Who Have Become Technoscientists

Humans have been subjected to the imperatives of biological evolution since they first appeared on the planet. Natural selection has determined the survival of our lineage, generating a specific form of adaptation. This particularity lies in the fact that our way of complying with biological evolutionary parameters involves the emergence of a new form of evolution: cultural evolution. Let us look at how this might have developed in a little more detail.

The process can be described as the conjunction of three elements: technical ability, self-awareness, and language, which generated two emergent properties in continuous feedback: human culture and individual linguistic self-awareness. The first of the three elements, the ability to use

M. Cano Soler (✉)
Neuroscience Program of Hospital del Mar Research Institute, Systems and Neurotherapies Group, Hospital del Mar Research Institute, Barcelona, Spain

M. Bosch (ed.), *Crucial Ethical Keys of Artificial Intelligence*,
https://doi.org/10.1007/978-3-032-22853-6_4

tools, is not unique to our species; it also exists in others with different evolutionary origins. Our closest relatives, chimpanzees and bonobos, use a wide range of tools (Sabater Pi, 1992), which suggests this was probably also the case with our last common ancestor (CHLCA). So where does the difference lie? Obviously, we turned what in other animals is a cultural complement for survival into the heart of our evolutionary development, opting to focus on technical production. Our survival improved, influencing natural selection processes, thanks to the enormous energy input generated by the capacity to exploit the environment. Moreover, this was not limited to material tools; it also included symbolic techniques essential for group cohesion (Geertz, 2005), strategic planning, and social and family organization. With this in mind, we can now examine two further points: firstly, the definition of technique; and secondly, self-awareness and language, the other two elements of cultural evolution.

We define technology as the capacity to materially and symbolically manipulate and transform what is available in the natural and social environment, with the aim of achieving proposed goals. Besides certain questions on the origin and cultural, etymological, and philosophical depths of the concept, technology—whether symbolic or material—implies rational, goal-based action. Such action requires a selection of means and resources, as well as the prioritization of the criteria for achieving the goals. Thus, this definition is inherent to the development of the human species from its beginnings, thus making it universal. We could say that we are a technical species, since technology holds the central and exclusive role necessary for the emergence of cultural evolution.

Continuing in this vein, it is important to emphasize that behind technology there necessarily lies rational thought. Since survival is the fundamental evolutionary imperative, instrumental rationality, in the form of hypothetical imperatives, directs technical production. The degree of development and sophistication of the technology this entails therefore requires a similar development in the species' degree of operational rationality. This, together with the enormous and growing supply of resources that its use *makes available*[1] to hominids, is accompanied by

[1] We deliberately use this Heideggerian term, taken from his work *The Question Concerning Technology* (Heidegger, 1994): modern technology, says Messkirch, *makes the world available as existence*, that is, as a "commodity". We fully agree with this idea, but, deep down, technology always makes the world available. Our evolution is proof of this,

a proportional increase in brain capacity and power. Here we have the first feedback effect: the brains most capable of technical production, being able to supply themselves with more resources, have greater chances of reproducing, being selected by biological evolution, and accelerating cultural evolution. We now have the foundations for the second of the three necessary elements mentioned above: self-awareness.

Although there are many different, even opposing, interpretations of self-awareness, we will focus here on one fundamental fact: establishing technology as an essential strategy of the species requires a sophisticated system that provides a rational understanding of the environment. In the case of our lineage, this is tied to self-awareness. Although other species can be described as self-aware, especially those that pass the Gallup test,[2] in humans, as mentioned above, the evolutionary process tended to select the appearance of brains that not only became larger, but also more complex.

However, before continuing, from the above discussion we may now define what we understand by technology, at least in relation to the first of the meanings we wish to assign to the concept. As its etymology indicates, technology is the application of rationality to technique. In line with the above explanation, the processes of neural and technical sophistication go hand in hand, so that these powerful brains can be devoted to improving technique. This is technology: the application of operational rationality to the improvement, sophistication, and development of technique (which, remember, can be material or symbolic, applied to the mastery of the natural environment or the modification of social environments). Thus technology, at least according to this first definition, consists of a recursive process in which rationality is applied to the conception, use, and extension of technology. At this point, and as will be seen with the second definition of technology, these objectives do not necessarily have to be rational in themselves. They may simply be associated with cultural processes. It is important to emphasize that, while initially the mandate

since it is technical capacity that allows us to survive by using everything around us for our benefit. Although, as we will see when discussing technoscience, it is true that this "modern technology" makes the world available in a different way, as "existences", i.e., as homogeneous and interchangeable products with the sole objective of monetizing reality.

[2] Despite the reasonable criticisms this test has received, it remains valid as evidence of the presence of a consciousness that knows itself, beyond mere sensory perception in interaction with the environment.

for survival sets in motion the technicity of the human species, later on, once such survival is sufficiently ensured, other drivers of technique and technology appear, drivers that we will call cultural.[3]

To sum up, biological evolution leads to cultural evolution. This is only possible through feedback between two fundamental emergent properties: individual self-awareness and the collective form of cultural organization. Three elements are necessary for this to occur, two of which we have already described: technical capacity or operational rationality and self-awareness itself. We are missing the third, the only one specific to humans and which functions as a catalyst for the aforementioned double emergence: language. Indeed, through complex processes of exaptation and genetic mutation, the human brain evolved into a complex linguistic mind. Parts of the brain shared with chimpanzees, such as Broca's and Wernicke's areas, are involved in the production and comprehension of language. This, together with genetic elements, such as the FOXP2 gene, and fundamental physiological transformations in the vocal apparatus, led to a new, specifically human form of communication: linguistic. Based on double articulation, the infinite possibilities of language open the door to the vastest social complexity known on the planet. Human societies do not develop solely on the basis of genetically encoded behaviors or vicarious learning. The explosion of complexity appears when these three elements—self-awareness, operational rationality, and language—interact, generating a universe where each individual acquires self-awareness, a consciousness that can only be developed within the group in which they are raised. In the words of Pascal Picq, the human being develops primarily in a "cultural womb" (Picq et al., 2009). Thus, as each individual is unique, the entire collective can act according to common cultural premises, without which such individual singularity would not be possible. This complex feedback, catalyzed by language, ceases to be a mere survival strategy and becomes a universe of meaning. We thus arrive at the essential core of this section: human beings live immersed in a symbolic-practical cultural framework that allows them to find that which is most precious: meaning. We do not refer here exclusively to the grand narratives of philosophy, religion, or even science, although, consciously or otherwise, they are present in the life of every human being. We essentially refer to everyday life, to that web of meaning that

[3] In line with what Ortega calls *Supernature* (Ortega y Gasset, 2002).

provides coherence to each person's life in any society and according to the parameters of any culture, each with its own worldview. The absolute vital necessity of this context[4] of meaning becomes evident in the most dramatic situations, such as the experience of the extermination camps recounted by Viktor Frankl in *Man's Search for Meaning* (Frankl, 2004): when this framework fails and mere survival looms, "dehumanization" emerges. This *supernature* (Ortega y Gasset, 2002), which cloaks human reality with a layer of meaning, is the fundamental framework that makes the human condition a habitable experience. Although it does not eliminate the pain, precariousness, or awareness of death inherent in a self-conscious linguistic being—i.e., one who knows themselves to be essentially vulnerable—it does offer a "narrative" in which to take refuge. The cultural narrative in which human experience is embedded is the core meaning of their experience of the world and of themselves. To the extent that it is cultural, or cosmic, it is necessarily social and collective, while also shaping all subjective experience. We are thus witnessing a transition from cultural organization, as a response to the need for survival, to cosmological organization, which responds to the need for meaning.

Let us turn to the final part of this section. We are now in a position to understand the remaining definitions: the second definition of technology and the second definition of technoscience. First, it should be noted that these two definitions, like the first definition of technique and the second definition of technology, are no longer universal. They are embedded in a worldview that arose during the historical process called Modernity and which culminated in the emergence of a new culture that still prevails today: capitalism.[5] If we look up the dictionary definition of technology, we find[6] a significant similarity across dictionaries in different languages: they all share a common element, whereby technology is always associated with industrial processes or the application of scientific knowledge to such processes. This already points to a highly relevant approximation to the current meaning of the term. By associating it closely to industrial processes, we no longer refer merely to its universal use as a recursive

[4] Context in the etymological sense of "fabric", "framework".

[5] We consider capitalism not only as an economic-political system but also as a culture, especially in the Wittgensteinian sense of "form of life".

[6] We have used the online versions of the following dictionaries: Royal Academy of the Spanish Language, Diccionari de l'Institut d'Estudis Catalans, Dictionnaire de l'Académie Française and Cambridge Dictionary.

process of reflection and improvement of technique, but as the application of such rationality to industry as we have known it since the Industrial Revolution. It is important to clarify that, from now on, when we use the term "industrial", we refer not only to the processes inherent to the various industrial revolutions, but also to the "spirit" of the form of life we call capitalism. This conception is specifically embedded in the capitalist worldview and, therefore, serves a specific purpose: the improvement and perfection of industrial production processes. Similarly, we can also define technoscience as the process by which scientific knowledge merges with technology in a process of inextricable feedback: in order to do science, it is necessary to increase the use and design of technology, but, at the same time, the applicability of technology to industrial processes defines technoscience.[7]

Technology, in the second sense, responds mainly to this impulse. However, the technological procedures applied for this purpose also have another objective, inseparable from the first: generating consumer products. Thus, technology today has a dual role, as it is not only embedded in production processes but has itself become an object of mass consumption. For this to occur, it must occupy a central place in people's lives, so central as to generate a ***data-driven economy***. The key difference is that, at its heart, this distinction is gradually fading, since by consuming technology we generate data, which, in turn, are the raw materials for the industrial processes of the Fourth Industrial Revolution. Ultimately, as consumers, we are products, seduced particularly by apps and programs designed to capture our attention, to keep us hooked on devices. This is because the data-driven economy requires ***an attention-based economy***: we are both the consumer and the consumed.

It is within this framework that new generations have grown and will grow up. Their world revolves around a technological universe whose goal is to capture their attention and generate data. The allure of this techno-scientific system is so great that it lies at the very heart of their existence, opening the door to numerous serious ethical problems that urgently need to be addressed. We will discuss this further below.

[7] An interesting analysis of this concept can be found in the work of Gilbert Hottois and Jean-Noël Missa, New Encyclopedia of Bioethics (Hottois & JN., 2005).

Morals and Ethics: Values, Culture, Society, and Rational Reflection

There are significant differences between ethics and morality. While perhaps being overly concise, we may say that morality is shared, social, and cultural. It establishes the norms required for group cohesion while simultaneously conditioning the collective's behaviors and values. On the other hand, ethics implies the possibility of reflecting and critically distancing ourselves from these moral norms, as well as seeking out their foundations and legitimacy. *Mutatis mutandis*, both are related to Daniel Kahneman's two types of thinking (Kahneman, 2012). Thus, as in fast thinking, morality can encompass everything from social and cultural prejudices to cognitive biases, including elements with a strong emotional charge. However, as in slow thinking, ethics requires the use of rationality to provide critical distance. To a large extent, it must also be grounded in individual autonomy and responsibility or, in certain circumstances, a degree of collective autonomy. We may say that morality encompasses much of the everyday worldview referred to above: what is "correct" and "normal" is what makes sense in the behavior of group members. When this normality is based on a process of naturalizing a certain use and production of technology that, as mentioned above, requires the data extraction in exchange for absorbing people's attention, we find ourselves facing a major ethical problem. As devices and programs, especially those using artificial intelligence—designed to hijack attention to generate monetizable data—become more sophisticated, we find entire populations of "digital natives" (and not just them) unable to look up from their screens. We also find this problem at increasingly younger ages. It is common to see very young children silently hypnotized by screens provided by their parents or close friends, often to keep them entertained. Several studies stress the need to control access to devices in children under six years of age, especially because of their impact on cognitive, linguistic, and emotional development, as indicated by the Spanish Association of Pediatrics (https://www.aeped.es/noticias/aep-actualiza-sus-recomendaciones-sobre-uso-pantallas-en-infancia-y-adolescencia).

From this perspective (the naturalization of unlimited and uncritical use of technological devices), we see how normalizing these habits can generate an alienated society subject to the designs of large corporations or totalitarian-leaning governments. The annulment of the capacity for critical reflection is a desideratum of all those who, throughout history, have sought to control populations and undermine their rights. With new technologies—most particularly with AI—this aspiration can become a reality. Such naturalization could generate a form of life centered on the monadic atomization of society, sanctioned by an extremely individualistic morality, that destroys social relations. If we consider the meaning of the concept of "form of life" in Wittgensteinian philosophy (Wittgenstein, 1988), we can better understand the scope of the danger discussed here. The concept refers to the configuration of moral and social rules that articulate what is valuable, good, and desirable regarding the unbridled use of technology. This paves the way to perceiving life through the screen, in the same way as the prisoners in Plato's cave observed projected shadows. The only truth is that which is contemplated through the mobile phone and manipulation is not perceived as such, since nothing outside the screen has credibility. Devices can thus be grafted onto human life to cultivate the fruits of alienation and solipsism. What is normal, and therefore correct, good, and desirable, is to fix one's gaze on the smartphone. The new matrix does not need to connect individuals with cables embedded in their bodies; the connection is wireless and, therefore, much easier to implement. Furthermore, just as in the classic film *Invasion of the Body Snatchers* (Siegel, 1956), its use spreads like an oil slick, as no one can escape it. Even government authorities close the door on analogue, while submitting to the dictates of the GAMAM,[8] generating two serious problems: first, the digital divide; and second, the need to use the apps they impose, further undermining consumer rights.[9]

This scenario can still be avoided, but it requires not only adequate legislation but also ethical implementation at all levels. From users to creators, ethics—as critical, autonomous, and rational thinking—is needed even more than legislation.

Is Technoscience Autonomous? Is It Neutral?

A major debate in the study of ethics and the philosophy of technology relates to two crucial aspects: its autonomy and its neutrality. Building on the previous section, the proceeding section tackles this issue.

[8] Google, Amazon, Meta Appel Microsoft.

[9] An example of this is the difficulty faced by many Linux users, who, at least in Spain, cannot access basic services such as digital signatures unless they complete the process through Microsoft and Google devices.

Let us begin with autonomy. Following the thought of Jacques Ellul (Ellul, 2003), first of all there is technique, not simply identifiable with the machine, but conceivable in two forms: the technical operation and the technical phenomenon. The former refers to what we defined above as technique, as well as the initial definition of technology. For Ellul, however, the technical phenomenon introduces a new perspective that, since the Industrial Revolution and incorporating quantification and efficiency, has led technique into a process of increasing autonomy, eliminating the capacity for human decision-making. According to the French author, the transition from one to the other occurs within the logic of the technical operation, which, from our understanding of technology in its first meaning, seeks the most efficient way to achieve its own objectives. This is where the technical phenomenon appears and expands throughout human reality, driven by the imperative of efficiency and guided by the specialist. This is achieved through three major areas in which the dominance of the technical phenomenon expands: economic technique, organizational technique, and human technique. Thus, the internal logic of technique obeys only itself, subjugating all social institutions, individuals, and specific sectors of society. Here, however, we must express our disagreement with the French author. According to the definitions provided in the first section, technique is universal, as is technology, understood as a reflection of technique. However, in its second definition, as technoscience, it is the product of a form of life, legitimized by a specific worldview, that arose with capitalism (as a culture and not a mere economic-political system). In Ellul's own terms, the transition from technical operation to technical phenomenon occurs through a profound cultural transformation and not solely through a change within technique itself. While stressing that this shift toward efficiency did indeed take place, what caused the metamorphosis in technology toward greater efficiency and quantification was not its own development but the production needs arising with the Industrial Revolution. A worldview emerged in which meaning, as defined in the first section, now focused on quantification, reification, monetization, labor, and chrematistics. This marks a process of global transformation in the conception of nature and of human beings themselves, centered on the economy,[10] in which technology is consequently transformed into technoscience. Following the

[10] Economics as chrematistics in the sense given to it by Aristotle in the first book of *Politics*.

path of Karl Polanyi (Polanyi, 2006) and leaving that of Jacques Ellul, the liberal movement that seeks to subject all society to market management drives technology to become technoscience servicing the needs of production and economic profit. In this way, the system that aspires to be autonomous[11] is the economic system, not the technical system. The logic that articulates our worldview, while incorporating technology at the heart of its imagination, is essentially one of accumulation in the form of economic wealth. As Alfred Crosby (Crosby, 1988) describes, at the end of the Middle Ages, the West shifted toward reducing reality to the quantifiable, expressed in the form of money. Driven by the pursuit of unlimited accumulation, all reality ends up falling into this process of quantification, and our current era marks the zenith of its splendor, through the aforementioned attention and data economies. In short, technoscience and the technologies it generates cannot be considered autonomous since, for several centuries, they have been dependent on the economic system, which aspires to being autonomous, without truly being able to, and dictating the rules of life. To a certain extent, the technical system intertwined with the economic system bears a certain resemblance to Mumford's megamachine (Mumford, 2017).

Given the above, can we claim that technology is neutral? Obviously, the answer must be no. Little else need be said on this question, since the old argument about "the neutrality of the knife"—that "it can be used to cut bread or to kill a person"—does not make sense, when viewed at a more profound level. Nevertheless, we shall briefly comment on it. A cutting tool belongs to the sphere of technologies essential to the human species, present even among the earliest hominids. Cutting, as a technical operation, is necessary for our food, building houses or making clothing, among many other operations essential to life. In this sense, the cutting instrument can clearly be used to take the life of another human being. But the creation of an AI does not respond to the same kind of universal need. Indeed, discourses that establish the history of technology as a linear process of continuous progress fundamentally fail to distinguish between one tool and another. In Stanley Kubrick's famous film, *2001: A Space Odyssey* (Kubrick, 1968), the transition from a bone in the hands of a hominid used to kill a fellow human being to the use of a spaceship is magnificently summarized in a scene of high aesthetic

[11] We say aspirational because in reality, as we will see, it does not completely annul human autonomy, although it greatly limits it.

and cinematic power, but with little value as an analysis of technology. The line is not direct; it is riddled with twists, turns, and transformations linked to cultural changes, transformations in forms of life, and the rules that articulate them. Thus, AI or computing, just like the internal combustion engine or nuclear power plants, responds to the parameters of our form of life and, consequently, their emergence responds to its needs. AI is not comparable to a knife as a tool, since its use encompasses a whole universe of meaning, while the cutting tool in turn responds to a universal need that, at times, can be used to kill.

In short, technology is neither autonomous nor neutral,[12] as it must be situated within the cultural framework and worldview in which it is generated and in which it causes decisive changes. This way of conceiving it highlights, firstly, the enormous complexity of our relationship with technology and, secondly, the fact that we are not dealing with a deterministic phenomenon over which we have no control. Technodeterminism often appears in the company of two contradictory but equally reductionist currents: techno-enthusiasm, which uncritically accepts everything technoscience has to offer, and technophobia, which irrationally rejects all technological proposals. Both positions are not only absurd but also dangerous: the former because it nullifies any critical reflection on technology; the latter because it throws the baby out with the bathwater, causing us to miss opportunities we have a duty to consider. Clearly, addressing technoscience requires ethical awareness on the part of all involved.

Responsibility of Creators and Users

The Creator's Perspective: Professional Ethics

There are four fundamental ethical dimensions in applied ethics. The first is civic or minimal ethics, as proposed by Adela Cortina (Cortina, 1986). Essentially based on human rights, it prevails in every democratic society and establishes the necessary requirements for coexistence, respect, and solidarity among fellow citizens. Its main objective is not to establish a model of the good life for all, but rather to generate the framework within

[12] As Melvin Kranzberg also indicated in the first of his principles on technology: it is neither good nor bad, but nor is it neutral (Kranzberg, n.d.).

which different conceptions of the good life can be harmonized and articulated. In this sense, it is characteristic of open and pluralistic societies in which people of different cultural backgrounds and values coexist. We may add that it should not only be limited, in a formal sense, to merely ensuring life projects are compatible; it must also consider the conditions that make such life projects possible. In this way, its mission is not only to ensure individual autonomy, but also that this can be realized by all. It is, therefore, an ethical mandate that every democratic society imposes upon itself, serving is the preliminary step and framework within which all policy should be developed. Thus, for example, the aforementioned digital divide represents an unacceptable fracture in terms of civic ethics.

Secondly, there are individual or maximal ethics. This considers the legitimacy of every person to pursue their life project based on their own conception of the good life, always within the framework of civic ethics. It is the individual who adheres to a personal ethical conception that they develop over the course of their life. Mutual coherence of the two ethical perspectives requires an interconnection that goes beyond the merely individual or collective. As the twentieth century and the first decades of the twenty-first century have dramatically taught us, unlimited development of one of the two extremes produces ethically unacceptable situations. Without the collective, the individual cannot exist, while the individual represents a multiplicity of life options that enriches and nourishes the collective with new opportunities.

The other two dimensions, which Begoña Román adds to the previous ones, are organizational ethics and professional ethics (Román, 2016). Organizational ethics seeks to involve organizations with their own ethical responsibility. This relates to their mission within society and how they frame their actions within civic ethics. In this sense, technology-creating companies should also fulfill the essential ethical commitment that binds them to their responsibility. However, this is not usually the case, and all too often we observe how the ethos of organizations becomes mere ethics washing. This is especially true of large corporations whose sole objective is profit-making. Thus, without ruling out the potentially positive impact of corporations truly embracing ethical principles in harmony with civic ethics, it is difficult to believe they will accept such limitations while their primary objective is still profit, unless required to do so by law. A restrictive law requires political commitments and well-established international legislation. While desirable, and recognizing positive steps taken in this direction,[13] this is beyond the scope of this paper, which is essentially an ethical perspective. Therefore, given its relevant ethical foundation, mention should be made, for example, of the Asilomar Conference and its 23 principles for the ethically responsible use of AI, the result of the "Asilomar Conference on Beneficial AI" in Asilomar, California (https://futureoflife.org/open-letter/ai-principles/).

The fourth dimension is professional ethics. Professionals' commitment to their own ethical principles is much stronger, especially among those in professional associations, governed by codes of ethics.[14] The ethical self-awareness of individual programmers and researchers can be significantly strengthened by such associations. We therefore argue that the first step in creating an AI, in particular, and a technoscience, in general, that respects the essential principles of civic ethics is to promote and disseminate professional ethics. As stated above, this might be possible through the creation of professional associations, but it could also be achieved by including ethics in the training of future generations of scientists and engineers. This should not be merely decorative and superficial; university curricula must include ethics both transversally, in all subjects wherever possible, and with specific courses on ethics throughout the curriculum. This, along with the promotion of professional associations, would have a valuable feedback effect: more conscientious professionals would create more codes of ethics, which, in turn, would contribute to greater ethical awareness.

[13] Proposals have been made by the EU, such as the European AI regulation (https://www.boe.es/buscar/doc.php?id=DOUE-L-2024-81079) and the OECD, which has established a group of experts on the subject (https://oecd.ai/en/about/network-of-experts). The problem is that the global race for AI hegemony, which is also the race for global economic and military hegemony, is hardly likely to comply with limiting guidelines, given the strategic importance of AI at all levels. The EU is a fragile island in this regard that, given its role in respecting human rights, must resist the challenge it currently faces. The short- and medium-term outlooks is not optimistic, but if the EU manages to stand firm against, above all, the USA and China, it may represent a credible alternative for solid international regulation.

[14] An example, the Code of Ethics for Computer Engineering: https://www.ccii.es/codigodeontologico

Complexity, Uncertainty, Ethics, and Technoscience (AI as a Paradigm)

In Funtowicz & Ravetz, 1993, Silvio O. Funtowicz and Jerome R. Ravetz published the article "Science for the Post-Normal Age" and the Spanish-language book *La ciencia postnormal. La ciencia con la gente*. In these works, the authors established the foundations for a new way of approaching technoscience with regard to the consequences and impacts of its development. Moving away from the "specialist paradigm"—i.e., someone capable of predicting the effects of the technology they develop and proposing appropriate solutions—they advocated for the need to incorporate the uncertainty and complexity inherent in new techno-scientific developments. To give an example: a mechanical engineer can determine the potential risks of an engine, since this technology matches a well-defined cause-effect model. However, when we talk about technologies such as AI, causal understanding and possible predictions are beyond the grasp of specialists. We are referring here, firstly, to the "black box" structure inherent to many AI systems and, secondly, to the difficulty of predicting the systemic effects of their large-scale application in most societies around the world. On top of this is another highly uncertain factor: the convergence of technologies, i.e., the extent of the combined effect of different technologies.[15] Funtowicz and Ravetz argue that the higher the uncertainty and the greater the stakes, the more important it is to involve all potentially affected stakeholders, so that a necessary direct proportion is established between uncertainty and the expansion of the decision-making community.

They assert that postnormal science, a concept clearly influenced by Kuhnian (Kuhn, 1994) thought, aims to extend the "community of equals" to all those affected by the development of technoscience. They use environmental problems as a paradigm, but this perspective can be applied to all techno-scientific processes with high uncertainty and potentially serious consequences. A specialist, such as a "mechanic", can take responsibility for his expert opinion because he is capable of understanding and anticipating the consequences of his decisions. By contrast, a specialist, whom we might call "complex", must always remain alert to the high degree of uncertainty in the processes they implement. Thus,

[15] You can view this interesting EU document at: https://op.europa.eu/en/publication-detail/-/publication/b75b4689-7224-4aae-aa02-9ebb6d25de87/language-en

they are not ethically entitled to make decisions that will have potentially unforeseen effects on third parties. What is essential here is not only the prudence inherent in professional ethics, as referred to in the previous section, but also the need to include all parties potentially affected by the potential impact in the decision-making process.

In some ways, this proposal implies accepting, as a professional ethical duty, the recognition of the epistemological limitations inherent in much of today's technology. This makes including uncertainty as an intrinsic element of technoscience in professional codes of ethics is an unavoidable necessity. AI is paradigmatic with regard to such uncertainty. We have already mentioned how it operates as a black box and the difficulty involved in predicting the systemic effects of unbridled application of this technology. Although efforts are being made to certify explainability—and there are various techniques for its implementation—it remains a significant problem. Many crucial areas of our lives are affected by its application, and the outlook is one of exponential growth. Some risks are already known: from social surveillance to the creation of autonomous weapons; from serious environmental issues, such as energy and water consumption, to the uncontrolled use of AI-powered smartphones, with the resulting serious impact on health (especially young people's mental health), privacy, and fundamental rights. The risks of uncontrolled AI, or AI driven solely by the profit motive, are far too high. But there are other, less well-known dangers: we have already referred to the potential systemic effects, but mention should also be made of the unexpected properties that could emerge if ever more aspects of our lives are left in the hands of AI. We do not need to resort to the science fiction idea of self-aware AI (an idea that is quite remote, if not practically impossible) to exercise caution over the possibility of critical situations spiraling out of control.

One of the best-known proposals for addressing all these problems is the incorporation of values into machines, a practice known as Ethics by Design. One such approach is found in the EU document "Ethics by Design and Ethics of Use Approaches for Artificial Intelligence".[16] This is undoubtedly a good and necessary approach to the problem. However, we must bear in mind that AI is being deployed globally,

[16] https://ec.europa.eu/info/funding-tenders/opportunities/docs/2021-2027/horizon/guidance/ethics-by-design-and-ethics-of-use-approaches-for-artificial-intelligence_he_en.pdf

which means we need effective and binding international legislation, as mentioned above, which currently seems impossible. Likewise, as we propose here, raising ethical awareness among the creators of techno-science, assuming epistemological uncertainty, along with promoting social participatory processes in decision-making regarding complex technologies should be compatible with Ethics by Design. There are precedents for informed social decision-making processes, such as consensus conferences or citizens' conferences, specifically designed to facilitate discussion and decision-making in complex contexts, supported and illustrated at all times by specialists.

Proposals for an Appropriate Use of AI

Clearly, technoscience always prevails in the form of *faits accomplis* and, for the most part, the interest behind its application is not necessarily the common good. The interests of industry have a much greater weight in its development and application than those of citizens. Indeed, the latter's only role is that of users, consumers, without ever having the opportunity to decide which technology would truly satisfy their interests and, above all, what risks they would be willing to accept in exchange for its implementation. The idea of informed social consent, borrowing from the model of informed consent used in healthcare, should be introduced to permit decision-making regarding technology. All stakeholders involved in the development and application of such technology should be able to engage in dialogue and social decision-making to assess its risks and benefits. Initiatives such as consensus conferences (Bourg & Boy, 2005), within the framework of postnormal science, are a model of decision-making based on deliberative processes that deepen democracy, recognition, social responsibility, and their compatibility with individual autonomy.

Involving young people in these deliberative processes is particularly important for two reasons. Firstly, it provides an excellent opportunity to enhance their development as responsible citizens engaged in processes of deepening and fostering democracy. Secondly, it allows them to consider not only the immediate advantages of technoscience, but also its potential negative impacts. While fostering critical thinking, allowing young people to see themselves not only as technology consumers but also as essential participants in reflecting on its application and development could promote a new way of conceiving technoscience itself. Accompanying this opportunity with changes in curricula at all educational levels, implementing subjects on ethical reflection regarding technology and its decisive importance in our form of life, might help bring about change in the current inertia. Assuming the role of passive agents, unaware of negative impacts, subject to the seductive and addictive effect of screens, reinforces the sense of overwhelming techno-determinism. This is true for all citizens, but it is especially serious for digital natives.

As mentioned earlier, we need to establish a middle ground between techno-enthusiasm and technophobia, while also avoiding the inherent techno-determinism. Here we return to Heidegger, particularly his reference to Hölderlin and the fragment from the poem Patmos (Heidegger, 1994, p. 16): "Where there is danger, there also grows what saves". This was also cited by Pope Francis, in his book *Let Us Dream Together: The Path to a Better Future* (Francisco, 2020), in a somewhat different sense: in the face of a crisis (such as the Covid-19 epidemic in which his work was produced) and in the worst of times, there is always a way out. Here we approach the excerpt from the perspective outlined at the beginning of this chapter: to a large extent, what "saved us" as a species was also what gave rise to us, namely cultural evolution. We are *as* we are and *what* we are because of it. We have spread across the entire planet and occupied all terrestrial ecosystems, and perhaps we will one day occupy other planets. The danger of extinction was largely overcome by our technical capacity, so we can interpret the poem from this perspective as well. The problem is that, paradoxically, what saved us is now leading us back toward danger. Like a circular path, we once again find ourselves in a critical situation: the excerpt can also be interpreted back to front.

Can technology save us? The answer is no; this would only be possible through cultural evolution, which goes beyond technology. If technoscience is born out of the capitalist form of life, changing the former without modifying the conditions that made it possible is unthinkable. We find ourselves in the situation Gramsci described as an "interregnum crisis": "The crisis consists precisely in the fact that the old is dying and the new cannot be born: in this interregnum, a great variety of morbid symptoms appear" (Gramsci, 1981). In a context where the problems generated by our form of life are now "glocal". No longer limited to local spheres, we need global consciousness, yet, at the same time, the problems are also very local, one might even say personal or subjective.

It is difficult for the vast majority of the world's population to understand that their use of a smartphone has global consequences, that their everyday gestures connect them inseparably as consumer to the status of a product; that their data becomes part of the foundation for training AI systems, which will not necessarily prioritize their interests, despite the appearance of individualized experience. We have mentioned only some of the challenges of technoscience, just touching on the true complexity it entails, but all these issues need to be considered in depth. As digital natives, the new generations have normalized the use of these devices, perhaps with no awareness of such risks.

Returning to Hölderlin's poem, by turning it back to front we point in the following direction: if cultural evolution propelled us as a species, allowed us to go beyond mere survival and permit us to think about the good life, then it is the only thing that can help us out of our current predicament. If the new generations do not bring about cultural change, the problem will perpetuate itself. To overcome the Gramscian dilemma, we must help the new to emerge, but through rational, ethical, and democratic guidance. Generating a new form of life does not necessarily mean moving closer to a better world, yet persevering with the old one is clearly too great a risk. Perhaps this is the most decisive moment in human history, the first in which we must consciously think together as a species. Whatever the case, changing our form of life alone will involve changing technoscience. A technoscience appropriate for life must be one that we can appropriate.

Conclusions

As a cultural species, our technology is directly related to the framework of meaning within which it develops. Thus, the problems it creates are also problems affecting our form of life, i.e., they are not merely technical problems. Therefore, moving toward a new technoscience implies seeking ways to change our form of life. To do so, we must address several fronts. Firstly, while reiterating this is not the specific topic of this chapter, mention must be made of the need for binding international legislation. Secondly, and without underestimating Ethics by Design, it is necessary to generate awareness of professional responsibility among all technology creators, over and above generally weak corporate ethics. More than in the machines themselves, ethics must be present in their developers, as an inescapable duty and integral aspect of technical knowledge. To further this path, we must not only promote the creation of professional associations but also build a culture of ethics at all educational levels: from primary school to university. The presence of ethics should not be seen as a mere complement but as structural and unavoidable in the development of professionals and citizens. Furthermore, fostering awareness of civic responsibility in the face of techno-scientific challenges in general, and those related to AI in particular, must begin by encouraging participation in reflection and decision-making regarding technology. Young people must be a part of such deliberation processes, so they realize that their role cannot be limited to mere users or consumers. Their future is at stake because so is the future of democracy itself. Through post-normal science, informed social consent, and consensus conferences, we can generate change. In the context of the high planetary complexity around us, such changes could end up being merely cosmetic. However, given this context, they could also provide starting conditions which, despite their apparently very limited scope, are like Edward Lorenz's butterfly wings (Lorenz, 1963). As he himself said, we should frame the butterfly effect as a question, not a statement, and in this sense, it is worth considering that perhaps, just perhaps, this could be one of the best ways to reverse the current situation.

References

Bourg, D., & Boy, D. (2005). *Conférences de citoyens, mode d'emploi*. Éditions Charles Léopold Mayer.

Cortina, A. (1986). *Ética mínima*. Tecnos.

Crosby, A, 1988, La medida de la realidad. La cuantificación y la sociedad occidental, 1250–1600.

Ellul, J. (2003). *La edad de la técnica*. Octaedro.

Francisco. (2020). *Soñemos juntos. El camino hacia un futuro mejor*. Plaza & Janés.

Frankl, V. (2004). *El hombre en busca de sentido*. Herder.

Funtowicz, S. O., & Ravetz, J. R. (1993). Science for the post-normal age. *Futures, Butterworth-Heinemann Ltd, 25*(7), 739–755.

Funtowicz, S. O., & Ravetz, J. R. (2000). *La ciencia postnormal*. La ciencia con la gente.

Geertz, C. (2005). *La interpretación de las culturas*. Gedisa.

Gramsci, A. (1981). *Cuadernos de la cárcel*. Ediciones Era.

Heidegger, M. (1994). *Conferencias y artículos*. Ediciones del Serbal.

Hottois, G. M., & JN. (2005). *Nova enciclopedia de bioética*. Universidade de Santiago de Compostela.

Kahneman, D. (2012). *Pensar rápido, pensar despacio*. Debate.

Kranzberg, M., Technology and history: Kranzsberg's laws Technology and Culture, Detroit, Michigan, Vol. 27, núm. 3, 544–560 1986.

Kubrick, S. (1968). *2001: A Space Odyssey*. Metro-Goldwyn-Mayer, Stanley Kubrick Productions.

Kuhn, T. S. (1994). *La estructura de las revoluciones científicas*. FCE.

Lorenz, E. N. (1963). Deterministic nonperiodic flow. *Journal of Atmospheric Sciences, 20*, 130–141.

Mumford, L. (2017). *El mito de la máquina*. Técnica y evolución humana.

Ortega y Gasset, J. (2002). *Meditación de la técnica*. Alianza Editorial.

Picq, P., Sagart, L., Dehane, G., Lestienne, C. 2009, La història més bonica del llenguatge, Edicions de 1984.

Polanyi, K. (2006). *La gran transformación*. Los orígenes políticos y económicos de nuestro tiempo.

Román, B. (2016). *Ética de los servicios sociales*. Herder.

Sabater Pi, J. (1992). *El chimpancé y los orígenes de la cultura*. Editorial Anthropos.

Siegel, D. (1956). *Invasion of the Body Snachers*. Alied Artist.

Wittgenstein, L. (1988). *Investigaciones filosóficas*. Editorial Crítica.

CHAPTER 5

Computational Ethics: What Can We Learn from Algorithmic Morality?

Gonzalo Génova

Computational Machines: A Mirror Where We Can Learn Something About Ourselves

> What we see now is like a dim image in a mirror.
> Then we shall see face to face.

These words, a literal quote of the First Epistle to the Corinthians (13:12), are heard at a crucial moment in *Ghost in the Shell* (Oshii, 1995), a cyberpunk film set in a technologically advanced future where the dividing line between humans and machines is increasingly blurred. The recurring image of the mirror in the movie shows cyborgs and humans as they look at each other and question themselves about their identity.

Each artifact of human manufacture, whether a pot, a meal, or a book, reflects some aspect of ourselves (Valera, 2022). The artifact is like a

G. Génova (✉)
Universidad Carlos III de Madrid, Madrid, Spain
e-mail: ggenova@inf.uc3m.es

M. Bosch (ed.), *Crucial Ethical Keys of Artificial Intelligence*,
https://doi.org/10.1007/978-3-032-22853-6_5

mirror, and by looking at it and reflecting on what we see in it (*reflection* is what happens in a mirror) we can learn important lessons. How much more so in the case of artificial intelligence systems that reproduce some of our cognitive capacities, i.e., tasks that it seemed only human beings could perform. In the words of Mitchell Waldrop (1987):

> The effort of understanding machine ethics may turn out to be invaluable not just as a matter of practicality, but for its own sake. The effort to endow computers with intelligence has led us to look deep within ourselves to understand what intelligence really is. In much the same way, the effort to construct ethical machines will inevitably lead us to look within ourselves and reexamine our own conceptions of right and wrong. (…) A computer (…) is like a mirror: The more we have to explain ourselves, the more we may come to understand ourselves.

If we transfer our way of reasoning to a machine, we can learn something about our own way of reasoning by observing how it works; we can learn what the consequences of certain principles or rules of reasoning are; we can take reasoning beyond what we can do without "leaving" our minds. We can detect conflicts or inconsistencies in our own ideas when we put them into a machine and observe—as if in a mirror—the consequences and logical implications of their development. In fact, this already happens with any reasoning or calculation we write on paper, on a screen, or in the sand on the beach.

A computational machine is one that calculates numbers from numbers, following a well-defined procedure or algorithm. The input numbers represent some condition (such as the probability of rain) and the output numbers represent some action (such as taking an umbrella before going out). Let us suppose, then, that we can program ethics into a computational machine, either with classical, explicit, programming, or with AI techniques that infer patterns of behavior from training data. That is, let us take seriously the possibility of computing ethical behavior based on measurable quantities in the machine's environment, evaluated using decision algorithms. How should this programming be done? What difficulties would it encounter?

This is the approach taken in this chapter. In each of the three following sections a concrete approach to computational ethics is analyzed, so that we humans can learn a lesson about human ethics from that approach. Finally, in the conclusions section I recapitulate these three "ethical lessons from AI", I point to the historical origin of algorithmic morality, and I suggest that the solution for humans is virtue ethics.

First Lesson: Ethics Is Not an Imitation Game[1]

The Imitation Game (Tyldum, 2014) is the title of the film that recounts the life of Alan Turing, and especially his outstanding participation in the deciphering of the German messages encrypted with the Enigma Machine at the Bletchley Park complex (Hinsley & Stripp, 1993). The expression "Imitation Game" is Turing's own, the first words of his 1950 article, *Computational Machines and Intelligence* (Turing, 1950), and is also the name of a Victorian aristocratic game, which consisted of a blind exchange of handwritten messages to try to guess whether the interlocutor was a woman or a man.

When Turing proposes his famous experiment—the Turing Test—to determine whether a machine can think, what interests him is the notion of intelligence as the ability to solve "closed" (i.e., computable) problems, whose paradigm would be the game of chess or code breaking. It is not that he did not care about ethical issues, of course he did, but possibly they did not fall within what he considered "intelligence".

Two Approaches for Artificial Moral Agents: Explicit and Implicit Ethics

The ethical behavior of machines has always been a favorite subject for more or less fanciful speculation, and most especially for science fiction. A paradigmatic example is Isaac Asimov (1942) and his legendary Three Laws of Robotics. When one comes to real technology, two main approaches have been tried. Allen et al. (2005) provide a framework to understanding strategies for designing artificial moral agents: top-down and bottom-up approaches to computing ethics. The idea behind *top-down approaches* is that moral principles or theories may be used as rules for the selection of ethically appropriate actions. The main problems found here are: which set of rules to select (such as the Ten Commandments, or Asimov's Laws of Robotics) and how to solve potential conflicts between rules. On the other hand, bottom-up approaches

[1] The argument in this section is developed with greater detail in (Génova et al., 2022) and (Génova et al., 2023).

do not (supposedly) impose a specific moral theory, but seek to provide environments in which appropriate behavior is selected or rewarded, with mechanisms that could resemble child development or biological evolution.[2]

The Three Laws of Robotics are an attempt to explicitly program an ethical code into a robot, what we might call *explicit ethics* (a kind of top-down approach). Classical, explicit programming is a procedural description of the instructions that a computational machine (a computer) has to follow in order to carry out a task, which can be adding two numbers, moving a package from one place to another, performing a cornea transplant... Classical explicit programming tries to decompose the problem into sequential instructions, repetitions, and alternative paths depending on certain conditions.

The truth is that trying to understand ethics in this way, enclosed within a code that is capable of considering all possible cases when confronted with them (which is what a program does) is quite problematic. This is why another approach has emerged in recent years, hand in hand with developments in artificial intelligence, which we can call *implicit ethics* (a kind of bottom-up approach). Researchers at Massachusetts Institute of Technology have developed an experiment in the domain of autonomous cars "to try to make machines more moral", which they have baptized as the *Moral Machine* (Awad et al., 2018).

The domain of autonomous vehicles is very much in the media, so it's well suited to make the Moral Machine project well known. But the same kind of techniques and way of reasoning developed here could presumably be applied not only to autonomous vehicles, but to many other different problems: who to select for a job, who to grant parole to, who to choose as the recipient of a transplanted organ, etc.[3]

The idea is to try to learn from the answers that ordinary people would give to driving dilemmas. *Since we don't know how to explicitly program the ethical code of an autonomous vehicle*, let's ask people: what would you do? In this situation, and in this other situation, and so on. Using AI techniques, information is extracted from people's answers, until a set of behavioral patterns is built. Something similar is done in other domains:

[2] In my opinion, however, a moral theory is always at least implicit in the way "appropriate" behavior is judged and rewarded.

[3] Of course, one may wonder if ethics is mainly about solving dilemmas, as if it were solving geometry problems... but let's leave that now.

since we don't know how to program with explicit rules how to recognize a human face, we ask people to recognize faces, and to distinguish whether they are smiling, angry, sad, or worried. Even bodily gestures can be recognized in this way: a friendly gesture between friends who have not seen each other for a long time, or between two people closing a deal, or a threatening gesture... All these are already known techniques that are working: let's try to apply them to extract moral knowledge from people's responses.

Problems of the Bottom-Up Approach

What are the problems with this approach to ethical issues? First, there is *the problem of explainability*, which is of great concern to researchers. In machine learning (which is just one branch among others of artificial intelligence) the end result is a formula, an algorithm, to recognize the face, the gesture, the handwriting, but you cannot explain why it works; there is no rational justification for the formula other than its very high success rate, its *effectiveness*. And of course, when the decision carries a strong ethical burden, the fact that it cannot be rationally justified is a serious problem, a very serious problem.

Another problem that arises again and again is *the problem of bias*. Ethical algorithms, it is said, have to avoid biases, whatever they are. Biases against women, against African-Americans, against those who dress unconventionally, and so on. But, then, what will happen if the population we are surveying in the experiment is biased? We will be reproducing the majority bias, and that is—we guess—not acceptable: if the majority is biased, it is not enough for us to *imitate* them, we have to avoid the bias, no matter how much the majority says so. It seems to me that this highlights a very interesting issue: we know that bias, or being biased, is a bad thing, regardless of what the majority says. In other words, *right and wrong is not what the majority says*, it is beyond that. This is not an original consideration: it is at the very origins of ethical reflection in Greek philosophy; the interesting thing is that artificial intelligence brings it back to the fore.

Another problem that arises, closely related to the previous one, is *the problem of the selection of the sample*, the selection of people to whom we ask, "Who would you run over?" Well, who are we asking, normal, ordinary people..., or sadists? And why shouldn't sadists be included in the survey? Aren't we biasing the sample? *And how do we know who are normal, ordinary people and who are sadists?* It is clear that we are already setting the ethical criterion in the selection of the sample: it is *a priori*, it is prior to the experiment. Even if we do not know it perfectly, in a way we already know what is good and what is bad before doing the experiment. It is not true that the experiment tells us the whole about ethics.

What I mean is that ethics does not consist in the imitation of typical or majority behavior. We do not teach ethics that way, nor do we want it to be taught that way. If a national or regional government were to include in its educational programs something like "Ethics Program: you boys and girls have to imitate the majority...", would we not rebel with tremendous indignation? The very seed of ethics is critical thinking, the refusal to conform to the dominant thinking, the commitment of one's own conscience to recognize for oneself what is right and what is wrong.

In short, ethics is not an imitation game. Ethics is not about following a code of conduct, as Asimov depicted with his Three Laws of Robotics. But neither is ethics about imitating the behavior of others.

Second Lesson: You Must Account for Consequences, But Not in the Way Proposed by Utilitarianism

Utilitarianism is a system of ethical thought constructed at the end of the eighteenth century by Jeremy Bentham (1780) and later developed—quite critically—by John Stuart Mill (1863). The utilitarian maxim or "greatest happiness principle" states that the best action is that which produces the greatest happiness and well-being for the greatest number of individuals involved. In Mill's words, "happiness is desirable, and the only thing desirable, as an end; all other things being only desirable as means to that end" (1863, ch. IV, p. 51).

Probably the main appeal of utilitarianism is that it avoids imposing absolute prohibitions and provides an ethical system where they are apparently not necessary. So, people who are reluctant to recognize absolute moral prohibitions are prone to explain their morality and justify their actions in utilitarian terms. I am not decrying this attitude: I readily admit that there are people of admirable moral rectitude who have serious difficulty accepting that there may be actions that are morally unjustifiable in themselves; unjustifiable even in extraordinary circumstances. What they think is, rather, that every action should be evaluated by weighing its consequences, its positive and negative effects, without *a priori* imposing any absolute prohibition.

What I do intend to argue is that utilitarianism cannot serve as a practical rule of conduct, that is, it will remain a vague orientation that cannot provide *precise* indications for action. Precise, in the sense of *computable*. In other words, however much it may trouble its adherents, it is not possible to take utilitarianism seriously.

The Calculation of Happiness

"The greatest happiness and well-being for the greatest number of individuals..." Can happiness be measured? Bentham thought so, and to achieve it he made a classification of pleasures and pains and even proposed a *felicific calculus*, a kind of hedonistic algorithm (Bentham, 1780). In this system the value of a pleasure (measured in *hedons*) is given by seven variables or attributes: Intensity, Duration, Certainty (of obtaining it), Propinquity (proximity in time), Fecundity (for other pleasures), pUrity (without mixture of pain) and Extent (how many individuals will be affected). In mathematical notation:

$$H = f(I, D, C, P, F, U, E)$$

A very simple way of relating these seven variables would be by means of a weighted average (like the final grade given to a student in a course, which depends, say, on 20% class exercises, 50% essay or individual work and 30% final exam):

$$H = a_1 \cdot I + a_2 \cdot D + a_3 \cdot C + a_4 \cdot P + a_5 \cdot F + a_6 \cdot U + a_7 \cdot E$$

Once the H value in hedons of a possible pleasure in sight has been calculated, it is compared with the other possible pleasures, and the one with the highest value is chosen. A very simple algorithm.

Too simple. It is certainly too much to assume that H can be calculated as a weighted average of several factors. It is also too much to assume that H is an increasing function of each and every one of these variables: for example, if I enjoy movies, is it worth twice as much in hedons a movie twice as long? And it is also too much to suppose that the coefficients $a_1...a_7$ are the same for all people: there will be those who value intensity more, others duration, others the certainty of getting it... Therefore, it is clear that the extent or number of people cannot be added as an extra summand; instead, H would have to be calculated for each of the individuals involved, each using his or her own set of coefficients. By the way, who are the individuals involved? The already almost 8,000,000,000 current inhabitants of the planet? Shouldn't the inhabitants of the future also be considered? (Of the past ones, certainly, we can forget, because nothing we do will change their "measure" of happiness).[4]

Maximizing a Function

"The greatest happiness and well-being for the greatest number of individuals..." Let's examine the problem from another point of view. As I have said, it is implausible that H is an increasing function of each of the attributes of a foreseen pleasure. I do not want to abuse mathematical terminology, but when a function is not simply increasing (mathematicians say "monotonically increasing"), then it presents "ups and downs" in the curve that represents it, i.e., maxima and minima (the maximum pleasure in the cinema is obtained when a movie lasts between 110 and 130 minutes, for example). Maxima and minima can be local or global, and there are relatively straightforward methods for calculating them in the case of a function that depends on a single variable, provided that the mathematical expression of the function is known. When the function depends on two variables, instead, we can represent the function as an undulating surface in three dimensions, where the two variables are represented as horizontal coordinates and the value of the function is the height above the plane.

Imagine a walk in the countryside: you come to a meadow with hills (local maxima) and hollows (local minima) stretching out in front of you. The global maximum will be the highest of the hills. Again, it is in principle possible to calculate where the hills and hollows lie, which is the highest and which is the lowest; but this is only feasible (a) when the mathematical expression of the height as a function of the horizontal coordinates is known, and (b) when this expression is also quite simple, which is a lot to assume in the case of the "felicific calculus".

[4] Others, like Peter Singer (1975), based on Bentham's ideas, want to include all sentient living beings in the equation. Reasoning in this way we could arrive at this: "the human being is the only one who can prevent a meteorite from wiping out all life on the planet, so human technological development is maximally beneficial for the life of all other living beings". I don't think animalists will like this conclusion at all.

On the contrary, if we are in the countryside and we do not have a map (we do not know the expression of the function), then in order to find out which is the highest hill there is no other way than to climb each of them, measure them, and keep the maximum value. If it is also foggy (i.e., we have no idea what the relief of the field is like beyond a few meters), we may believe that we have found the highest hill after a few trials, and yet still be far from the optimal result.

The situation becomes impossible for the felicific calculus, which depends not only on thousands of millions of variables (remember the variables could have different weight for each subject), but also has no simple mathematical form. It is simply not a computable function, and a trial-and-error procedure is of no use (because the landscape is foggy).[5]

The Seduction of the Measurable

As I said at the beginning, I believe that part of the attraction of utilitarianism is that it avoids imposing absolute prohibitions. But I think there is also another important factor, which is the seduction of the measurable. Modern science and technology have a well-earned prestige, and they are inconceivable without the development of rigorous procedures for measuring and comparing magnitudes. Utilitarianism, then, is a form of *technification of ethics*, based on defining measurable magnitudes that are taken as inputs in a decision algorithm. That which is not measurable is thus ignored, and that which is measurable acquires disproportionate importance. But the fact is that a function that cannot be calculated efficiently cannot serve as the basis for a decision algorithm.

On the other hand, an inherent characteristic of utilitarianism, linked precisely to the fact that there are no absolute prohibitions, is that it is capable of justifying the harm of a few for the benefit of many (Anscombe, 1958). I can justify an expropriation to build a hospital on that land. This would be a moderate harm with a large associated benefit: who will object? But I can also justify monstrous damages in exchange for ridiculously small benefits, as long as the number of beneficiaries is huge. I can justify turning a person's life into a spectacle—remember *The Truman Show* (Weir, 1998)—if it will bring a little joy to the lives of billions of

[5] Another, even stronger, reason for the non-computability of a decision based on computing outcomes, when the outcomes themselves are a consequence of the decision (in a kind of vicious circle) is explained in detail in (Alfonseca et al., 2021).

viewers. If the utilitarian does not want to admit monstrosities, then absolute bans must be put in place. "Ah, no monstrosities!" There's your absolute ban.

The alternative to utilitarianism is not an "ethics of rules" (Génova et al., 2007) that bypasses the assessment of the consequences of action, of course not. As Robert Spaemann (1982, p. 49) puts it, to act is to want to produce consequences:

> There is in fact no system of ethics which absolutely disregards the consequences of actions, because it is not possible to define an action without making reference to particular effects. Action means 'bringing about effects'. If for example you regard all lies as being in principle reprehensible, this does not mean that you are disregarding consequences. What you are really doing is taking into account one consequence only, the very consequence that makes a lie a lie, the deception or misleading of another person. Without this consequence there would be no lies, otherwise telling fairy-tales would be telling lies.

Of course, *consequences must be taken into account, but not in the way proposed by utilitarianism* ("the greatest happiness and well-being for the greatest number of individuals"), with an appearance of mathematical seriousness behind which there is nothing more than a chimera that cannot be taken seriously: a mirage.

Third Lesson: The Decision About Right/Wrong Action Is Not Computable from Descriptions/Rules

In this section I want to address the Kantian ethical imperative from the point of view of computability and artificial intelligence. More specifically, I try to answer the question of whether the categorical imperative can serve as a basis for programming ethical machines.

Algorithmic Morality

In a paper on the ethical behavior of robots, Malle and Scheutz (2019) make this claim: "Moral action, we suggested earlier, is action in compliance with moral norms". Their approach to morality consists in applying general rules to particular cases (i.e., an *algorithmic morality*); ethical machines apply the morality that has been programmed into them. This consideration of morality as a mere mechanical, deductive application of universal rules is a worrisome approach; they completely disregard the essence of ethics as the proper exercise of freedom (Sols, 2021).

I am afraid that, unfortunately, for many of those who work in robotics, the ethics of human beings themselves is not the "proper exercise of freedom", but "doing the right thing and avoiding the wrong thing" (whether or not this is done freely is secondary). It is an *impersonal ethics*, and that is why it does not shock them that we can talk about the ethics of robots: how to program them to do "the right thing".

The Categorical Imperative

The categorical or unconditional imperative is a central concept in Kantian ethics and of all subsequent modern deontological ethics (Johnson & Cureton, 2022). It claims to be an autonomous (not dependent on any religion or ideology) and self-sufficient commandment, capable of governing human behavior in all its manifestations. Immanuel Kant used the term for the first time in his *Grounding for the Metaphysics of Morals* (1785).

A *conditional or hypothetical imperative* is that which depends on something other than the imperative itself, such as "if I want to pass the exam, I must study": the obligation to study is not absolute, but rather a function of the desire to pass. The conditional imperative is a convenience, which is accepted for utility, for authority, or for fear of punishment (which is nothing more than another form of utility). A *categorical imperative* is the opposite: that which does not depend on anything else to be valid, but is valid in itself, such as "tell the truth". If the force of this obligation came only from the possible positive or negative consequences for the agent, then it would not be a categorical imperative, but a conditional one: I tell the truth because it is convenient for me, and only when it is convenient for me. (Convenience for society in general, instead of only "for me", does not change this conditional character; the categorical imperative seeks to be detached from any convenience, even for society.)

According to Immanuel Kant, *heteronomous morality* is made of conditional imperatives, while *autonomous morality* is made of categorical imperatives. Although the expression "categorical imperative" sounds very solemn, in reality it is nothing more than the other side of "autonomous morality" (which, on the other hand, has a good press). Kant provides several formulations of the categorical imperative. The best known is the so-called formula of the universal law (Kant, 1785): "Act only according to that maxim whereby you can at the same time will that it should become a universal law".

As might be expected, for Kant what is truly moral is obedience to unconditioned imperatives, acting "because it is right", not "because I expect a benefit". Personally, I judge this contribution to be very positive and correct. On the other hand, I consider that this Kantian formulation of the categorical imperative is a sterilizing reduction of "the good" to "the universal" (which is a logical property, not an ethical one). If goodness is not recognized for itself, neither can it be recognized because it is logical or universalizable, nor because it is useful or convenient, nor for any other reason. However, I would now like to examine an additional difficulty I find in attempting to judge concrete acts in the light of a universal rule.

Universal Statements

A universal statement is one whose subject is universally quantified, such as "every man is mortal". In propositional logic notation:

$$\forall x.man(x) \rightarrow mortal(x)$$

Needless to say, here "man" is "human being". Action rules are not exactly the same as statements of facts or properties, although they can be formulated in a similar way. A rule of action such as "one must always tell the truth" can be formulated as "telling the truth is always obligatory" (here the adverb "always" serves as a universal quantifier). In his *Elementa juris naturalis* (written between 1669 and 1671, unpublished) Gottfried Wilhelm Leibniz is the precursor of *deontic logic*, which is the part of logic that deals with reasoning about rules and obligations (Leibniz, 1671). The first plausible system of deontic logic was proposed by G. H. von Wright (1951).

A good student pointed out to me years ago that rules such as "telling the truth *to your friend* is always obligatory", or even "telling the truth to your friend *on Tuesdays from three to five* is always obligatory" are also universal. That is, we can add as many clauses to the rule as we want; the rule will be arbitrarily complicated, but it will still be *formally* universal. The student felt that this was cheating, and I agreed (and agree) with him. Rigorously defined *logical universality* allows rules that are universal and at the same time as *complicated, intricate, twisted*, as we want them to be.

Possibly this is not what Kant had in mind; he would want for the categorical imperative a rule that is not only *universal*, because it has a universal quantifier, but one that is also *simple*. Which opens us to the problem of the vagueness of the definition of a "simple" rule.

A computational system will try to represent concrete acts by measurable, quantifiable variables, as it does with any other aspect of the real world. If we consider that two variables are sufficient (for the sake of simplicity), then we can represent these specific acts as dots on a two-dimensional diagram: for example, white dots for "good" acts and black dots for "bad" acts. We can also draw dividing lines to separate regions of acts evaluated as good from regions of acts evaluated as bad. Each dividing line expresses a "universal moral rule", an imperative, that separates two categories of acts (good or bad) according to their conformance to the rule, i.e., the imperative. The imperative is universal because it does not point to this or that concrete act, but rather to a category of acts defined by their verbal expression, their defining formula.

An extremely simple universal rule would be a straight line, for example, "thou shalt not kill". However, if we rework it to say "thou shalt not kill *human beings*", or "thou shalt not kill *innocent* human beings", formally it remains universal, although we could possibly no longer represent it as a straight line, because it is subjected again and again to successive complications that twist it more and more. Each nuance we add to the commandment becomes a new curve in that line: thou shalt not kill people who are in good health; thou shalt not kill people of your tribe; thou shalt not kill rich people; thou shalt not kill...

Indeed, once we admit curved lines of arbitrary complexity, it turns out that we can cope with any distribution of "good" and "bad" points, provided that the equation of the curve is sufficiently complex. In other words, we can make any particular behavior "justified" under the guise of a universal maxim (the "good" side of the curve equation). Apparently, because in reality...

The Undecidable

Let us now consider that the *description* of a category of acts that we want to (computationally) evaluate as good or bad can be considered analogous to a logical proposition whose truth or falsity we want to prove, or to a computer program that we want to know whether it will finish its execution in a finite time.

Well, invoking Kurt Gödel (1931) and Alan Turing (1936), we know that in every coherent logical system there are unprovable propositions; or, equivalently, that there cannot exist a single computer program that can determine *a priori* whether any other program will finish its execution or will "hang" (become stuck in an infinite loop). In other words, a single universal maxim, however complicated, cannot serve to evaluate the morality of all categories of acts. *The Kantian categorical imperative is not computable, any more than utilitarianism was.*

Obviously, I am not saying that some *particular* acts, even some *categories* of acts, cannot be evaluated. Certainly you can, just as you can prove some logical propositions and evaluate some programs. What I am saying is that you cannot evaluate *all* acts and categories with a *single* moral rule, within a single universal system.

Let us take, for example, the statement "Amy has killed Benny" (a particular act), whose moral evaluation we would entrust to a program that contrasts it with a universal rule (for these purposes, it is indifferent whether the rule is simple or an arbitrarily complicated combination of rules). So, what Gödel and Turing have shown is that *there cannot be a universal rule* capable of evaluating all statements of that style. A single universal rule, a single program, cannot evaluate *all propositions* describing morally qualifiable acts. It will be able to judge some acts as good, and some acts as bad, but there will remain a set of acts that cannot be judged according to that rule (technically, a set of morally *undecidable* acts).

A Fractal Theory of Good and Evil

But this is not the end of the story, because the difference between the description of an act finally evaluated as good, and an act finally evaluated as bad, *can be ridiculously small.* Exactly as it happens with logical propositions and computer programs, which can be arbitrarily complex, so that a single different symbol among thousands or millions of equal symbols (say, changing once '+' for '-') can make the difference between a true and a false proposition, a program that stops and one that does not.

Thus, *the descriptions of good and bad acts* (the clouds of black and white dots in that two-dimensional diagram) *are not separated in zones delimited by well-defined curves*, not even if they are curves as complex as necessary. The verbal descriptions of one act and another are intricately intertwined, and need not be easily distinguishable with a rule. Perhaps the Gospel parable of the wheat and the tares (Matthew, 13:24–30) is the best informal explanation I know of this.

According to Gödel (1931), in a logical system the set of propositions is not clearly delimited by a dividing line between true and false statements. They are intimately mixed, *fractally* (Mandelbrot, 1982), and alongside the infinite true and false propositions there are also infinitely many that are undecidable (Blum & Smale, 1993; Penrose, 1989). Similarly, there is no clear dividing line between good and bad human acts based on their verbal description. *There is no universal algorithm for distinguishing good from bad, just as there is no universal algorithm for distinguishing true from false.*

The good and the bad are fractally intertwined. The difference between the saint and the scoundrel—as seen and measured from the outside—can be minimal, because *corruptio optimi pessima* (the corruption of the best is the worst of all). The worst liar is the one who best feigns to tell the truth. The worst criminal is the one who manages to appear to be a saint. As Lord Byron wrote in his *Don Juan* (1822):

> And, after all, what is a lie?
> 'Tis but the truth in masquerade.

Lord Byron, by the way, was the father of Ada Lovelace, whom he abandoned as a newborn.[6]

Conclusion: The Exhaustion of Deductive Rationalist Ethics

As shown in the preceding sections, three major lessons can be drawn from the attempt to program ethical behavior into a computational machine:

- We can learn some ethics by copying the behavior of others, but ethics is not just an imitation game.

[6] Ada Lovelace, Charles Babbage's close collaborator, is usually considered the first computer programmer (Hammerman & Russell, 2016).

- Consequences must be taken into account when evaluating the morality of actions, but not in the way proposed by utilitarianism.
- There is no universal algorithm for distinguishing right from wrong, just as there is no universal algorithm for distinguishing true from false.

Well then, does this mean that we should not look at the behavior of others to learn ethics, that we should not take foreseeable consequences into account, or that we should not know and follow moral norms? Not at all. It simply means that the approaches to algorithmic ethics examined are radically insufficient to guide moral behavior. It means that *ethical behavior is not computable*. If the best option among several were computable, how could it not be mandatory? If it were computable and mandatory, what would be left for the will, apart from being a blind driver to act in the manner dictated by the computation?

The fact that the decision is not computable does not mean either that free will chooses *arbitrarily* among the available options. Undoubtedly, free will chooses guided by imitation, outcomes and norms; but this guidance is not the result of a mechanical and deductive process. *Free will is rational, but not mechanical*. It is not true what Modernity claims: that all mediation between knowledge and action is deductive and mechanical, as in normativism and utilitarianism. Understanding this may be a bit more difficult than it should be for us, the sons and daughters of the Enlightenment.

If ethical behavior is not computable, it means that something is missing. Indeed, there is an important element at play that algorithmic ethics does not consider: *prudence*, the ancient moral virtue that the Greeks (especially Aristotle) called *phronesis*, the type of wisdom or intelligence concerned with practical action. *Prudence mediates between knowledge and action, but not deductively*. That kind of practical reason—prudence—is not the algorithmic application of universal rules to particular cases.

This is interesting because of the reflection we are forced to make in the *mirror* of artificial intelligence. Artificial intelligence, and the acting power we are giving it, forces us to rethink ethical issues. I am not so much concerned about the humanization of the robot, as about the robotization of the human: the reduction of robotic (and human!) ethics to compliance with a set of "rules to be good". If general (or strong) artificial intelligence were to become a reality (which I do not believe) the solution for their moral behavior would not be in programmed ethics, *just as the solution for human persons is not the ethical programming of their consciences*.

Algorithmic morality was invented long before artificial intelligence was born; it is not an invention of contemporary computer scientists in their attempt to program ethical behavior. It is rather the offspring of modern rationalistic philosophy, when it attempts to mathematize ethics, as exemplified by the famous optimistic and naïve words of Leibniz (1685):

> The only way to rectify our reasonings is to make them as tangible as those of the Mathematicians, so that we can find our error at a glance, and when there are disputes among persons, we can simply say: Let us calculate, without further ado, to see who is right.

In my view, machine ethics is an interesting new way to show the exhaustion of deductive rationalist ethics (MacIntyre, 1981). The solution to this exhaustion lies in virtue ethics, which has experienced an interesting revival since the second half of the twentieth century. In the end, the perspectives of imitation, utilitarianism, and normativism must always be tempered by prudence in order to bear fruit, whereas when set aside from virtue ethics, they produce monsters (Marcos, 2011). But virtue ethics is not a computable function either. Don't expect from me to announce a "virtuous algorithm": that simply cannot exist. What can exist are virtuous programmers, who virtuously program machines to be instruments for good.

References

Alfonseca, M., Cebrián, M., Fernández Anta, A., Coviello, L., Abeliuk, A., & Rahwan, I. (2021). Superintelligence cannot be contained: Lessons from computability theory. *Journal of Artificial Intelligence Research, 70*, 65–76.

Allen, C., Smit, I., & Wallach, W. (2005). Artificial morality: Top-down, bottom-up, and hybrid approaches. *Ethics and Information Technology, 7*(3), 149–155.

Anscombe, G. E. M. (1958). Modern moral philosophy. *Philosophy, 33*(124), 1–19.

Asimov, I. (1942). Runaround. *Astounding Science Fiction, 29*(1), 93–103.

Awad, E., Dsouza, S., Kim, R., Schulz, J., Henrich, J., Shariff, A., Bonnefon, J.-F., & Rahwan, I. (2018). The moral machine experiment. *Nature, 563*, 59–64.

Bentham, J. (1780). *An introduction to the principles of morals and legislation*. T Payne and Sons.

Blum, L., & Smale, S. (1993). The gödel incompleteness theorem and decidability over a ring. In M. W. Hirsch, J. E. Marsden, & M. Shub (Eds.), *From topology to computation: Proceedings of the smalefest*. Springer.

Génova, G., González, M. R., & Fraga, A. (2007). Ethical education in software engineering: Responsibility in the production of complex systems. *Science and Engineering Ethics, 13*(4), 505–522.

Génova, G., Moreno, V., & González, M. R. (2022). A lesson from AI: Ethics is not an imitation game. *IEEE Technology and Society Magazine, 41*(1), 75–81.

Génova, G., Moreno, V., & González, M. R. (2023). Machine ethics: Do androids dream of being good people? *Science and Engineering Ethics, 29*, 10.

Gödel, K. (1931). Über formal unentscheidbare Sätze der Principia Mathematica und verwandter Systeme I. *Monatshefte für Mathematik und Physik, 38*, 173–198.

Hammerman, R., & Russell, A. L. (Eds.). (2016). *Ada's legacy: Cultures of computing from the victorian to the digital age*. Association for Computing Machinery and Morgan & Claypool Publishers.

Hinsley, F. H., & Stripp, A. (Eds.). (1993). *Codebreakers: The inside story of Bletchley Park*. Oxford University Press.

Johnson, R., & Cureton, A. (2022). Kant's moral philosophy. In E. N. Zalta & U. Nodelman (Eds.), *The stanford encyclopedia of philosophy* (Fall 2022 ed.) Available at https://plato.stanford.edu/archives/fall2022/entries/kant-moral/

Kant, I. 1785. *Grundlegung zur Metaphysik der Sitten / Grounding for the Metaphysics of Morals* (J.W. Ellington, Trans.). Hackett, Indianapolis. Available at https://archive.org/details/groundingformet000kant/page/n5/mode/2up

Leibniz, G. W. (1671). Elementa juris naturalis (unpublished). In *Leibniz-Edition, Die Akademie Ausgabe, Reihe VI, Philosophische Schriften, 1990*. Walter de Gruyter GmbH.

Leibniz, G.W. 1685. The art of discovery. In P.P. Wiener (Ed.), *Leibniz: Selections*, 1951, Scribner, p. 51.

MacIntyre, A. 1981. *After Virtue: A Study in Moral Theory* (2nd ed., 1984, 3rd ed. 2007), University of Notre Dame Press, Notre Dame, Indiana.

Malle, B. F., & Scheutz, M. (2019). Learning how to behave. In O. Bendel (Ed.), *Handbuch maschinenethik*. Springer Reference Geisteswissenschaften. Springer.

Mandelbrot, B. (1982). *The fractal geometry of nature*. Macmillan.

Marcos, A. (2011). Prudencia, verdad práctica y razón postmoderna. In A. R. Pérez Ransanz & A. Velasco (Eds.), *Racionalidad en ciencia y tecnología* (pp. 119–134). UNAM.

Mill, J.S. 1863. Utilitarianism. Parker, Son, and Bourn. Facsimile text available at https://archive.org/details/a592840000milluoft/page/n3/mode/2up.

Oshii, M. 1995. Ghost in the shell.

Penrose, R. (1989). *The emperor's new mind*. Oxford University Press.

Singer, P. (1975). *Animal liberation: A new ethics for our treatment of animals*. Random House.

Sols, J. (2021). *Ética de la inteligencia artificial: el caso de los soldados robot*. Universidad de Monterrey.

Spaemann, R. 1982. Moralische Grundbegriffe. C.H. Beck, München. *Basic Moral Concepts* (T.J. Armstrong, 1989, Trans.).

Turing, A. M. (1936). On computable numbers, with an application to the entscheidungsproblem. *Proceedings of the London Mathematical Society, 2*(42), 230–265.

Turing, A. M. (1950). Computing machinery and intelligence. *Mind, 59*, 433–460.

Tyldum, M. 2014, The imitation game.

Valera, L. (2022). *Espejos*. Filosofía y nuevas tecnologías.

von Wright, G. H. (1951). Deontic logic. *Mind, 60*(237), 1–15.

Waldrop, M. M. (1987). A question of responsibility. *AI Magazine, 8*(1), 28–39.

Weir, P. 1998. The truman show.

CHAPTER 6

Ethical Principles for the Use of Artificial Intelligence (AI) in Education

Oscar-Yecid Aparicio-Gómez

Introduction

The integration of artificial intelligence (AI) into education is profoundly transforming how knowledge is taught and acquired. This technological revolution holds the promise of optimizing learning efficiency, personalizing education, and democratizing access to high-quality resources. However, alongside these opportunities, significant ethical challenges arise that must be addressed to ensure that AI implementation in education is both beneficial and equitable. This chapter focuses on the fundamental ethical principles that should guide the use of AI in educational settings, offering a framework to responsibly navigate these challenges.

In recent years, AI has assumed an increasingly prominent role in education, from personalizing learning experiences to automating administrative tasks. Adaptive learning platforms, virtual assistants, and automated assessment systems exemplify how AI is being leveraged to enhance

O.-Y. Aparicio-Gómez (✉)
Ed&TIC Research Center, Bogotá, Colombia
e-mail: oaparicio@editic.net

M. Bosch (ed.), *Crucial Ethical Keys of Artificial Intelligence*,
https://doi.org/10.1007/978-3-032-22853-6_6

the educational experience. However, the rapid adoption of these technologies raises critical questions about their regulation and ethical use. The need for a clear ethical framework has never been more urgent, as the decisions made today will have lasting implications for future generations. In this context, it is imperative to establish ethical principles that guide this transformative process.

One of the most critical ethical principles in the use of AI in education is equity and justice. AI has the potential to reduce inequities by providing access to personalized educational resources tailored to individual student needs, irrespective of socioeconomic background. However, without careful implementation, AI risks exacerbating existing inequalities, particularly if access to these technologies is uneven or if the algorithms reflect inherent biases. It is essential to ensure that all students have equitable access to AI-powered educational tools and that these tools are designed to promote inclusion and diversity. This approach not only seeks distributive justice but also procedural justice in the design and application of these technologies.

Accountability is another key principle for ensuring the ethical and beneficial use of AI in education. This involves establishing clear mechanisms of responsibility for all stakeholders involved in the development and deployment of AI technologies. Best practices include creating policies that define the roles and responsibilities of developers, educators, and administrators, as well as implementing monitoring and evaluation systems to ensure the ethical and effective use of AI. Accountability also entails the ability to rectify errors and adjust practices when negative impacts are identified. This principle is closely linked to the need for transparency, as accountability is only achievable when processes are visible and understandable.

Transparency is critical for building trust in AI systems used in education. Students, parents, and educators must understand how these systems operate, how decisions are made, and what data is used in the process. Transparency not only fosters trust in the technology but also enables users to critically evaluate the effectiveness and ethics of AI systems. This requires developers to adopt open and explainable design practices, ensuring that algorithms are interpretable and that decisions can be audited and justified. Thus, transparency serves as a foundational pillar supporting both fairness and accountability.

Privacy is another essential consideration in the ethical use of AI in education. AI systems must comply with existing data protection regulations, and privacy safeguards should be integrated from the design phase. This includes minimizing data collection, employing anonymization techniques, and obtaining informed consent from users. Protecting privacy is not only an ethical imperative but also crucial for maintaining user trust in AI systems.

Human autonomy is a fundamental value that must be preserved in the implementation of AI in education. AI systems have the potential to influence students' decision-making processes, and it is vital that these systems empower students to make informed choices about their learning. This requires providing students and educators with clear, understandable information about how AI systems function and how they may impact educational experiences. Fostering autonomy also means ensuring that students retain control over their participation in digitalized environments. Preserving autonomy is essential to ensure that AI is used in ways that respect the dignity and freedom of learners.

The principles of beneficence and non-maleficence are equally critical to ensure that AI in education maximizes benefits while minimizing potential risks. Beneficence involves using AI to enhance student learning and development, offering tools tailored to individual needs and facilitating access to educational opportunities. Non-maleficence, on the other hand, requires avoiding harm—whether physical, psychological, or social—to students and other stakeholders. This includes designing AI systems that do not perpetuate biases or inequalities and that safeguard the privacy and security of personal data. By adhering to these principles, we can ensure that AI is used in ways that benefit all learners while minimizing potential risks.

The ethical principles discussed in this chapter are essential for guiding the responsible use of AI in education. By adopting an ethical and human-centered approach, we can ensure that AI contributes positively to student learning and development while upholding core ethical values. Collaboration among educators, technology developers, policymakers, and the broader education community is crucial for addressing ethical challenges and maximizing the transformative potential of AI in education. These principles not only provide a framework for the ethical implementation of AI but also ensure that the technology is used in ways that respect and promote the rights and well-being of all students.

Equity and Justice in AI-Powered Education

In the contemporary educational landscape, the integration of AI presents both significant challenges and opportunities. Among these challenges, the ethical principles of equity and justice emerge as fundamental considerations. These principles aim to ensure that the implementation of AI in educational settings does not perpetuate or exacerbate existing inequalities. Instead, they seek to promote equitable access to AI-enhanced technologies and resources while mitigating discriminatory biases in AI systems (Alfredo et al., 2024).

Equity in education extends beyond the provision of equal access; it involves addressing pre-existing disparities and actively working to reduce them. When applying AI in education, it is essential to consider the socioeconomic, cultural, and geographic factors that may influence the accessibility and effectiveness of these technologies. For instance, rural or low-income communities often face additional barriers in accessing the advanced technological infrastructure required to fully leverage AI systems in learning (Song et al., 2024). Ensuring equity necessitates investment in appropriate technological infrastructure and the provision of ongoing support to guarantee that all students can benefit from AI tools in a fair and equitable manner.

Justice, on the other hand, refers to the imperative of ensuring that AI systems in education do not perpetuate or amplify existing injustices. AI algorithms can be inherently prone to bias if they are not meticulously designed and trained (Tebenkov & Prokhorov, 2021). Consequently, it is crucial to implement rigorous design and auditing practices to identify and mitigate potential discriminatory biases. This requires a critical examination of data collection methods, the relevance of selected features, and the decision-making processes based on AI outputs. Additionally, clear ethical policies and standards must be established to ensure that AI systems in education respect the rights and dignity of all students, regardless of their ethnicity, gender, ability, or socioeconomic status (Dawkins, 2014).

An illustrative example of how equity and justice can be impacted by AI in education is the use of algorithms for automated assessment. If these algorithms are not trained on a representative dataset encompassing diverse contexts, they may produce biased results that favor certain groups while inadvertently excluding others. This not only compromises the fairness of the assessment process but may also have significant repercussions on students' educational and career trajectories (Teke & Kavzoglu, 2024).

Addressing these ethical challenges requires close collaboration among educational institutions, technology developers, policymakers, and other stakeholders. This includes the active involvement of the educational community in shaping policies and implementing practices that promote equity and justice in the use of AI. By adopting an inclusive and consultative approach, the specific needs and concerns of diverse communities can be better identified, paving the way for solutions that foster equitable access and genuine justice in the application of AI in education (Aparicio Gómez et al., 2022).

Moreover, it is essential to incorporate ethical principles such as transparency and accountability into the design and implementation of AI systems in education. Transparency ensures that students, educators, and other stakeholders understand how AI systems operate and how they may influence educational outcomes (Song et al., 2024). Accountability, in turn, ensures that developers and users of AI in education are held responsible for their decisions and actions, particularly in cases where negative impacts or injustices may arise (Floridi, 2014).

The role of AI in personalizing education must also be examined through the lens of equity and justice. AI-powered personalized learning systems have the potential to tailor educational experiences to individual student needs, thereby enhancing learning outcomes (Chiappe & Lee, 2017). However, this personalization must be carefully managed to avoid inadvertently reinforcing existing biases or inequalities. For example, if AI systems are trained on biased data, they may perpetuate stereotypes or restrict opportunities for certain student groups (Shoaib et al., 2024).

The ethical deployment of AI in education also demands a commitment to continuous evaluation and improvement. This involves not only assessing the effectiveness of AI systems in achieving educational objectives but also monitoring their impact on equity and justice. Regular audits and feedback mechanisms can help identify areas where AI systems may fall short and provide opportunities for corrective action (Weckert, 1996).

Furthermore, the integration of AI in education must be accompanied by efforts to educate students and educators about the ethical implications of AI technologies. This includes fostering digital literacy and critical thinking skills to enable individuals to understand and navigate the complexities of AI-driven systems. By equipping students and educators with the knowledge and skills to interact with AI ethically, we can promote a more equitable and just educational landscape (Johnson, 2001).

By adopting robust ethical principles and striving for inclusive policies and transparent practices, we can harness the transformative potential of AI to significantly enhance education while safeguarding and promoting the core values of equity and justice in our increasingly digitized societies. The collaboration of all stakeholders—including educators, policymakers, technology developers, and the broader community—is essential to ensure that AI serves as a tool for positive change rather than a source of further inequality (Adler & Antezana, 2018).

Responsibility for the Implementation of AI in Education

The rapid expansion of AI in education has sparked significant debates and ethical concerns, underscoring the urgent need to establish clear principles of responsibility and accountability. These principles are essential to mitigate inherent risks and ensure that AI systems in education operate ethically and beneficially for all stakeholders involved (Sankey, & St. Hill, R., 2008). In the context of educational AI, responsibility extends to multiple key actors: developers who design and program the systems, vendors who implement these solutions in educational environments, and end-users—such as students, teachers, and school administrators—who interact with these technologies. Each of these actors plays a critical role in the lifecycle of AI systems, from their conception and development to their implementation and practical use in classrooms (Tracy & Carmichael, 2013).

Developers of AI systems for education bear the primary responsibility for ensuring that their technologies adhere to rigorous ethical standards. This involves not only creating accurate and efficient algorithms but also addressing ethical considerations such as fairness, transparency, and privacy. Developers must understand how their design decisions influence educational outcomes and user experiences (Forbes-Riley & Litman, 2010). Similarly, vendors facilitating the implementation of AI systems in educational settings are responsible for ensuring that these technologies are deployed ethically and responsibly. This includes providing adequate user training, ongoing technical support, and continuous monitoring of system performance. Vendors must also be prepared to address any ethical issues that arise during the implementation and use of educational AI (Sharma & Singh, 2022).

A crucial aspect of accountability in educational AI is the ability to take responsibility for decisions and actions related to these systems. This requires establishing clear mechanisms to monitor and evaluate the impact of AI on student learning and development. Developers and vendors must demonstrate that their technologies not only enhance educational efficiency but also promote equity and well-being for all students, regardless of socioeconomic or cultural background (Alfredo et al., 2024). Furthermore, effective procedures must be in place to identify and rectify potential errors or biases in AI systems. Since AI algorithms can continuously learn and adapt based on input data, they may develop biases or unintended errors that disproportionately affect certain student groups. Early identification and swift corrective action are essential to maintaining the integrity and effectiveness of AI systems in education (L. Yuan, 2019).

To ensure accountability, clear policies and regulations must be established at institutional and governmental levels. These should define ethical and legal standards for developers, vendors, and users when designing, deploying, and using AI technologies in education (Nijenhuis-Voogt et al., 2018). Regulations should also address issues related to the collection and use of students' personal data, ensuring that privacy and data protection rights are upheld. Additionally, independent oversight and auditing mechanisms should be implemented to ensure compliance with ethical standards and to safeguard the interests of students and the broader educational community (Adler & Antezana, 2018).

Transparency is a cornerstone of trust in AI systems. It entails making the processes and decision-making mechanisms of AI systems understandable and accessible to all stakeholders. This transparency extends beyond revealing algorithms or code; it also involves explaining how data is collected, processed, and utilized to inform decisions (Teke & Kavzoglu, 2024). For students, teachers, and administrators, this means having access to the technical underpinnings of AI systems and understanding how these systems impact learning, assessment, and educational administration. In practice, transparency requires developers and vendors to adopt open and explanatory design practices. Algorithmic decisions must be traceable and comprehensible to users, preventing algorithmic opacity from undermining trust and acceptance of these technologies in educational environments (von Feigenblatt et al., 2024).

Transparency also necessitates the implementation of effective auditing and oversight mechanisms. This includes conducting robustness testing and ethical impact assessments to ensure that AI systems are not only accurate and efficient but also fair and ethical in their application within educational settings (Marwala, 2021). Audit procedures should be accessible and comprehensible to stakeholders, enabling them to critically evaluate how AI influences educational processes and learning experiences. On a broader level, transparency addresses ethical concerns related to power and autonomy. The deployment of AI systems in education affects not only individual student experiences but also power dynamics within educational institutions. Clarity about how automated decisions are made helps mitigate the risks of algorithmic biases that could perpetuate existing inequalities or restrict educational opportunities for certain student groups (Woschank et al., 2020).

Beyond technical understanding, transparency also involves openness and honesty in communicating about the use of AI in education. This includes actively disclosing privacy and data management policies and educating users about their rights and choices regarding the collection and use of their personal data. Students and parents should be informed about how data collected through AI platforms is used to enhance the educational experience and how they can exercise control over their personal information (Russell & Tegmark, 2016). Finally, fostering responsibility and accountability in the use of AI in education requires ongoing education and awareness efforts. All stakeholders, from developers to end-users, must be trained and informed about the ethical challenges associated with AI implementation in educational settings. This includes instruction on fundamental ethical principles, the identification of potential algorithmic biases, and the adoption of practices that promote fairness and transparency in the design and deployment of AI systems (Cioffi et al., 2020).

Transparency as a Guarantor of Trust in the Use of AI in Educational Contexts

In the contemporary digital age, the rapid advancement of AI has permeated nearly every facet of modern life, including education. While AI promises enhanced efficiency and personalized learning, it also raises critical ethical concerns, particularly regarding transparency. Transparency is a cornerstone of ethical AI use in education, ensuring that users understand how these systems operate and the processes underlying their decisions (Yuan, 2019). This principle goes beyond merely disclosing source code or algorithms; it encompasses clarity about data collection, processing, and utilization, as well as the rationale behind automated decisions. For students, educators, and administrators, transparency is essential not only for accessing technical information but also for comprehending how AI systems influence learning, assessment, and institutional administration (Sutton & Barto, 2018).

Transparency in practice involves several critical dimensions. First, it requires developers and providers of AI systems to adopt open and explanatory design practices. Algorithmic decisions must be traceable and interpretable, ensuring that users can understand the reasoning behind system outputs. This mitigates the risk of algorithmic opacity, which can undermine trust and acceptance in educational settings. For instance, educators and students should be able to discern why an AI system recommends specific content, assessments, or learning pathways (van der Rijst et al., 2019). Second, transparency necessitates robust audit and oversight mechanisms. These include rigorous testing for accuracy, fairness, and ethical impact, ensuring that AI systems operate equitably within educational contexts. Audit procedures must be accessible and comprehensible to stakeholders, enabling them to critically evaluate how AI influences educational processes and outcomes (Traxler, 2018).

Transparency also addresses broader ethical concerns related to power dynamics and autonomy in education. The deployment of AI systems can reshape institutional power structures and individual experiences. Clear insights into automated decision-making processes help mitigate risks such as algorithmic bias, which could exacerbate existing inequalities or restrict educational opportunities for marginalized groups (Song et al., 2024). Trust is a pivotal factor in the successful adoption of AI technologies in education. Transparency fosters trust by ensuring stakeholders understand how AI systems function and the rationale behind their decisions. When users perceive AI systems as transparent and accountable, they are more likely to engage with and trust these technologies (Pantano & Di Pietro, 2012). Moreover, transparency empowers stakeholders to make informed decisions by providing the necessary information to evaluate the benefits and risks of AI integration in educational practices (Johnson, 2001).

Despite its importance, achieving transparency in AI systems is fraught with challenges. One major obstacle is the inherent complexity of AI algorithms, which can be difficult for non-experts to comprehend. This complexity often results in a lack of transparency, as users struggle to interpret the decision-making processes of AI systems (Tamás & Koltai, 2020). Additionally, the proprietary nature of many AI technologies restricts access to underlying algorithms and data, creating a "black box" effect. Overcoming this barrier requires a commitment to open and transparent practices from developers and technology providers (Alexandron et al., 2016). To address these challenges, several strategies can be employed. One approach is the development and implementation of explainable AI (XAI) techniques, which aim to make AI systems more interpretable for users. XAI can demystify complex algorithms and provide clear explanations of decision-making processes (Tamás & Koltai, 2020). Another strategy involves establishing clear guidelines and standards for AI transparency. Such frameworks can guide developers and vendors in prioritizing transparency throughout the design and deployment of AI technologies (Floridi, 2014).

As AI continues to evolve and integrate into educational contexts, the importance of transparency will only grow. Future advancements in AI will likely introduce new challenges and opportunities for transparency, necessitating ongoing efforts to ensure that AI systems remain accountable and understandable (Sutton & Barto, 2018). Transparency is a foundational principle for building trust in the use of AI in education. By prioritizing transparency, we can ensure that AI systems are deployed ethically and responsibly, fostering trust among all stakeholders. Through sustained efforts to enhance transparency, we can harness the transformative potential of AI to improve education while safeguarding the rights and interests of students, educators, and the broader educational community (Grinbaum, 2012).

Privacy in the Design of AI Systems for Education

The integration of AI into various domains, including education, presents significant ethical challenges, particularly concerning privacy and data protection. Ensuring that AI systems in educational settings respect individual rights and adhere to stringent ethical standards is crucial (Yuan et al., 2024). Protecting the privacy of students and other users is a paramount ethical imperative. AI systems often collect and process sensitive information, such as academic performance, behavioral patterns, learning preferences, and even biometric data. If mismanaged, this data can compromise individuals'privacy and security (Smith et al., 2014).

To mitigate these risks, educational institutions and technology developers must implement robust data-protection measures from the initial design phase of AI systems. This includes strict compliance with legal frameworks like the General Data Protection Regulation (GDPR) in the European Union, as well as adherence to local data-protection laws in other regions (Leonardi & Treem, 2020). A proactive approach to risk management is also essential, involving the identification of potential vulnerabilities and the development of clear privacy and security policies to address potential threats (Pantano & Di Pietro, 2012). Privacy is not just a legal obligation but a fundamental right that must be upheld to maintain trust in AI systems. In educational contexts, where students' personal and academic data are at stake, the implications are particularly significant. Misuse or mishandling of such data can lead to breaches of confidentiality, identity theft, and other forms of harm (Smith et al., 2014).

Moreover, perceptions of privacy can significantly influence the willingness of students and educators to engage with AI technologies. If users perceive their data as insecure, they may hesitate to adopt AI systems, hindering the effectiveness and widespread implementation of these technologies in education (Castro & Zermeño, 2020). Designing AI systems that respect privacy involves several key strategies. One effective approach is the adoption of privacy-by-design principles, which integrate privacy considerations into the development process from the outset. This ensures that privacy is not an afterthought but a foundational component of the system's architecture (Cuzzocrea, 2014). Similarly, implementing data minimization techniques—collecting only the data necessary for the intended purpose—can reduce the risk of privacy breaches and enhance the overall security of the system (Leonardi & Treem, 2020).

Transparency is another critical principle. Users must be clearly informed about what data is collected, how it is used, and with whom it is shared. This transparency fosters trust in AI systems and enables individuals to provide informed consent regarding the handling of their personal data (Jorzik et al., 2024). In educational settings, transparency is especially vital, as it allows students, parents, and educators to make informed decisions about their engagement with AI technologies. By providing clear and accessible information about data practices, educational institutions can cultivate a culture of trust and accountability (Floridi, 2014).

Responsible data management in educational AI extends beyond initial data collection to include secure storage, anonymization where feasible, and the secure deletion of data when it is no longer needed. AI systems should minimize the collection of personal data and employ robust encryption and protection methods to safeguard sensitive information (Heller & Bry, 2021). Furthermore, educational institutions must establish clear policies and internal procedures for managing data security incidents. This includes the ability to respond promptly to breaches, notify affected parties, and collaborate with regulatory authorities as necessary (Pantano & Di Pietro, 2012).

A critical aspect of data protection in educational AI is addressing algorithmic biases—prejudices that may be inadvertently built into AI systems, leading to unfair or unjustified discrimination. These biases can have profound implications for student privacy and educational equity (Song et al., 2024). To tackle this issue, AI developers must implement techniques to identify and mitigate biases throughout all stages of system development. This includes selecting representative and diverse datasets, conducting rigorous bias testing, and implementing continuous feedback and correction mechanisms (Harris, 2021).

To strengthen privacy protection in educational AI systems, it is essential to prioritize education and awareness initiatives among all stakeholders. This includes providing targeted training for educators and administrative staff on best practices in data protection, as well as educating students and parents about their rights and responsibilities concerning online privacy and the use of educational technologies (Bhatia, 2011). Educational institutions should develop comprehensive resources and training programs to equip stakeholders with the knowledge and skills required to navigate the complexities of data privacy in

AI-driven environments. By fostering a culture of privacy awareness, institutions can ensure that all users are well-informed and empowered to safeguard their personal information effectively (Nissenbaum, 2010).

Privacy considerations must be integrated into the design of AI systems for education, as this represents a critical ethical imperative to ensure the responsible and effective deployment of these technologies. Adopting privacy-by-design principles, implementing robust data protection measures, and promoting transparency and accountability are essential steps for safeguarding the privacy and security of students and other users. These efforts not only mitigate risks but also build trust in AI applications within educational settings. By addressing these challenges, we can harness the transformative potential of AI to enhance educational outcomes while upholding the fundamental rights and values that are central to a just and equitable society (Graetz et al., 2020).

Preserving Human Autonomy in AI Systems in Educational Settings

In the emerging context of AI integration in education, the principles of participation and autonomy stand as essential pillars for the formulation of ethical practices. These principles emphasize not only the inclusion of all stakeholders in decision-making processes regarding AI implementation but also the promotion of autonomy and empowerment among individuals affected by these technologies (Floridi, 2014). Effective participation extends beyond merely informing stakeholders about decisions; it requires the active involvement of students, parents, teachers, and educational communities in the design, development, and continuous evaluation of AI systems in education. This democratic approach enhances the legitimacy of decisions and incorporates diverse perspectives and contextual insights that may be overlooked by AI developers and designers (Rebola & Gonsher, 2018).

The inclusion of students in decision-making is particularly critical, as they are the primary beneficiaries and end-users of AI-based educational technologies. Their active participation not only grants them a voice in shaping these technologies but also cultivates critical thinking and ethical evaluation skills, preparing them for an increasingly digital and automated world (Ezzaim et al., 2024). Similarly, parents play a vital role as advocates for their children's interests. Involving parents in decisions about educational AI ensures that concerns regarding privacy, equity, and personal development are addressed, while fostering collaboration between schools and families to support student learning and well-being (Kaur et al., 2023).

Teachers, with their deep understanding of classroom dynamics, are indispensable in the development of AI educational tools. Their involvement ensures that these technologies are practical and effective in real-world educational settings, positioning them as complementary tools rather than replacements for traditional teaching methods. Collaboration with teachers not only enhances administrative efficiency but also enriches students' learning experiences (Tiwari, 2022). Additionally, the broader educational community—including school administrators, support staff, and other professionals—must be engaged to ensure that AI decisions reflect the values and needs of the entire school community. This diversity of perspectives can uncover challenges and opportunities that might otherwise be overlooked, leading to the design and implementation of more ethical and effective AI systems (Song et al., 2024).

Beyond participation, the principle of autonomy in educational AI focuses on empowering individuals to make informed and responsible decisions about their interaction with these technologies. This entails educating students, teachers, and parents about the ethical foundations of AI, its potential impacts, and how they can maintain control over their participation in digital environments (Leonardi & Treem, 2020). Promoting autonomy also requires providing clear and accessible information about how AI systems operate, what data they collect, how it is used, and how these technologies influence educational experiences. Such transparency not only builds trust in AI but also enables users to make informed decisions about their engagement (Jorzik et al., 2024).

To achieve these objectives, education policies and institutional practices must actively support participation and empowerment. This could involve establishing advisory committees with diverse stakeholder representation, implementing professional development programs on AI ethics and technology for educators, and adopting transparent and responsible data practices (Floridi, 2014). However, several challenges hinder the realization of autonomy in AI systems. A significant barrier is the inherent complexity of AI technologies, which can make it difficult for non-experts to understand their functioning and implications, thereby limiting users' ability to exercise autonomy (Tamás & Koltai, 2020). Additionally, poorly managed AI systems risk exacerbating inequalities by privileging certain groups over others. Addressing this issue demands a commitment to equity and inclusion in AI design and implementation (Alexandron et al., 2016).

To enhance autonomy, several strategies can be employed. Developing user-friendly interfaces can make AI technologies more accessible and understandable, empowering users to engage with these systems more effectively (Tamás & Koltai, 2020). Providing comprehensive training and resources—such as workshops, seminars, and online courses on AI ethics, data privacy, and digital literacy—is another key approach to equipping users with the necessary knowledge and skills (Jones, 2019).

As AI continues to evolve and integrate into educational contexts, the importance of autonomy will only grow. Future advancements in AI will likely present new challenges and opportunities, necessitating ongoing efforts to ensure that AI systems remain empowering and inclusive (von Feigenblatt et al., 2024). In conclusion, participation and autonomy are not only critical ethical principles for the responsible use of AI in education but also foundational to creating an inclusive, transparent, and learner-centered educational environment. By actively involving all stakeholders and fostering autonomy, we can ensure that AI integration in education is both technologically effective and ethically responsible, ultimately delivering social and educational benefits (Jonas, 1984).

Beneficence and Non-maleficence in the Implementation of AI in Education

In the contemporary educational landscape, the integration of AI holds significant promise for transforming teaching and learning processes. However, this technological advancement also introduces a series of ethical and practical challenges that must be addressed with meticulous care and thoughtful reflection. Among the fundamental ethical principles guiding the development and implementation of AI in education, beneficence and non-maleficence stand as cornerstones to ensure that the benefits outweigh potential risks (Floridi, 2014).

The principle of beneficence entails an ethical obligation to act in the best interest of students, maximizing their opportunities for learning and development. AI in education offers tools and systems capable of intelligently adapting to individual student needs, providing personalized and adaptive educational resources that can significantly enhance comprehension and retention of material. These systems can accurately identify each student's strengths and weaknesses, offering immediate and personalized feedback. This capability is particularly valuable in educational settings with large student populations and limited time for individualized teacher intervention (Marín et al., 2018).

Moreover, AI technologies can enrich the learning experience by delivering interactive and engaging educational content. For instance, AI-powered platforms can simulate real-world scenarios, enabling students to apply theoretical knowledge in practical contexts. This experiential learning approach can deepen understanding and foster critical thinking skills (Sumarni & Kadarwati, 2020). Additionally, AI can enhance educational accessibility, enabling students with diverse learning styles, abilities, and special needs to fully participate in the educational process. This is crucial for promoting equity in education and reducing disparities often present in traditional education systems. For example, AI-driven tools can provide real-time translations, speech-to-text services, and personalized learning paths, making education more inclusive and accessible to all students (Song et al., 2024).

However, alongside these benefits, it is imperative to address the potential risks and ethical challenges associated with the use of AI in education. The principle of non-maleficence emphasizes the obligation to avoid causing harm, whether physical or psychological, to students or other stakeholders in the educational context. One of the primary risks lies in the development of AI systems that may perpetuate or amplify existing social and educational biases, thereby exacerbating pre-existing inequalities rather than mitigating them (Song et al., 2024). To counteract this, AI systems in education must be designed and developed with a strong focus on equity and justice, ensuring that they do not discriminate against or exclude any group of students. This necessitates the use of ethically designed algorithms that are transparent, explainable, and auditable to identify and correct potential biases. Transparency in the design and operation of these systems is essential to ensure that users—including students, teachers, and parents—understand how decisions are made and how data is utilized (Gebru et al., 2020).

Furthermore, protecting the privacy and security of students' personal data is critical to upholding the principle of non-maleficence. AI systems must comply with current data protection and privacy regulations, ensuring that the collection, storage, and use of data are conducted ethically and securely, with informed consent obtained where necessary (Leonardi & Treem, 2020). Educational institutions and technology developers must implement robust data protection measures, such as encryption, anonymization, and secure data storage, to safeguard sensitive information. Clear policies and procedures should also be established to manage data breaches and ensure accountability in the event of a security incident (Sclater, 2014).

To ensure that the benefits of AI in education outweigh the potential risks, it is essential to establish a robust ethical framework and responsible governance. This requires collaboration among diverse stakeholders, including educators, researchers, technology developers, policymakers, and the broader education community. Ongoing ethical dialogue and critical evaluation of AI applications in education are crucial for identifying and addressing emerging ethical dilemmas (Floridi, 2014). Ethical guidelines should be developed to provide a clear framework for the responsible use of AI in education. These guidelines can outline best practices for data management, algorithm design, and user engagement, ensuring that AI systems align with ethical principles and societal values (Weckert, 1996).

The ethical training of professionals involved in the design, implementation, and use of AI in education also plays a pivotal role in promoting responsible practices. Educators must be equipped with the knowledge and skills necessary to ethically integrate AI into their pedagogical practices, fostering a thoughtful and critical use of technology to enhance the educational experience without compromising fundamental ethical principles (Johnson, 2001). Training programs should cover topics such as AI ethics, data privacy, and digital literacy, providing educators with the tools needed to navigate the complexities of AI technologies. By cultivating a culture of ethical awareness, educational institutions can ensure that AI systems are used in ways that benefit students and uphold their rights (Doshi-Velez & Kim, 2017).

Beneficence and non-maleficence are essential ethical principles that should guide the implementation of AI in education. By prioritizing these principles, we can ensure that AI technologies are leveraged to enhance learning and development while minimizing potential risks and harms. Through collaboration, ethics training, and the establishment of a robust ethical framework, we can harness the transformative potential of AI to improve education and promote equity and justice for all students (Asefi & Imani, 2018).

Conclusions

The increasing integration of AI in education represents an unprecedented opportunity to transform teaching and learning processes. However, this technological advancement also introduces significant ethical challenges that must be addressed to ensure that AI implementation is both beneficial and equitable. In this chapter, we have examined the fundamental ethical principles that should guide the use of AI in educational settings, offering a framework for responsibly navigating these challenges.

One of the central themes discussed is the role of equity and justice in AI-mediated education. AI has the potential to reduce inequities by providing access to personalized educational resources tailored to individual student needs, irrespective of socioeconomic background. However, there is also a risk that AI could exacerbate existing inequalities if access to these technologies is uneven or if the algorithms reflect inherent biases.

To address these concerns, it is imperative to ensure that all students have equitable access to AI-powered educational tools and that these tools are designed to promote inclusion and diversity. This requires the implementation of policies that guarantee equitable access to technology and foster diversity in algorithm development. Key measures include collecting representative data, conducting rigorous testing to identify and mitigate biases, and involving diverse communities in the design and development of AI technologies to ensure that multiple perspectives and needs are considered.

Accountability is another critical principle emphasized in this chapter. To ensure the ethical and beneficial use of AI in education, it is essential to establish clear accountability mechanisms for all stakeholders involved in the development and implementation of AI technologies. This includes creating policies that define the responsibilities of developers, educators, and administrators, as well as implementing monitoring and evaluation systems to ensure the ethical and effective use of AI. Best practices also involve the ability to rectify errors and adjust practices when negative impacts are identified. This demands a commitment to continuous improvement, adaptation, and learning from past mistakes. By establishing a robust accountability framework, we can ensure that AI benefits all learners while minimizing potential risks.

Transparency is equally vital, as it not only builds trust in AI technologies but also enables users to critically evaluate their effectiveness and ethical implications. Achieving transparency requires adopting open and explainable design practices, ensuring that algorithms are interpretable and that decision-making processes can be traced and justified. This includes documenting decision-making procedures clearly and providing accessible information about data usage. By fostering transparency, we empower users to make informed decisions about their engagement with digitalized environments.

Privacy protection is another cornerstone of ethical AI implementation. It is essential that AI systems comply with existing privacy regulations and that data protection measures are integrated from the design phase. This involves minimizing data collection, employing anonymization techniques, and obtaining informed consent from users. Additionally, clear policies for data management and security incident response must be established. By safeguarding student privacy, we can ensure that AI is used in ways that respect their rights and dignity.

Promoting autonomy is also crucial. This entails providing students and educators with clear, understandable information about how AI systems operate and how they may influence educational experiences. Fostering autonomy further involves ensuring that students retain control over their participation in digitalized environments. This includes offering options to personalize learning experiences and the ability to opt out of certain activities if desired. By preserving student autonomy, we can ensure that AI respects their freedom and capacity to make informed decisions.

The principles of beneficence and non-maleficence are essential to ensure that AI in education maximizes benefits while minimizing risks. Beneficence involves leveraging AI to enhance learning and development, while non-maleficence requires avoiding harm, such as perpetuating biases or compromising privacy. This entails designing AI systems that do not reinforce existing inequalities and that protect the privacy and security of personal data. Ongoing assessments of AI's impact on education are also necessary to identify and mitigate potential risks. By prioritizing beneficence and non-maleficence, we can ensure that AI is used in ways that benefit all students while minimizing potential harms.

The ethical principles discussed in this chapter provide a foundation for the responsible use of AI in education. By adopting an ethical and human-centered approach, we can ensure that AI positively contributes to student learning and development while safeguarding core ethical values. Collaboration among educators, technology developers, policymakers, and the broader education community is essential to addressing ethical challenges and maximizing the transformative potential of AI in education. These principles not only offer a framework for ethical AI implementation but also ensure that the technology respects and promotes the rights and well-being of all students. By adhering to these principles, we can build an educational future in which AI serves as a powerful tool for the common good, advancing equity, justice, and human development across all levels of the education system.

References

Adler, A. H., & Antezana, C. N. (2018). Research ethics and teacher trainers. *Revista Electronica de Investigacion Educativa, 20*(3), 1–10. https://doi.org/10.24320/redie.2018.20.3.1776

Alexandron, G., Armoni, M., Gordon, M., & Harel, D. (2016). Teaching nondeterminism through programming. *Informatics in Education, 15*(3), 1–23. https://doi.org/10.15388/infedu.2016.01

Alfredo, R., Echeverria, V., Jin, Y., Yan, L., Swiecki, Z., Gašević, D., & Martinez-Maldonado, R. (2024). Human-centred learning analytics and AI in education: A systematic literature review. *Computers and Education: Artificial Intelligence, 6*, 100215. https://doi.org/10.1016/j.caeai.2024.100215

Aparicio Gómez, O. Y., Ostos Ortiz, O. L., & Mesa Angulo, J. G. (2022). La convergencia de aprendizajes en el metaverso. *Revista Interamericana de Investigación Educación y Pedagogía RIIEP, 15*(2), 385–398. https://doi.org/10.15332/25005421.7879

Asefi, M., & Imani, E. (2018). Effects of active strategic teaching model (Astm) in creative and critical thinking skills of architecture students. *Archnet-IJAR, 12*(2), 209–222. https://doi.org/10.26687/archnet-ijar.v12i2.1340

Bhatia, A. L. (2011). Adolescents' roles in science, technology and ethics. In *Ethics issues and reflections* (pp. 165–171). Nova Science Publishers, Inc..

Castro, M. P., & Zermeño, M. G. G. (2020). Challenge-based learning: Innovative pedagogy for sustainability through e-learning in higher education. *Sustainability (Switzerland), 12*(10), 4063. https://doi.org/10.3390/SU12104063

Chiappe, A., & Lee, L. L. (2017). Open teaching: A new way on e-learning? *Electronic Journal of E-Learning, 15*(5), 369–383.

Cioffi, R., Travaglioni, M., Piscitelli, G., Petrillo, A., & De Felice, F. (2020). Artificial intelligence and machine learning applications in smart production:

Progress, trends, and directions. *Sustainability (Switzerland), 12*(2), 492. https://doi.org/10.3390/su12020492

Cuzzocrea, A. (2014). Privacy and security of Big Data: Current challenges and future research perspectives. In *PSBD 2014 - Proceedings of the 1st International Workshop on Privacy and Secuirty of Big Data, Co-Located with CIKM 2014* (pp. 45–47). https://doi.org/10.1145/2663715.2669614

Dawkins, M. A. (2014). Ethics, wearable technology, and higher education: Toward a new point-of-view angle on interactive instruction. In *Human Rights and ethics: Concepts, methodologies, tools, and applications* (Vol. 3, pp. 1581–1596). IGI Global. https://doi.org/10.4018/978-1-4666-6433-3.ch087

Doshi-Velez, F., & Kim, B. (2017). Towards a rigorous science of interpretable machine learning. *arXiv*. https://doi.org/10.48550/arXiv.1702.08608

Ezzaim, A., Dahbi, A., Haidine, A., & Aqqal, A. (2024). Enabling sustainable learning: A machine learning approach for an Eco-Friendly multi-factor adaptive E-learning system. *Procedia Computer Science, 236*, 533–540. https://doi.org/10.1016/j.procs.2024.05.063

Floridi, L. (2014). *The ethics of information*. Oxford University Press.

Forbes-Riley, K., & Litman, D. (2010). Metacognition and learning in spoken dialogue computer tutoring. In *Lecture notes in computer science (including subseries lecture notes in artificial intelligence and lecture notes in bioinformatics), 6094 LNCS (PART 1)* (pp. 379–388). https://doi.org/10.1007/978-3-642-13388-6_42

Gebru, T., Morgenstern, J., Vecchione, B., Vaughan, J. W., Wallach, H., Daumé III, H., & Crawford, K. (2020). Datasheets for datasets. *Communications of the ACM, 64*(12), 86–92. https://doi.org/10.1145/3458723

Graetz, N., Woyczynski, L., Wilson, K. F., Hall, J. B., Abate, K. H., Abd-Allah, F., Adebayo, O. M., Adekanmbi, V., Afshari, M., Ajumobi, O., Akinyemiju, T., Alahdab, F., Al-Aly, Z., Rabanal, J. E. A., Alijanzadeh, M., Alipour, V., Altirkawi, K., Amiresmaili, M., Anber, N. H., et al. (2020). Mapping disparities in education across low- and middle-income countries. *Nature, 577*(7789), 235–238. https://doi.org/10.1038/s41586-019-1872-1

Grinbaum, A. (2012). *Ethics of information technology*. Cambridge University Press.

Harris, J. (2021). Ethics in AI and data science: Exploring the challenges of bias and fairness. https://doi.org/10.1007/978-3-030-69978-9

Heller, N., & Bry, F. (2021). Human computation for learning and teaching or collaborative tracking of learners' misconceptions. *Intelligent Systems and Learning Data Analytics in Online Education, 2021*, 323–343. https://doi.org/10.1016/B978-0-12-823410-5.00015-2

Johnson, D. G. (2001). *Computer ethics* (4th ed.). Prentice Hall.

Jonas, H. (1984). *The imperative of responsibility: In search of an ethics for the technological age*. University of Chicago Press.

Jones, K. M. L. (2019). Learning analytics and higher education: a proposed model for establishing informed consent mechanisms to promote student privacy and autonomy. *International Journal of Educational Technology in Higher Education, 16*(1), 24. https://doi.org/10.1186/s41239-019-0155-0

Jorzik, P., Klein, S. P., Kanbach, D. K., & Kraus, S. (2024). AI-driven business model innovation: A systematic review and research agenda. *Journal of Business Research, 182*, 114764. https://doi.org/10.1016/j.jbusres.2024.114764

Kaur, P., Kumar, H., & Kaushal, S. (2023). Technology-assisted language learning adaptive systems: A comprehensive review. *International Journal of Cognitive Computing in Engineering, 4*, 301–313. https://doi.org/10.1016/j.ijcce.2023.09.002

Leonardi, P. M., & Treem, J. W. (2020). Behavioral visibility: A new paradigm for organization studies in the age of digitization, digitalization, and datafication. *Organization Studies, 41*(12), 1601–1625. https://doi.org/10.1177/0170840620970728

Marín, S. Q., Cádiz, M. M. M., Vázquez, R. R., Páez, J. A. P., & Méndez, J. A. C. (2018). Design of a pedagogical route for the evaluation of competencies through the electronic portfolio in distributed and heterogenous environments of learning. *Revista Espanola de Orientacion y Psicopedagogia, 29*(3), 25–44. https://doi.org/10.5944/reop.vol.29.num.3.2018.23319

Marwala, T. (2021). Rational machines and artificial intelligence. *Rational machines and artificial intelligence.*, 1–257. https://doi.org/10.1016/B978-0-12-820676-8.09990-7

Nijenhuis-Voogt, J., Meijer, P. C., & Barendsen, E. (2018, October 4). Context-based teaching and learning of fundamental computer science concepts: Exploring teachers' ideas. *ACM International Conference Proceeding Series.* https://doi.org/10.1145/3265757.3265772

Nissenbaum, H. (2010). *Privacy in context: Technology, policy, and the integrity of social life*. Stanford Law Books.

Pantano, E., & Di Pietro, L. (2012). Understanding consumer's acceptance of technology-based innovations in retailing. *Journal of Technology Management and Innovation, 7*(4), 1–19. https://doi.org/10.4067/S0718-27242012000400001

Rebola, C. B., & Gonsher, I. (2018). Discursive engineering design: A speculative framework for designing technological innovation. *Proceedings of International Design Conference, Design, 5*, 2495–2504. https://doi.org/10.21278/idc.2018.0195

Russell, S. J., & Tegmark, M. (2016). *Life 3.0: Being human in the age of artificial intelligence.* Penguin.

Sankey, M., & St. Hill, R. (2008). The ethics of designing for multimodality: Empowering nontraditional learners. In *Ethical Practices and Implications in Distance Learning* (pp. 126–154). IGI Global. https://doi.org/10.4018/978-1-59904-867-3.ch010

Sclater, N. (2014). Code of practice for learning analytics. *Jisc*. https://www.jisc.ac.uk/guides/code-of-practice-forlearning-analytics

Sharma, A., & Singh, U. K. (2022). Modelling of smart risk assessment approach for cloud computing environment using AI & supervised machine learning algorithms. *Global Transitions Proceedings, 3*(1), 243–250. https://doi.org/10.1016/j.gltp.2022.03.030

Shoaib, M., Sayed, N., Singh, J., Shafi, J., Khan, S., & Ali, F. (2024). AI student success predictor: Enhancing personalized learning in campus management systems. *Computers in Human Behavior, 158*, 108301. https://doi.org/10.1016/j.chb.2024.108301

Smith, H. J., Dinev, T., & Xu, H. (2014). Information privacy research: An interdisciplinary review. *MIS Quarterly, 35*(4), 989–1015. https://doi.org/10.2307/41409970

Song, Y., Weisberg, L. R., Zhang, S., Tian, X., Boyer, K. E., & Israel, M. (2024). A framework for inclusive AI learning design for diverse learners. *Computers and Education: Artificial Intelligence, 6*, 100212. https://doi.org/10.1016/j.caeai.2024.100212

Sumarni, W., & Kadarwati, S. (2020). Ethno-stem project-based learning: Its impact to critical and creative thinking skills. *Jurnal Pendidikan IPA Indonesia, 9*(1), 11–21. https://doi.org/10.15294/jpii.v9i1.21754

Sutton, R. S., & Barto, A. G. (2018). *Reinforcement learning: An introduction*. MIT Press.

Tamás, A., & Koltai, T. (2020). Application of learning curves in operations management decisions. *Periodica Polytechnica Social and Management Sciences, 28*(1), 81–90. https://doi.org/10.3311/PPso.14136

Tebenkov, E., & Prokhorov, I. (2021). Machine learning algorithms for teaching AI chat bots. *Procedia Computer Science, 190*, 735–744. https://doi.org/10.1016/j.procs.2021.06.086

Teke, A., & Kavzoglu, T. (2024). Exploring the decision-making process of ensemble learning algorithms in landslide susceptibility mapping: Insights from local and global explainable AI analyses. *Advances in Space Research, 78*(8), 3765–3785. https://doi.org/10.1016/j.asr.2024.06.082

Tiwari, S. P. (2022). Emerging technologies: Factors influencing knowledge sharing. *World Journal of Educational Research, 9*(2), 69–79. https://doi.org/10.22158/wjer.v9n2p69

Tracy, F., & Carmichael, P. (2013). Research ethics and participatory research in an interdisciplinary technology-enhanced learning project. In *Ethics and academic freedom in educational research* (pp. 41–53). Taylor and Francis. https://doi.org/10.4324/9781315872711

Traxler, J. (2018). Distance learning—Predictions and possibilities. *Education Sciences, 8*(1). https://doi.org/10.3390/educsci8010035

van der Rijst, R., Baggen, Y., & Sjoer, E. (2019). University teachers' learning paths during technological innovation in education. *International Journal for Academic Development, 24*(1), 7–20. https://doi.org/10.1080/1360144X.2018.1500916

von Feigenblatt, O. Federico., & Aparicio Gomez, O. Yecid. (2024). Artificial intelligence and education. Editorial Octaedro. ISBN 978-8410282049.

Weckert, J. (1996). *Computer ethics: The key issues*. Macmillan Press.

Woschank, M., Rauch, E., & Zsifkovits, H. (2020). A review of further directions for artificial intelligence, machine learning, and deep learning in smart logistics. *Sustainability (Switzerland), 12*(9), 3760. https://doi.org/10.3390/su12093760

Yuan, L. (2019). Discussion on the application of computer big data in internet learning. In *Proceedings - 2019 12th international conference on intelligent computation technology and automation, ICICTA 2019* (pp. 482–486). https://doi.org/10.1109/ICICTA49267.2019.00109

Yuan, Y., Li, Y., Nie, J., Chao, X., & Li, J. (2024). An individual adaptive ubiquitous learning paradigm: Focusing on the collection and utilization of academic emotions. *Computers in Human Behavior, 156*, 108228. https://doi.org/10.1016/j.chb.2024.108228

CHAPTER 7

Education and Artificial Intelligence: Critical and Ethical Guidelines for Times of Algorithms

Ferran Sánchez Margalef

Introduction

The exponential advancement of artificial intelligence (AI) in the educational field has inaugurated a new era in the configuration of teaching and learning processes. From adaptive systems that personalize content to automated assessment platforms and intelligent virtual tutors, AI is redefining the means, relationships, and goals of pedagogical action. This transformation, beyond its instrumental aspect, implies a profound redesign of the material and symbolic conditions of human formation. In this context, ethical and axiological questions cease to be accessory and move to the center of the educational debate, for "ethics has played a strong role in education for many years, most obviously via the codes of professional practice that teachers are expected to act within. In the early days of AI, ethical issues around education tool design and deployment

F. Sánchez Margalef (✉)
University of Barcelona, Barcelona, Spain
e-mail: ferran.sanchez@ub.edu

M. Bosch (ed.), *Crucial Ethical Keys of Artificial Intelligence*,
https://doi.org/10.1007/978-3-032-22853-6_7

were not uppermost in the minds of designers: simply making the systems work effectively was the maingoal" (du Boulay, 2022: p. 13).

This work is situated in the field of applied ethics in education, understood as a practical discipline that articulates normative principles with concrete pedagogical decisions, situated and oriented toward the common good, since it seeks to contribute to the formation of ethically responsible and critical subjects in environments mediated by intelligent technologies. This applied-ethical approach is necessary at a time when AI technologies are modifying frameworks of subjectivation, forms of control and evaluation, and the distribution of power in educational spheres. As Ruha Benjamin (2019) warns, algorithmic infrastructures can become systems of encoded injustice and domination. For this reason, they must be questioned from an ethical perspective committed to equity and dignity, for, as we have been pointing out, "ICTs have a huge ethical, legal, and political significance, yet one with which we have begun to come to terms only recently" (Floridi, 2015, p. 2).

From an ethical-pedagogical point of view, this study is based on a relational and critical applied ethics that draws from different traditions, such as the ethics of care (Gilligan, 1982; Tronto, 1993), which emphasizes the centrality of vulnerability, interdependence, and responsibility in the construction of ethical bonds. This perspective is especially relevant in educational contexts mediated by AI, where the risk of dehumanization and relational fragmentation intensifies. Secondly, we also draw on philosophical traditions that promote a practical and hermeneutical ethics, oriented toward the development of situated moral judgment through argumentation, deliberation, and interpretation of conflicts (Nussbaum, 2011; Ricoeur, 1990). From this perspective, educating in ethics does not consist in applying abstract principles, but in cultivating the capacity to deliberate with others from a reflective, empathetic, and contextualized position. This ethics allows us to address in depth the moral dilemmas that emerge in everyday decisions related to the use of AI in education.

Beyond this, critical pedagogy (Freire, 1970) conceives education as a political practice oriented toward emancipation, and warns about the risks of reproducing unjust power structures through technological means, such as when the oppressors increasingly appropriate science as an instrument for their ends: of technology as an indisputable force for maintaining the oppressive "order" with which they manipulate and crush (Freire, 1970, pp. 40–41). From this approach, AI in education is not merely an instrument, but a field of symbolic and political struggle that must be re-signified from an ethical and pedagogical commitment. In addition, we also incorporate Kohlberg's ethics of justice (1981, 1984), since the aim is to foster students' moral reasoning so that they can relate more critically and autonomously to AI through activities that confront them with moral dilemmas and invite them to listen to reasoning different from their own.

New Ethical Challenges in Education with Artificial Intelligence

The entry of artificial intelligence (AI) into education should not be analyzed merely as a technical evolution, but rather as a structural transformation of the frameworks in which human formation takes place. Indeed, the increasing use of technologies capable of making decisions, personalizing content, or assessing performance without direct human mediation forces us to rethink fundamental questions about judgment, responsibility, and moral agency in educational contexts. In this sense, the introduction of technologies that promise to replace aspects of that interaction (through algorithms that personalize, recommend, assess, or guide trajectories) directly affects the way we conceive moral formation, student autonomy, and the role of the educator as an ethical agent.

The automation of pedagogical decisions such as content selection, performance prediction, or student classification poses a risk of depersonalization, transcendence, and reflection. In the words of Gert Biesta (2015), the educational act must preserve a moment of interruption, where the other is not reduced to a set of data or an expected pattern, but welcomed in their unpredictability: "Philosophy might also deny the need for transcendence and shield itself off for any possible interruption, thus trying to maintain its self-chosen self-sufficiency. While philosophy might perhaps be forgiven for such a strategy, I do not think that this is a viable option for philosophy of education—if, that is, philosophy of education does not wish to collapse into a philosophy of learning in which teaching has no place" (p. 52). However, the use of AI may tend toward "programming learning" rather than opening it up. Thus, AI-mediated education runs the risk of replacing pedagogical judgment—always situated, ethically dense, and affectively involved—with automated calculation.

Moreover, the very notion of educational agency, in which intelligent algorithms may turn the recipient into a passive learner, is challenged. The act of educating, which has always belonged to the realm of what is properly human, is being displaced by AI toward the technological, changing the ontological foundations of what it means to form an autonomous subject, as educational decisions (what to learn, when, at what pace) are increasingly shaped by algorithmic systems. Likewise, in the past "ethics was a matter of rational and disembodied autonomous subjects, rather than a matter of social beings. And responsibility for the effects brought about by technological artefacts was attributed to their designer, producer, retailer or user" (Floridi, 2015, p. 8). However, nowadays, technology dilutes responsibility among the corporations that design the products, the governments that promote them, the families who demand innovation, the institutions that purchase the products, and the teachers who use them.

A new field of questions thus opens up around the educational experience itself: what happens when the formative process becomes an algorithmic sequence of stimuli and responses? If educational agency is eroded by the automation of decisions, the nature of the pedagogical experience is also transformed, ceasing to be an ethical-relational event and becoming a technical operation of optimization. This shift compels us to rethink the very moral architecture of learning. At this point, it is necessary to analyze how technological mediation reconfigures the student's subjectivity and their ability to exercise judgment, to question, to disagree, or to resist, since formation takes place in an environment saturated with automated prescriptions, strategic incentives, and guided trajectories.

Therefore, an ethical and pedagogical response is required that matches the technological challenge, for as Dong and Li (2024) warn, these systems not only automate responses, but are also capable of improving through interaction with the user. This type of digitally hypermediated pedagogical experience turns the user into an active agent in shaping their own informational path, while simultaneously surrounding them with a set of emerging issues linked to privacy, surveillance, and autonomy, introducing a series of practical ethical tensions that must be critically addressed through pedagogical action. It will only be possible to harness the pedagogical advantages and possibilities of technology to the extent that ethical education plays a central role and, consequently, to the extent that human beings learn to deal with it: it is not only about incorporating technology, but about educating subjects capable of living with ethical awareness in contexts mediated by artificial intelligence, defending their dignity, their rights, and their capacity for judgment.

We now identify some of the most relevant:

Algorithmic Opacity and the Loss of Teacher Control

Many AI-based systems operate as "black boxes," whose internal processes are neither understandable nor auditable by teachers. This generates a displacement of pedagogical authority: decisions that were previously deliberately made by teachers—such as feedback, identifying difficulties, or assessment—can now fall into the hands of opaque systems. Ben Williamson (2017) has documented how platforms like ClassDojo introduce logics of gamification and surveillance without teacher deliberation or participation:"ClassDojo is not merely a tool for measuring behaviors, but a technology of psycho-compulsion and behavior modification that encourages teachers to award positive value and feedback to behaviors deemed appropriate to developing a growth mindset" (p. 450).

Undoubtedly, this compromises the teaching role in its more maternal sense of caring for students, but also complicates the teacher's position as a mediator between the learner and their environment, blurring their educability. In this regard, it is necessary to educate students so that when they face new technological challenges, they do so responsibly and autonomously, since in many contexts they find themselves alone in front of algorithms that make decisions about their performance, behavior, or progress without any comprehensible explanation or human pedagogical judgment.

Digital Surveillance and the Erosion of Privacy

Many AI tools collect and process large amounts of personal data, often without genuine informed consent from users. This massive datafication can lead to forms of educational surveillance incompatible with an ethics based on respect for basic individual freedoms. Shoshana Zuboff (2019) has warned of the shift toward a surveillance capitalism that turns educational environments into data markets, where students are treated as objects of informational extraction. In this way, the educational space ceases to be a protected realm and becomes just another node within the infrastructures of algorithmic extraction under the logic of capitalism. Evidently, this logic not only compromises students' privacy but also alters pedagogical relationships, introducing mistrust, self-surveillance, and pressure for constant performance.

The Reproduction of Biases and Social Injustices

Artificial intelligence systems are not neutral. Although they are often presented as objective and technical tools, in reality they are deeply conditioned by human decisions involved in their design, programming, training, and implementation. These decisions include data selection, assumptions built into the models, and the goals guiding their use. As Cathy O'Neil (2016) has pointed out, algorithms can become real weapons when they conceal under a veil of mathematical rationality patterns of discrimination already present in society.

Similarly, Eubanks (2018) also argues that they can reproduce and generate inequalities and exclusion. They are, in that sense, opinions embedded in code. Far from correcting inequalities, these systems tend to reproduce and amplify them, especially when they operate without clear mechanisms of transparency, ethical oversight, or accountability. In the educational field, this issue becomes particularly serious. Algorithmic decisions can determine everything from access to specific programs to opportunities for personalized intervention. When the data used reflect historical structural inequalities—for example, in the representation of ethnic minorities, women, or people with disabilities—the results produced by the system may consolidate and reproduce biases instead of mitigating them.

The Dehumanization of the Educational Experience

The integration of artificial intelligence systems into educational environments poses an increasing risk of dehumanizing teaching-learning processes. Although many technological developments are presented under a mask of "personalization" of learning, this personalization is often a simulation based on reducing the subject to a series of quantifiable data, such as responses, interaction times, behavior patterns, and scores. This model fits within what Han (2015) calls "digital psychopolitics," a form of control in which apparent freedom hides forms of algorithmic manipulation. When the subject is treated as a database to be managed, the affective, ethical, narrative, and communal dimensions of learning tend to disappear. Education thus becomes a mechanical adaptation process to externally defined goals, where the criterion of efficiency replaces that of integral formation.

Reducing education to mere technical training is not only impoverishing but also politically dangerous. As Nussbaum (2001) has insisted, among the key competencies for today's world are those related to cultivating "narrative imagination [understood as the capacity to put oneself in the place of the other, to understand the fragility of the human condition, and to engage ethically with the common good] and critical reflection to experience full democratic citizenship" (pp. 30–31).

This humanistic dimension of education is absent in most automated systems. Algorithms do not understand suffering, exclusion, or meaning. They do not dialogue or empathize. For this reason, an education mediated exclusively by AI runs the risk of becoming a pedagogy without a face and without a community, without tradition. As Freire (1970) states, "there is a kind of narration sickness. The dominant tone of education is this one: narrating, always narrating" (p. 51). However, we may fall into the danger of reproducing a commodified and digitalized education, where data replaces the living word, and where learning is reduced to a unidirectional transfer of information—without dialogue, without praxis, without transformation.

Moreover, authors such as Biesta (2010) have pointed out that the educational act always implies an intersubjective relationship in which the other is recognized as someone unique and unrepeatable. Biesta, in particular, warns against the growing "learnification" of education, that is, its transformation into an individualistic, instrumentalized process oriented solely toward performance or, in other words, "the tendency to replace a language of education with a language that only talks about education in terms of learning" (Biesta, 2010, p. 5). In this sense, AI systems, if not carefully designed from a relational ethics perspective, may reduce education to a process of information transmission, ignoring the processes of subjectivation, emancipation, and recognition that shape it. Thus, a pedagogy that includes an ethics of care and human relationships (Gilligan, 1982; Noddings, 2003) can hardly be replaced by artificial intelligence without a human perspective, since this involves contemplation of the other, attention, presence, and a situated response to the other's concrete needs.

How to Educate in Values in AI-Mediated Contexts

One of the most relevant consequences of the educational use of artificial intelligence is the reorganization of the space in which students make decisions, exercise their reasoning, and refine their ethical sense. Algorithmic mediation tends to reduce ambiguity, simplifying options and optimizing trajectories, which may imply a decrease in the active exercise of ethical judgment. In this scenario, it is essential to maintain formative spaces where learners can think critically about the consequences of their decisions, including those involving interaction with automated systems. The introduction of AI in education not only transforms the means of accessing knowledge, but also deeply alters the axiological frameworks from which decisions are constructed. In this new environment, ethical judgment is mediated by technological architectures that filter, rank, and present information according to computational logics, which raises the challenge of how to educate ethical sensitivity when the digital environment tends to make moral conflict invisible or simplified, and to dissolve responsibility in automated systems.

A key strategy consists in incorporating ethical exercises into curricular modules, as this can have a positive effect on students' moral attitudes and prepare them to better navigate the ethical dimensions they will face in the future (Kopec et al., 2023). The literature on moral education highlights the importance of contextualizing ethical learning in realistic situations, where students can activate processes of moral deliberation and reflection on agency, responsibility, and the common good (Rest et al., 1999). Therefore, the exercises must go beyond the simple presentation of rules, including complex dilemmas that trigger cognitive dissonance and promote the transition to more advanced stages of moral judgment according to the neo-Kohlbergian model.

Moral Dilemmas

In particular, participation in dilemmas involving intelligent technologies, with open-ended and value-laden consequences, allows students to develop competencies for decision-making in uncertain contexts, thereby strengthening their ethical and professional training. For example, analyzing a case in which an educational recommendation system excludes certain students due to implicit biases in the data, or discussing whether it is legitimate for an AI to select candidates for a scholarship based on performance predictions and listening to the students' moral reasoning, can help them advance in their moral reasoning and judgment, as validated by Blatt and Kohlberg (1975), who, after leading a discussion group in a class for an extended period exposing students to moral dilemmas, observed that half of the students progressed in their moral development. This approach is based on the constructivist premise that moral judgment develops through interaction with significant ethical challenges in an environment that combines emotional support and cognitive stimulation. Guided group discussion, when conducted systematically, enables processes of decentering the self and fosters reasoning from impersonal perspectives, which is crucial for advancing toward post-conventional moral structures (Power et al., 1989).

Additionally, digital simulations can be used to represent real decision-making environments with ethical variables involved. Tools such as MIT Moral Machine (participatory and online) or environments designed on educational platforms allow students to face choices where efficiency, justice, privacy, equity, or well-being intersect, while also serving to collect information about the users themselves and their moral decision-making, as demonstrated by the study published by Awad et al. (2018), using precisely MIT Moral Machine, in which they gathered a large amount of information about cultural differences reflected in the ethical values of people across different continents. These types of platforms not only allow training in ethical deliberation competencies but also make visible how sociocultural biases shape the frameworks from which moral decisions are made. Thus, ethical learning is not limited to the individual dimension but is framed within an intercultural critical pedagogy, in which the analysis of collected data can open spaces for reflection on diversity, globalization, and epistemic justice.

Role-Playing Games

It is also relevant to implement simulated role-playing games through gamified activities as a strategy to foster moral judgment in educational contexts mediated by artificial intelligence. These activities allow students to adopt differentiated roles—for example, AI programmers, teachers, students, or institutional managers—within simulated scenarios that present complex ethical dilemmas. Through these simulations, participants must make value-based decisions under conditions of uncertainty, thereby reactivating processes of contextualized ethical deliberation. As

Narvaez (2010) states, "deliberation permits one to step back from the current flow of events to consider additional information and alternative cues, facts, and paths from those to which one first attends" (p. 170), which is essential for the development of elevated moral judgment. In this context, ethical gamification can be understood as a dialogical-experiential methodology that activates processes of moral metacognition. Since it enables the assumption of multiple perspectives, role-playing strengthens the development of skills such as moral empathy, anticipation of consequences, evaluation of alternatives, and systemic ethical thinking—key aspects in complex moral education (Thompson, 2014).

The pedagogical value of role-playing lies in its ability to promote moral empathy and cognitive decentering, essential elements in the development of ethical judgment. Richmond et al. (1990) observed that participation in social roles significantly contributed to the development of students' ethical reasoning, showing a direct impact on their DIT (Defining Issues Test) scores, indicating moral judgment development. This immersion fosters a deep understanding of conflicting values and allows for a critical analysis of the consequences of algorithmic decisions on users' autonomy, equity, or privacy.

Socratic Debates

Complementarily, the inclusion of Socratic debates helps reinforce the reflective and dialogical dimension of moral judgment. Grounded in maieutics and guided by open-ended questions, these debates do not aim to impose a correct answer but to foster critical inquiry and the reasoned articulation of diverse positions. As Nussbaum (2010) notes, "such courses, through both content and pedagogy, will stimulate students to think and argue for themselves, rather than defer to tradition and authority—and they believe that the ability to argue in this Socratic way is, as Socrates proclaimed, valuable for democracy" (pp. 47–48), thus reinforcing the pedagogical value of these dialogical practices in students' ethical formation. In the current context, in which intelligent systems tend to automate decisions that were previously subject to human deliberation, the Socratic method emerges as a counter-hegemonic pedagogy that reclaims the value of questioning, argumentation, and individual responsibility. Questions such as the delegation of educational decisions to AI systems or the attribution of moral responsibility to algorithms serve as catalysts for collective reflection on the normative assumptions underlying technological practices in educational settings. To question, to inquire, and to seek the truth inherent in this technocratic and power-operating logic constitutes, therefore, one of the ethical duties in a democratic society.

Favero et al. (2024) demonstrated that a Socratic chatbot designed to foster critical thinking can significantly promote reflection and intellectual autonomy, showing how interventions based on the Socratic method can strengthen moral judgment in learning environments. In AI-mediated environments, ethics must be integrated through deliberative, experiential, and critical pedagogical approaches, aimed at empowering students as moral agents capable of responsibly inhabiting a technologically complex world.

Developing Ethical Competencies in Digital Environments

Educating in values in contexts mediated by artificial intelligence cannot be limited to the isolated analysis of ethical dilemmas: it requires selecting a set of principles and developing a network of deeply contextualized ethical competencies that enable the student to act as an active moral subject in complex and evolving technological ecosystems. In this way, we wish to highlight the following ethical competencies for relating to and ethically dealing with AI.

Equity and Justice: Competency to Design and Evaluate Inclusive Systems

The principle of equity demands ensuring that AI systems do not reproduce structural inequalities but instead actively contribute to reducing them. This requirement translates into the ability to identify algorithmic errors, analyze the representativeness of the data used, and design inclusive tools: "El principio de equidad exige asegurar que los sistemas de IA no reproduzcan desigualdades estructurales, sino que contribuyan activamente a reducirlas. Esta exigencia se traduce en la capacidad para identificar sesgos algorítmicos, analizar la representatividad de los datos utilizados y diseñar herramientas inclusivas" (Cantero & Bosoer, 2025, p. 55).

This competency requires integrating into the educational curriculum a critical literacy on how algorithmic biases operate, both in their technical and social dimensions. Students must learn to detect how certain statistical patterns can reinforce historical structures of inequality, and how the lack of diversity in training data or development teams can result in exclusionary automated decisions. Moreover, working on this competency implies promoting an intersectional sensitivity that considers the intersecting effects of gender, ethnicity, class, or disability. From the perspective of algorithmic justice, it is essential that future professionals are capable of proposing mechanisms for correction, ethical impact assessment, and participatory system redesign, in line with frameworks proposed by UNESCO (2021a, 2021b) or the European Commission (2020).

Responsibility: Competency to Establish Accountability Mechanisms

Ethical responsibility in AI contexts involves not only attributing consequences but also anticipating impacts and establishing control and prevention mechanisms. This competency requires that teachers and students be able to map the actors involved in the development and application of a technology, distribute responsibilities, and design review and reparation protocols in case of harm. In this sense, AI accountability includes being answerable for both the intended and unintended effects of automated decisions (UNESCO, 2021a, 2021b). Developing this competency allows not only ethical action but also the ability to demand it within institutional frameworks.

Furthermore, this competency requires understanding that responsibility cannot rest solely with technical developers but must be distributed among the different agents involved in the design, implementation, and use chain. In educational contexts, this includes institutions, teachers, technology providers, and curriculum designers. Educating in responsibility involves teaching how to map actors, decision chains, and zones of ethical ambiguity. It also involves knowing how to develop ethical review protocols, establish risk indicators, and activate reparation mechanisms in case of unintended impacts. As Floridi and Cowls (2019) have argued, the culture of responsibility must be proactive and preventive, not reactive. In teacher training, this competency can be addressed through the analysis of real cases, the design of codes of conduct, and institutional simulations.

Transparency: Competency to Interpret and Communicate Algorithmic Processes

The principle of transparency takes pedagogical form as the ability to understand, translate, and explain how an AI system works. This competency is linked to the development of critical thinking, digital literacy, and the capacity for accountability. Grosz et al. (2019), in proposing the Embedded EthiCS model, highlighted the importance of teaching students to identify ethical issues embedded in algorithmic systems and explain how they arise from design choices. In this way, a culture of critical interpretation of automated decisions affecting learning is strengthened. Furthermore, another important issue, closely related, is explainability, that is, understanding how these systems make decisions, since "la explicabilidad asegura transparencia en las operaciones de IA, permitiendo a los usuarios ver qué datos utiliza la IA y cómo procesa esos datos para llegar a una decisión. Cuando los sistemas de IA pueden explicar sus decisiones, se facilita determinar la responsabilidad por estas decisiones, particularmente importante cuando una decisión conduce a consecuencias negativas" (Galiana et al., 2024, p.180).

Developing this competency involves teaching students to dismantle algorithmic opacity through a functional and ethical understanding of systems. It is not enough to use the platforms: one must learn to question their logic of operation, their decision criteria, and their implicit assumptions. To this end, it is useful to combine basic technical analysis with philosophical reflection on the notion of agency, causality, and moral intelligibility.

Privacy: Competency to Ethically Manage Data

Protecting privacy in digital environments requires that students and teachers understand the information flows involved in AI systems, be able to assess their risks, and make informed decisions about the treatment of their data. The associated ethical competency includes knowing how to request consent, apply data minimization principles, and understand the legal and moral implications of informational exposure. Being such a fundamental issue that affects human intimacy itself, becoming one of the cores of dignity, it is necessary to work to ensure that users of online content are aware and knowledgeable about algorithms, how they operate, and the repercussions they may have for themselves in terms of data collection and use (Kivinen et al., 2022).

This competency must integrate content related to the regulatory framework, but also promote an ethical understanding of privacy as a relational and not merely individual right. Ethical education should address how data is collected, stored, transferred, and inferred from our activity, highlighting the risks of surveillance, bias, or manipulation. It is crucial to educate students to recognize when they are giving up their data, under what conditions, and what limits should be established—especially in educational contexts. Privacy must be presented as a basic condition for fair, free, and respectful interaction with technology.

Moreover, real scenarios should be incorporated in which popular educational platforms are analyzed and their privacy policies critically assessed, as well as their effects on student autonomy, the family environment, and the school community.

Autonomy: Competency to Promote Digital Agency and Self-Determination

There is a significant risk to personal autonomy when information and personal data are managed and modeled through algorithmic logics. This form of digital governance affects individual decision-making, subtly and often unconsciously guiding behaviors and choices, with the goal of producing certain outcomes or inducing specific behaviors (Cotino, 2017). This process can be intensified by the generation and diffusion of negative emotional dynamics in the digital environment (Zafra, 2018). Preserving autonomy requires fostering in subjects the ability to make informed decisions about their interaction with intelligent technologies. This includes developing the competency of self-regulation, reflective ethical thinking, and critical awareness of systems that influence academic choices, trajectories, or evaluations. Therefore, this competency aims to train students not only to use technology but to understand its logic and deliberate on its appropriateness.

To strengthen this competency, training should include analysis of algorithmic personalization mechanisms and their effect on subjective agency. Students need to understand how "engagement" is generated, how recommendation systems work, and to what extent these condition their decisions or cognitive reinforcements. The aim is to promote a reflective autonomy, capable of resisting behavioral programming and acting with independent judgment in hypermediated environments. Ethical education in AI must, therefore, teach how to maintain inner margins of freedom, to take critical distance, and to exercise will in the face of persuasive technologies. This also involves working on habits of attention, concentration, and emotional self-regulation in the face of platforms designed to capture time, attention, and action.

Digital autonomy is thus connected with the idea of a strong ethical subject, not subordinate to the automatisms of technological design nor to the commercial logics that structure many current educational platforms.

Beneficence and Non-maleficence: Competency to Assess Impacts and Prevent Harm

Acting ethically in AI-mediated environments also means anticipating both the benefits and potential risks of its implementation. This competency requires developing an evaluative perspective that allows for analyzing side effects, unintended discrimination, or forms of invisible suffering: "Ello vale tanto para quienes desarrollan y configuran la IA, como para sus resultados. Incluye evitar los daños accidentales (uso excesivo), así como los daños deliberados ("uso indebido")" (Cotino, 2019, p. 37), and, precisely when faced with hypothetical consequences, the principles of precaution and responsibility are necessary.

The principle of non-maleficence demands an anticipatory ethics that teaches how to foresee the unintended effects of any technology implemented in the classroom. This competency is not limited to the technical analysis of consequences but must also incorporate an emotional and social dimension. Assessing harm is not only about identifying errors: it is about understanding their human and collective effects. Therefore, developing this competency requires incorporating ethical and social indicators and participatory evaluation techniques. On the other hand, the principle of beneficence demands an orientation toward the common good, educational justice, and student well-being, beyond technical efficiency or performance. Educational AI cannot be limited to improving outcomes; it must demonstrate that it improves formative conditions in a broader sense. This competency can be developed through impact assessment exercises, retrospective case studies, and ethical simulations of technological decisions.

Conclusions

The progressive integration of artificial intelligence systems into educational environments entails a profound transformation of the conditions under which moral judgment is formed, knowledge is constructed, and citizenship is exercised. We are not simply facing a methodological change or a technological innovation, but rather a structural mutation in the forms of interaction, deliberation, and decision-making in the educational domain. Algorithmic mediation, by operating on data, learning trajectories, and available options, introduces a rationality oriented toward efficiency, prediction, and optimization that may come into tension with pedagogical principles such as autonomy, equity, deliberation, and justice.

This context imposes the need to rethink the aims of education through an ethical lens. It is not about opposing artificial intelligence, but about subjecting it to scrutiny from a critical pedagogy that reclaims the formative meaning of the educational experience. AI cannot assume the role of moral authority nor replace the judgment of human subjects; its role, at best, is instrumental and subsidiary. Therefore, it is urgent to design educational environments in which students not only understand how technologies work but also develop the capacities necessary to deliberate ethically about their uses and consequences.

Throughout this chapter, various pedagogical strategies have been developed for this purpose. The use of complex ethical dilemmas, digital simulations, role-playing games, and Socratic debates are formative practices that create spaces where moral judgment is exercised in a situated and dialogical manner. These strategies activate students' ability to recognize value conflicts, make reasoned decisions, and assume the consequences of their choices.

The second line developed has been the formulation of a framework of fundamental ethical competencies for ethical education in relation to artificial intelligence. A structure based on six key dimensions has been proposed: equity, responsibility, transparency, autonomy, privacy, and justice. These dimensions should be understood as competencies that require continuous, situated, and context-sensitive training. Working on them involves mobilizing both conceptual content and deliberative experiences and demands the active involvement of teachers, institutions, and regulatory frameworks. Ethics cannot be reduced to drafting codes of conduct: it must be inscribed in a formative praxis that transforms pedagogical relationships and institutional logics.

In this sense, the underlying challenge is not merely technical or curricular, but profoundly political and axiological. What is at stake is the model of the subject that education seeks to shape in a technologically conditioned world. Against an adaptive vision that promotes passive compatibility with intelligent systems, a strong conception of the moral subject is asserted: capable of judgment, critique, resistance, and creation. Educating in ethics in AI-mediated contexts thus means educating for a democracy that does not delegate its sovereignty to automatisms but is renewed in every act of critical deliberation.

Ultimately, artificial intelligence in education can become an opportunity to reactivate the ethical meaning of pedagogical practice, as long as it is not subordinated to technocratic logics or corporate interests. As Gozálvez (2011) has noted, "la educación tecnológicamente matizada es una oportunidad para la ampliación y el enriquecimiento del campo de la experiencia, ampliación que, sin embargo, ha de ser un acicate para la ciudadanía de los alumnos, los futuros constructores de la realidad social y humana. Al fin y al cabo, la tecnología ha de ser vista como lo que es, un medio, un instrumento para usos y fines muy diferentes, que van desde el solipsismo o la endogamia digital hasta un civismo-en-red, profundamente democrático" (p. 134). This statement synthesizes the spirit of the present chapter: only an ethical, critical, and deliberative education will allow artificial intelligence to truly become a tool in the service of emancipation and not yet another device for functional normalization.

References

Awad, E., Dsouza, S., Kim, R., Schulz, J., Henrich, J., Shariff, A., et al. (2018). The moral machine experiment. *Nature, 563*(7729), 59–64. https://doi.org/10.1038/s41586-018-0637-6

Benjamin, R. (2019). *Race after technology: Abolitionist tools for the new Jim code.* Polity Press.

Biesta, G. (2010). *Good education in an age of measurement: Ethics, politics, democracy.* Routledge.

Biesta, G. (2015). *The beautiful risk of education.* Routledge.

Blatt, M. M., & Kohlberg, L. (1975). The effects of classroom moral discussion upon children's level of moral judgment. *Journal of Moral Education, 4*(2), 129–161.

Cantero, M., & Bosoer, L. (2025). *REDemocracIA: Guía para una aproximación democrática a la inteligencia artificial en Iberoamérica.* School of Transnational Governance. European University Institute (EUI).

Cotino, L. (2017). Big data e inteligencia artificial: Una aproximación a su tratamiento jurídico desde los derechos fundamentales. *Dilemata, 24*, 131–150.

Cotino, L. (2019). Ética en el diseño para el desarrollo de una inteligencia artificial, robótica y big data confiables y su utilidad desde el derecho. *Revista Catalana de Dret Públic, 58*, 29–48.

Dong, Q., & Li, L. (2024). Exploring the role of both online and offline knowledge sources and artificial intelligence in information management for digital libraries. *Profesional de la información, 33*(6), e330608. https://doi.org/10.3145/epi.2024.ene.0608

du Boulay, B. (2022). Artificial intelligence in education and ethics. In O. Zawacki-Richter & I. Jung (Eds.), *Handbook of open, distance and digital education* (pp. 1–16). Springer Nature Singapore.

Eubanks, V. (2018). *Automating inequality: How high-tech tools profile, police, and punish the poor*. St. Martin's Press.

European Commission. (2020). White paper on Artificial Intelligence: A European approach to excellence and trust. European Commission. https://commission.europa.eu/publications/white-paper-artificial-intelligenceeuropean-approach-excellence-and-trust_en

Favero, L., Pérez-Ortiz, J. A., Käser, T., & Oliver, N. (2024). *Enhancing critical thinking in education by means of a Socratic chatbot [Preprint]. ArXiv*. https://doi.org/10.48550/arXiv.2403.13989

Floridi, L. (2015). *The onlife manifesto: Being human in a hyperconnected era*. Springer.

Floridi, L., & Cowls, J. (2019). A unified framework of five principles for AI in society. *Harvard Data Science Review, 1*(1). https://doi.org/10.1162/99608f92.8cd550d1

Freire, P. (1970). *Pedagogía del oprimido*. Herder.

Galiana, L. I., Gudino, L. C., & González, P. M. (2024). Ética e inteligencia artificial. *Revista Clínica Española, 224*(3), 177–181. https://doi.org/10.1016/j.rce.2023.10.004

Gilligan, C. (1982). *In a different voice: Psychological theory and women's development*. Harvard University Press.

Gozálvez, V. (2011). Educación para la ciudadanía democrática en la cultura digital. *Comunicar, 36*(1), 1–15.

Grosz, B. J., Grant, D., Vredenburgh, K., Behrends, J., Hu, L., Simmons, A., & Waldo, J. (2019). Embedded EthiCS: Integrating ethics broadly across computer science education. *Communications of the ACM, 62*(8), 54–61. https://doi.org/10.1145/3341163

Han, B.-C. (2015). *Psicopolítica: Neoliberalismo y nuevas técnicas de poder*. Herder.

Kivinen, K., Aslama Horowitz, M., Havula, P., Härkönen, T., Kiili, C., Kivinen, E., et al. (2022). *Digital Information Literacy Guide*. EDMO NORDIS project. UE–Faktabaari.

Kopec, M., Magnani, M., Ricks, V., Torosyan, R., Basl, J., Miklaucic, N., et al. (2023). The effectiveness of embedded values analysis modules in Computer Science education: An empirical study. *Big Data & Society, 10*(1), 20539517231176230. https://doi.org/10.1177/20539517231176230

Narvaez, D. (2010). Moral complexity: The fatal attraction of truthiness and the importance of mature moral functioning. *Perspectives on Psychological Science, 5*(2), 163–181. https://doi.org/10.1177/1745691610362351

Noddings, N. (2003). *Caring: A feminine approach to ethics and moral education* (2nd ed.). University of California Press.

Nussbaum, M. C. (2001). *El cultivo de la humanidad. Una defensa clásica de la reforma en la educación liberal*. Editorial Andrés Bello.

Nussbaum, M. C. (2010). *Not for profit: Why democracy needs the humanities*. Princeton University Press.

Nussbaum, M. C. (2011). *Creating capabilities: The human development approach*. Harvard University Press.

O'Neil, C. (2016). *Weapons of math destruction: How big data increases inequality and threatens democracy*. Crown.

Power, F. C., Higgins, A., & Kohlberg, L. (1989). *Lawrence Kohlberg's approach to moral education*. Columbia University Press.

Rest, J. R., Narvaez, D., Bebeau, M. J., & Thoma, S. J. (1999). *Postconventional moral thinking: A neo-Kohlbergian approach*. Lawrence Erlbaum Associates.

Richmond, S. S., Anderson, K. L., & Morris, J. D. (1990). Social role playing and moral judgment development. *Social Research, 4*(1), 21–34. https://doi.org/10.1007/BF01049391

Ricoeur, P. (1990). *Soi-même comme un autre*. Éditions du Seuil.

Thompson, D. (2014). The role of moral reasoning and moral emotions in ethics education for future teachers. *Journal of Moral Education, 43*(4), 414–431. https://doi.org/10.1080/03057240.2014.943161

Tronto, J. C. (1993). *Moral boundaries: A political argument for an ethic of care*. Routledge.

UNESCO. (2021a). *AI and education: Guidance for policymakers*. Retrieved May 14, 2025, from https://unesdoc.unesco.org/ark:/48223/pf0000376709

UNESCO. (2021b). *Recommendation on the ethics of artificial intelligence*. Retrieved May 16, 2025, from https://unesdoc.unesco.org/ark:/48223/pf0000381137

Williamson, B. (2017). Decoding ClassDojo: Psycho-policy, social-emotional learning and persuasive educational technologies. *Learning, Media and Technology, 42*(4), 440–453. https://doi.org/10.1080/17439884.2017.1278020

Zafra, J. (2018). Tenemos que cambiar el modelo: Toda la economía se basa en manipular personas. Entrevista a jaron lanier. *Telos, 109*, 26–34.

Zuboff, S. (2019). *The age of surveillance capitalism: The fight for a human future at the new frontier of power*. PublicAffairs.

CHAPTER 8

Person, Relationships, and AI. Metaphysical Foundations

Abel Miró i Comas

To my wife Assumpta

A Contemporary Problem: The Personal Character of AI

The term "Artificial Intelligence" (AI) was first used in the summer of 1956 at a conference held at Dartmouth University on computer intelligence (*Darmouth Summer Research Project on Artificial Intelligence*). Great scientists such as J. McCarthy, M. Minsky, C. Shannon, A. Newell and H. Simon gathered there, and defined AI as "The science and engineering of making intelligent machines" (Poole & Mackworth, 2010). A more recent conceptualization has led to defining it as the area of computer science the goal of which is to *emulate* the cognitive functions of human beings through the use of computational systems (Manyika

A. Miró i Comas (✉)
Universitat Internacional de Catalunya, Barcelona, Spain
e-mail: amiro@uic.es

M. Bosch (ed.), *Crucial Ethical Keys of Artificial Intelligence*,
https://doi.org/10.1007/978-3-032-22853-6_8

et al., 2017). The difference between the two definitions is not minor: in the first, the character of intelligence is *truly* attributed to the artifact; in the second, the machine is relegated to the condition of a mere "imitator" of intelligent subjects.

No matter which definition we take, it is undeniable that the development of this technology has made it possible for some actions that were previously considered exclusive to personal beings—such as writing an academic article, generating images with a certain "artistic" character or holding a conversation—to be carried out by a machine. This situation presents an anthropological problem with strong ethical implications: Can we affirm that something *is* a person just because it, in certain aspects, acts *like* a person? Is *resembling* a person a sufficient condition for *being* a person?

To answer this question—very relevant today—we must refer to a metaphysical question that is perennially present: What is a person?

A False Conception of the Person: The Person as a Relationship

Some current trends, when examining the concept of person, leave aside its substantial character, to put in the foreground the operation or the relationship (Canals, 2004). This is the attitude, for example, of contemporary Personalism: "Personalist anthropology discovers and values the singular freedom, the dignity of each subject, and places it above impersonal structures. Mounier personifies this trend. He is the one who discovers the three radical relationships of the person: vocation, communion, commitment (Lobato, 1987)".

The person, according to Personalism in general, is not a "thing", a "substance", it does not possess its own essential characteristics by virtue of which man can act freely, in a personal way. It is through his acts that the individual becomes a person. It is something that man must conquer, a self-creation: "The person is not an essential principle or constituent, the root of all personal properties. It is not the origin of a process, but the end of a totally free self-creating activity. In short, man is not a person by nature, but through his freedom he can become a person, thus achieving maximum dignity (Forment, 1994)".

According to the general conception of Personalism, man as such is just an "individual", a mere part of the human species and is devoid of all originality and "authenticity". However, when man "chooses" to become a person—according to some authors, with an intellectual option, according to others, with a voluntarist option—and achieves it, then he ceases to be vulgar.

Personalist authors consider the person from an ethical perspective. When they affirm that it is necessary to become a person, what they really mean is that it is necessary to be a *good* person, understanding this goodness in the sense of a conformity between one's actions and an ultimate end, set by a moral system which they often do not make explicit: "A person is a spiritual being constituted as such by a form of subsistence and independence in its being; it maintains this subsistence thanks to its adherence to a hierarchy of values freely adopted, assimilated and lived through a responsible commitment and a constant conversion; this way, it unifies all its activity in freedom and unfolds, through creative acts, the singularity of its vocation (Mounier, 1936)".

The ethical direction of the personalist doctrine has led some of its defenders, such as Maurice Nédoncelle, to affirm that the relationship with the other is the foundation of the personal self: "To have a self it is necessary to be loved by another self, and at the same time to love it; it is necessary to be conscious, even if it is obscure, of the other and of the relationships that unite the terms of this spiritual network. The communion of consciousnesses is the primitive fact, the *cogito* has a reciprocal character (Nédoncelle, 1942)".

Any attempt to attribute a substantial character to the person is disqualified by personalists because they consider that it denies the interpersonal openness of the human being. In accordance with ethics, which is at the basis of their metaphysics, they characterize the person by the relationship. The person is not something that is given to some entities, but something that is constituted in the interpersonal relationship.

However, this position presents some difficulties, as Forment notes. The first has to do, precisely, with the possibility of opening up to the other: "it seems to be forgotten that in all communication there is always someone who communicates, and, therefore, the anteriority of the subject. There is a radical impossibility of communication, if aptitudes for it are not admitted, in subsistent subjects. It is necessary that they are constituted by a being that confers on them faculties, intellectual and loving, that make their communication possible (Forment, 1994)".

Secondly, any dialogue is impossible if the interlocutors, before being "for-an-other", are not "in-themselves": "They are subsistent in rational nature before being ones who dialogue. Hence it is not possible for someone to become a person by dialoguing, nor to give the personal being to someone through dialogue (Forment, 1994)".

And, finally, as Canals observes, it is also problematic to affirm that by virtue of a relationship of friendship is how friends are constituted as persons: "Would the esteem and praise of a 'friend' be serious if all that could be said was 'my friend', without affirming of him, in himself and 'absolutely' all that perfection for which he is dear to me and for which I enter in him in a relationship of friendship? (Canals, 1994)".

From the position described, which places at the core of the person the operation and the relationship, avoiding any "substantial" element, an alarming consequence follows, which completely escapes the original intention of personalists: the obligation to attribute the condition of personal being to an artifact that acts like a person—that converses amicably like a person, that can write a novel or a philosophical essay.

Let us note how a doctrine, which was born with the noble end of affirming "the primacy of the human person over material needs and over the collective mechanisms that sustain its development (Mounier, 1936)", can end up attributing the condition of "person" to one of these mechanisms that should be at the service of the development of the human person, that is, to a computer. This is how a humanist philosophy, if it does not have a firm metaphysical foundation, can end up leading, in practice, to a "radical anti-humanism (Sadin, 2018, 2023)". A humanism without Metaphysics is virtually a weapon against man.

To resolve this insufficiency of contemporary "personalisms", we propose to return to the canonical definition of person formulated by Boethius (480–524) in his *Liber de persona et duabus naturis contra Eutychem et Nestorium*.

The Person Not as a Relationship But as a Substance. Boethius' Definition of Person

The philosophical consideration of "person" appeared from a theological need. The Christian faith, in order to formulate the two main mysteries contained in Revelation—that of the Trinity and that of the Incarnation—necessitated the notion of "person": in God there are three persons and a single substance or nature (Trinitarian mystery); in Christ there are two natures—one divine and the other human—but a single person (Christological mystery). Thus, the study of the person, despite it belonging to the strictly rational or philosophical realm, was aroused by a religious or theological motivation.[1]

It is relevant to take this into account since Boethius, as the title of his opuscule indicates, presents his philosophical characterization of the person in the context of a theological discussion against two heresies, that of Eutyches and that of Nestorius. The first maintained that in Christ there is only one nature, in such a way that the human nature of Jesus was absorbed by the divine nature; the second not only affirmed that in Christ there were two natures, but also two persons (Canals, 2015).

Faced with this situation, Boethius is forced to philosophically clarify the relationship between the notions of "nature" and "person". The word "nature" has several meanings, which had already been examined by Greek philosophy. The one that is relevant for the Christological problem and, in turn, for the metaphysics of the person, is the following: "Nature has, further, another meaning according to which we speak of the different nature of gold and silver, wishing thereby to point the special property of things; this meaning of nature will be defined as follows: 'Nature is the specific difference that gives form to anything [*unamquamque rem informans specifica differentia*]' (Boethius, *Liber de persona et duabus naturis*, chap. 1)". Boethius affirms that both Nestorius and the Catholics maintain that there are two natures in Christ, understanding the notion of "nature" in the indicated sense, since neither of them thinks that the same specific differences befit God and man.

In order to define what is proper to the person, it is essential to investigate in what way it is distinguished from nature: "For if every nature has person, the difference between nature and person is a hard knot to unravel; or if person is not taken as the equivalent of nature but is a term of less scope and range, it is difficult to say to what natures it may be extended, that is, to what natures the term person may be applied and what natures are dissociated from it. For one thing is clear, namely that nature is a substrate of Person, and that Person cannot be predicated apart from nature (Boethius, *Liber de persona et duabus naturis*, chap. 2)".

We already have a *first conclusion*: every person is a nature or, formulated negatively, there is no person outside of natural things.

[1] "Aristotle did not have any principle to distinguish the *suppositum* from the singular nature; and we would not have it either if we had not had the opportunity to investigate it, instructed by the mysteries of faith (Suárez, F., *Disputationes Metaphysicae*, XXXIV, s.3, n.18)".

Now it is necessary to determine what kind of nature the person is: "Since Person cannot exist apart from nature and since natures are either substances or accidents and we see that a person cannot come into being among accidents (for who can say there is any person of white or black or size?), it therefore remains that Person is properly applied to substances (Boethius, *Liber de persona et duabus naturis*, chap. 2)".

Second conclusion: the person is a substantial nature, that is, a nature that exists by itself and in itself, and not in a subject different from it, as is proper of accidental natures.

But what kind of substance is the person? Boethius presents a classification of the different types of substances: "But of substances, some are corporeal and others incorporeal. And of corporeals, some are living and others the reverse; of living substances, some are sensitive and others insensitive; of sensitive substances, some are rational and others irrational. Similarly of incorporeal substances, some are rational, others the reverse (for instance the animating spirits of beasts); but of rational substances there is one which is immutable and impassible by nature, namely God, another which in virtue of its creation is mutable and passible except in that case where the Grace of the impassible substance has transformed it to the unshaken impassibility which belongs to angels and to the soul (Boethius, *Liber de persona et duabus naturis*, chap. 2)".[2]

Next, Boethius excludes, from the previous catalogue, those substances that cannot be persons: "Now from all the definitions we have given it is clear that Person cannot be affirmed of bodies which have no life (for no one ever said that a stone had a person), nor yet of living things which lack sense (for neither is there any person of a tree), nor finally of that which is bereft of mind and reason (for there is no person of a horse or ox or any other of the animals which dumb and unreasoning live a life of sense alone), but we say there is a person of a man, of God, of an angel (Boethius, *Liber de persona et duabus naturis*, chap. 2)".

We now have the *third conclusion*: the person is a rational substance.

Finally, following Aristotle, Boethius distinguishes between the first substance, that is, the concrete individual, which cannot be predicated of another (e.g., *this* stone), and the second substance, that is, the universal

[2] The will of the angel and of man, by grace, can be fixed on that which constitutes their ultimate good, their supernatural happiness, that is, God. In the case of man, this fixation can only occur after the present life; in the case of the angel, after the first election.

nature, which can be predicated of many individuals, at least hypothetically (e.g., stone): "Again, some substances are universal, others are particular. Universal terms are those which are predicated of individuals, as man, animal, stone, stock and other things of this kind which are either genera or species; for the term man is applied to individual men just as animal is to animals, and stone and stock to individual stones and stocks. But particulars are terms which are never predicated of other things, as Cicero, Plato, this stone from which this statue of Achilles was hewn, this piece of wood out of which this table was made. But in all these things person cannot in any case be applied to universals, but only to particulars and individuals; for there is no person of a man if animal or general, only the single persons of Cicero, Plato, or other single individuals are termed persons (Boethius, *Liber de persona et duabus naturis*, chap. 2)".

This brings us to the *fourth and final conclusion*: the person is a particular substance, a primary substance.

We now have a definition of person: "The person is an individual substance of rational nature [*Persona est naturae rationalis individua substantia*] (Boethius, *Liber de persona et duabus naturis*, chap. 3)".

Extreme Individuality of the Person

Commenting on Boethius' definition, Thomas Aquinas notes that the person not only has individuality, but also an extreme individuality. It is the most individual of all individual realities and, precisely for this reason, the worthiest, the most perfect. When a person is lost, something more unique or irreplaceable is lost than when a stone, a plant or an animal is lost. This thesis can be justified for three reasons.

Firstly, because within the genus of substance, the person is a "first" or singular substance: "substance is here taken in a general sense, as divided into first and second, and when *individual* is added, it is restricted to first substance [*substantia prima*] (Thomas Aquinas, *Summa Theologiae*, I, q. 29, a.1, ad 2)". The "first substance" or "individual" can also be called a "hypostasis" or "*suppositum*".

The word "substance", considered in itself, without any further determination, has a generic meaning that can be applied to two different things: "first substance" and "second substance". "Second substance", at the same time, can refer to both the "*abstract*" and "*concrete*" substance. The former contains the totality of essential principles, but is devoid of individuating principles; thus, for example, the name "humanity" includes the essential principles of man, but since it excludes any reference to that by virtue of which this humanity is concretized in a singular man, the "humanity" of *this* or *that* man cannot be predicated. "Humanity" is a part of what is in the individual, and the part can never be predicated of the whole (I certainly cannot say of a cat that it is its tail). The "*concrete* substance", on the other hand, is predicated as a whole, because it contains all the principles found in the individual, that is, the essential and the individuating.[3] The latter, if it expresses the individuating principles indeterminately, is called "common concrete substance" (e.g., "man"); if it expresses them determinately and explicitly, it is called "individual concrete substance" (e.g., "Socrates" or "Plato") (Thomas Aquinas, *De ente et essentia*, chap. 3; *Summa contra gentiles*, IV, chap. 81).

In short, the word "substance" expresses both the "second substance", which can be predicated of many, and the "first substance", which can only be predicated of a singular individual. If the term "person" expresses what is maximally singular in the reality of things, we should not be surprised that Boethius, in his definition of person, adds the qualifier "individual" next to the term "substance", thus implying that the substance to which he is alluding here is something irreplaceable, unique, unrepeatable, which cannot be said of the "second". Socrates is unrepeatable, but he is as much a man as Plato.

The *second reason* to affirm that the person is the supreme individuality is based on its substantial character: "Although the universal and particular exist in every genus, nevertheless, in a certain special way, the individual belongs to the genus of substance. For substance is individualized by itself [*individuatur per seipsam*]; whereas the accidents are individualized by the subject, which is the substance; since *this* particular

[3] What do these individuating principles, by virtue of which the human essence is singularized, consist of? The Angelicus answers: "the principle of individuation is matter (Thomas Aquinas, *De ente et essentia*, chap. 1)". Later, he clarifies that he is not speaking of "prime matter", but of "*materia signata*" or "designated matter", which is the one affected or determined by the accident of quantity: "We should notice, therefore, that the principle of individuation is not matter taken in just any way whatsoever, but only designated matter. And I call that matter designated which is considered under determined dimensions [*sub determinatis dimensionibus*]. Such matter is not placed in the definition of man as man, but it would be placed in the definition of Socrates, if Socrates had a definition. Rather, it is non-designated matter which is placed in the definition of man; for this bone and this flesh are not placed in the definition of man, but bone and flesh absolutely. These latter are man's non-designated matter (Thomas Aquinas, *De ente et essentia*, chap. 1)".

whiteness is called *this*, because it exists in *this* particular subject (Thomas Aquinas, *Summa Theologiae*, I, q. 29, a.1, in c)".

The "singular" or "individual substance" individuates itself in a double sense: *either* because it is already individual and does not need to be individualized—as is the case of angelic substances, in which two individuals of the same species cannot be found—[4];*or* because it is singularized thanks to the addition of individuating principles, which contract the specific essence, but which are part of the same "individual substance". Let's see it from an example: the archangel Gabriel is individuated by his own specific essence, which is not shared and cannot be shared by another; he is the only individual of his species. Socrates, on the other hand, is individuated by principles that contract the human essence—which is shared by many—to a unique and unrepeatable version of it. Although these principles are accidental to man as man, they are essential to Socrates as Socrates. In both cases, the substance is individuated by itself. Accidents, on the other hand, are not individuated by themselves in either sense, but by the "first substance" in which they exist. Obviously, the one individuated by itself is more singular than the one individuated by virtue of another.

Rationality and Person

So far, we have indicated two reasons by virtue of which the person is what is maximally individual in all of nature: (1) the fact that it is a "first substance" and not a "second substance"; and (2) the fact that it is a substance and not an accident. All this, however, can be found in Socrates as well as in a cloud or a rabbit. We still lack a third element to be able to speak rigorously of the person: rationality.

Rational substances possess a greater degree of singularity than non-rational substances, because they can impose on themselves their own ends, they can give their lives their own direction, their actions are not completely determined by nature or environmental circumstances. Persons have a biography, while animals only have biology (Canals, 1987): "Further still, in a more special and perfect way, the particular and the individual are found in the rational substances which have dominion over

[4] In angels, therefore, it makes no sense to distinguish between the "*common concrete essence*" and the "*singular concrete essence*". The cause of this is that the "principle of individuation" is matter, from which angels are completely separate.

their own actions; and which are not only made to act, like others [*non solum aguntur, sicut alia*]; but which can act of themselves [*per se agunt*]; for actions belong to singulars. Therefore also the individuals of the rational nature have a special name even among other substances; and this name is *person*. (Thomas Aquinas, *Summa Theologiae*, I, q. 29, a.1, in c)".

In rational substances, individuals belong to the genus of substance "in a more special and perfect way (Thomas Aquinas, *Summa Theologiae*, I, q. 29, a.1, in c)". That is why they are distinguished from the rest with the special name of "person". For this reason: "the term *individual substance* is placed in the definition of person, as signifying the singular in the genus of substance; and the term *rational nature* is added, as signifying the singular in rational substances (Thomas Aquinas, *Summa Theologiae*, I, q. 29, a.1, in c)".

The individual or "first substance", that Boethius refers to in his definition of person, can also be called "*suppositum*". As Aquinas says: "'*suppositum*', however, is a singular in the genus of substance, which is called 'hypostasis' or 'first substance' (Thomas Aquinas, *Quodlibet II*, q.2, a.2, in c)". Every person is a "*suppositum*", although not every "*suppositum*" is a person. To be one, it should also possess a rational nature, that is, a nature capable of imposing itself its own ends.

In the *Disputed Questions on the Power of God*, Thomas Aquinas also expresses the peculiarity of the person, already indicated in the definition of Boethius: "Therefore, just as the word 'hypostasis' according to the Greeks or 'first substance' according to the Latins is the special name of an individual in the genus of substance [*nomen individui in genere substantiae*], even so the word 'person' is the special name of an individual of rational nature, so that person is a special name under both these heads ['hypostasis' and 'first substance']. Hence, to indicate that it is in a special manner an individual in the genus of substance, it is stated that it is 'an individual substance'; and to indicate that it is in a special manner an individual of rational nature, it is added, 'of rational nature' (Thomas Aquinas, *De Potentia Dei*, q.9, a.2, in c)". To distinguish this "individual substance" or "*suppositum*" from all the others, the word "person" is used.

Let us suppose that AI is a "*suppositum*" or "individual substance"—a problematic affirmation because, as we have seen, Boethius circumscribes substance to the sphere of natural realities, so that human works are relegated to the condition of accidental configurations—[5]can we legitimately apply the qualifier of "rational" to it? Or put another way: is AI really intelligent? The Mexican philosopher Manuel Ocampo answers, relying on the doctrine of Aquinas: "Human intelligence as a faculty is not a purely passive power, but is mainly an active power (*Summa Theologiae*, I, q.54, a.4, in c); that is, real capacity to move another, while AI can only be a passive power, that is, capacity to be moved by another (*Summa Theologiae*, I, q.2, a.3) (Ocampo, 2024)".

The activities carried out by AI are proper to a moved agent, whereas those of an intelligent substance are proper to an agent with a certain capability to move itself. Therefore, AI cannot perform the two fundamental operations of human intelligence, because these require an intrinsic capacity for movement, an active power. The first of these operations is the abstraction of the universal essence of singular sensible objects, the "*simplex apprehensio*" (Sanguinetti, 1992): "technology is not capable of performing the first operation of the human mind, which consists of separating the universal essence of concrete entities, thanks to the agent intellect, elaborating ideas or concepts (Ocampo, 2024)". And the second operation, judgment, allows the intellect to consider the essence apprehended in the first operation "*sub ratione entis*", as a being, as present in the extra-mental reality: "Neither is [AI] capable of making judgments in the strict sense and in a formal way, but only materially, uniting, separating or combining terms, copulas and accommodating propositions that have been elaborated by human intelligence or processed by the artefact (Ocampo, 2024)". It is proper of human judgment to compose and divide representations. However, this activity constitutes, as Manuel Ocampo indicates, only the material aspect of our judgment; the formal consists of taking a position with respect to the reality of things, in a commitment of the subject—even the self-defined relativists—with respect to the truth.

[5] The block of Carrara marble on which Michelangelo Buonarroti sculpted his *Pietà* is a substance; however, the figure that the Italian sculptor imprinted on it is an accident belonging to the genus of quality. All of man's artistic and technical activity is circumscribed within the horizon of accidents. Our works do not sustain themselves—otherwise we would have to say that we have created them out of nothing—but on materials that are given to us by nature.

A corpse, moved by electrical impulses, could raise an arm or a leg, but no one would think of saying that it is alive because it does not move by itself; all its movement depends exclusively on an external impulse. Likewise, AI cannot be considered "rational" just because it generates propositions similar to those we form, uniting, separating and combining terms. Its language is not the exteriorization of an intellectual and, therefore, vital act, but an external act originated by another external act, just as the movement of a billiard ball is caused by the impact of another ball. For all this, we can affirm that between AI and human intelligence there is not a sufficient similarity that allows us to rigorously apply the term "intelligence" to both. AI is not intelligent.

"*Esse*" as a Formal Constituent of the Person

Rational nature individualized by dimensional quantity is not yet a concrete man; it is not yet a "*suppositum*" or "individual substance"; in short, it is not yet a "person". The essence of Socrates is not yet Socrates. What, then, is the individual essence of each man lacking to become "this" man, that is, a personal being? Aquinas responds as follows: "'*Esse*' belongs to the very constitution of the person [*esse pertinet ad ipsam constitutionem personae*] (Thomas Aquinas, *Summa Theologiae*, III, q.19, a.1, ad 4)".[6]

The word "person", as Forment points out in an extensive monograph recently published, differs from all other nouns—both common and proper—in that without the mediation of something essential, it points directly to "*esse*". Only in a mediate or indirect way, the word "person" signifies the essence that is the subject or receptacle of "*esse*". This essence, in the case of the person, according to Boethius' definition, is of a rational type: "all other nouns always refer to essential, general or individual characteristics. The person is the term that names the essentially inexpressible individual foundation, the act of being (Forment, 2023)".

But what is this mysterious element that is not only an intrinsic constituent principle of the person, but also its formal constituent; that to which the word "person" directly points? What should we understand by "*esse*"? This classical passage from Aquinas helps us to understand this notion, which is the keystone of his entire philosophical system: "'*Esse*' is

[6] See also: Thomas Aquinas, *Summa Theologiae*, III, q.17, a.2, in c; Thomas Aquinas, *Summa Theologiae*, III, q. 35, a.1, in c.

the most perfect of all things [*perfectissimum omnium*], for it is compared to all things as that by which they are made actual; for nothing has actuality except so far as it exists. Hence '*esse*' is that which actuates all things [*actualitas omnium rerum*], even their forms [*ipsarum formarum*] (Thomas Aquinas, *Summa Theologiae*, I, q.4, a.1, ad 3)".[7]

What makes an individual of human nature—composed of soul, body and individuating principles—a person, is not something that is part of his nature or essence; it is its proper "*esse*", which actualizes the essence of *this* man in particular—not the essence of man in general, which only exists in our mind—and converts it into a being. More precisely, it converts the individual essence into a being that possesses the act of "*esse*" in its most eminent degree, that is to say, in the degree proper to the spirit, which is the only substantial being that possesses the perfections of intelligence and free will.[8]

It is true that, even in non-personal realities—such as the stone, the sunflower, or the cow—the act of "*esse*" is the foundation of all their perfections; this case, however, cannot be compared with that of the person. In infra-personal realities, their perfections are claimed by the essence; they are, ultimately, essential perfections.[9] Even though all existing stones are unique and unrepeatable examples of the same specific nature—gold, marble, agate, *et sic de caeteris—in* them the repeatable, universalizable, conceptualizable element prevails above the individual, ineffable element, which makes "this" stone "this" stone.

Non-personal things, as Forment points out, "are esteemed for the essence they possess. In them, everything is ordered, including their singularity, to the specific properties and operations of their natures.

[7] See also: Thomas Aquinas, *Quaestiones disputatae de anima*, a.1, ad 17; Thomas Aquinas, *Quaestiones disputatae de anima*, a.6, ad 2; Thomas Aquinas, *De Potentia*, q.7, a.2, ad 9; Thomas Aquinas, *De Potentia*, q. 7, a.2, ad 9; Thomas Aquinas, *De Potentia*, q.7, a.2, ad 5.

[8] "Person, therefore, is constituted intrinsically by a material constituent, the individual concrete essence or nature, and a formal constituent, the proper '*esse*' provided to it. It is thus a complete substance and as such subsistent or with an '*esse*' of its own, and, because it is involved in the degree of the spirit, it is rational or intellectual (Forment, 2025a)".

[9] "As also in non-personal realities being is its formal constituent, it must be noted that the person differs from them by his greater degree of possession of '*esse*'. Although, in all entities, their perfections are ultimately resolved in the act of being, they are expressed by their essence. On the other hand, the person, without the mediation of something essential, directly refers to '*esse*', to the entity act (Forment, 2025a)".

Hence individuals are only of interest insofar as they are carriers of it (Forment, 2025a)". In other words, the stone that I am seeing right now through the window is more "a *stone*" than "*this* stone". The rose-bush that I have planted in the garden is more "a *rosebush*" than "*this* rosebush". The swallow that stopped on the neighbors' roof is more "a *swallow*" than "*this* swallow". What is most valuable in the stone, the rosebush and the swallow is not what differentiates them from other individuals of the same species, but what they have in common with them. If I were to exchange them for another with the same characteristics, the difference would not be too pronounced; nothing too important would be lost.

Persons, on the contrary, are valuable for their own individuality, for what they have that is unique. If I love my wife, it is not for what she has in common with other women, so that I can easily replace her with this one or that one. I love her for what sets her apart from all others, for what makes her unique, inimitable: "in non-personal things, all the individuals of the same species are interchangeable. However, unlike all other singular entities, each human person is an absolutely unique individual, unrepeatable and irreplaceable (Forment, 2025a)".

That which the person possesses that is singular, absolutely incommunicable, is more perfect and more worthy than those aspects of it that can be expressed in generic or specific terms, that is, in terms that signify a universal essence. This man is more perfect and more worthy by virtue of being "this" man—that is, because he is a person—than by virtue of being "a man" or "an animal". The greatest singularity is also the greatest perfection and, for this reason, Thomas Aquinas says that "'person' signifies that which is most perfect in all nature [*perfectissimum in tota natura*] (Thomas Aquinas, *Summa Theologiae*, I, q. 29, a.3, in c)". It is worth noting that this is not affirmed of an abstract person, but of each one in particular: "this" person in particular is the best and most excellent thing that exists in all of nature or material world. Each person is superior to everything that exists in this world and to its sum.

Let us note how, in Saint Thomas, there is a close connection between his way of understanding the person, which is "that which is most perfect in all nature (Thomas Aquinas, *Summa Theologiae*, I, q. 29, a.3, in c)", and his way of understanding the "*esse*", which is "the most perfect among all things (Thomas Aquinas, *De Potentia*, q.7, a.2, ad 9)", "the perfection of all perfections (Thomas Aquinas, *De Potentia*, q.7, a.2, ad 9)", "the most perfect of all (Thomas Aquinas, *Summa Theologiae*, I, q.

4, a.1, ad 3)". The "*esse*" is found in the person more intensely than in non-personal beings, and this is precisely the basis of its absolute incommunicability, of its maximum individuality, of its supreme perfection and dignity.

The proper "*esse*", which converts nature or rational essence into a personal being, is not a physical reality, like a stone or an apple. It is a metaphysical reality, which cannot be grasped by the senses, and which escapes any attempt of the intelligence to fix it in a concept. However, this does not mean that we know absolutely nothing about the "*esse*": we have an obscure, mysterious knowledge of it, not of an essential order, but of an experiential and intimate order. Thanks to this knowledge, which we can call "existential", we do not know *what* we are; we simply know that we *are*: "[The knowledge of our "*esse*"] is possible, because each person's own "*esse*" is revealed to him in his intellectual consciousness, in the intellectual perception of what is or exists, of that of which he has absolute certainty and whose object, his own "*esse*", he indicates with the word "I" (Forment, 2025a)".

Without "I"—which is a transparency of the personal "*esse*" that we perceive actually in every act of thought (Forment, 2025b)—there is no person; and without person there is no "I". The notion of person immediately refers to the "*esse*" participated in a maximum degree of perfection, dignity, nobility and perfectibility, to the "*esse*" that can reflect upon itself, to the "*esse*" of a spiritual substance; only it can be mysteriously perceived by the subject who possesses it. This is why Aquinas considers that the formal constituent of the person is what is most intimate and profound in the rational subject, his heart, his "*esse*".

A Practical Consequence: The Case of Eugenia Kuyda

After losing her best friend in an accident, Russian-born engineer Eugenia Kuyda developed a program capable of simulating his way of speaking and interacting. To achieve this, she uploaded into this program all the information she had about her friend in her emails and WhatsApp messages. Kuyda's ultimate goal was to "copy", "reply", or "imitate" her friend. This claim, besides the ethical problems it may raise and which have recently been studied by Magdalena Bosch (Bosch et al., 2022), is based on a metaphysical misunderstanding: what was most valuable in the friend and, therefore, what Kuyda particularly regretted losing, is precisely what made him someone different from everyone else, what made his way of talking, of being affable, of laughing... unique; in short, everything that was individual or inimitable about him and that had its root in his personal "*esse*". If this—that is, his "self"—could be reproduced, communicated, multiplied, it would not have as much value and, consequently, the pretension of "replicating" it in a "chatbot" would be meaningless.

The hamburger I ate yesterday, although I cannot eat it again today, I do not particularly regret it, because I can eat another one. Likewise, there would be no reason to regret the loss of a friend, if what is proper of him could be replicated in another—like the recipe for the hamburger. The missing hamburger does not matter, what is important is that what I have in front of me is precisely that: a hamburger. Basically, by trying to "replicate" the friend, what I am doing is treating him as if he were a non-personal reality—like a hamburger—as a mere bearer of an essence that can be universalized and, therefore, as something of little value.

We are faced with an unsustainable position: neither what is proper of the friend is replicable, nor what is replicable is proper of the friend. To pretend to reproduce what is most valuable and perfect in a person—that is, his personal character—means falling into the contradiction of wanting to imitate what is inimitable. But even if the personal character of the friend could be imitated, we would fall into another absurdity: what we intended to imitate would cease to be what is most valuable and perfect in the friend and, consequently, it would cease to be something worthy of imitation.

Conclusion

The cause of all this confusion is ignorance of what a person is. If we consider that the essential constituent of the person consists in the relationship, as personalists claim, we will be forced to agree with Eugenia Kuyda when she claims to have produced an "artificial friend". The "chatbot" that she has created, and which she has marketed under the name *Replika*, simulates a conversation with another human being quite accurately; if the person is constituted in the relationship with the other, we will have no choice but to attribute a personal character to the program. But, as we have seen, in order to communicate, it is essential to be something first: a substance. For this reason, we consider that it is urgent to return to Boethius' definition of the person as an "individual substance of a rational nature (Boethius, *Liber de persona et duabus naturis*, chap. 3)" in order to face the great ethical challenge that the AI implies. We also consider that this definition has to be interpreted as Aquinas does, taking into account that the formal constituent of the person is not something of an essential order, but the act of "*esse*", which is the foundation of the supreme individuality of the person. An error in the consideration of the person entails serious ethical consequences, as we clearly see in the previous example: it leads to treating a person as a non-personal being and a non-personal being as a person. It leads to treating the highest as if it were the lowest and the lowest as if it were the highest. And this is not a minor confusion.

References

Aquinas, T. (1888-1906). *Sancti Thomae de Aquino opera omnia iussu leonis XIII P. M. edita, vols. IV–XI. Summa theologiae cum commentariis caietani.* Ex Typographia Polyglotta.

Aquinas, T. (1918-1930). *Sancti Thomae de Aquino opera omnia iussu leonis XIII P. M. Edita, vols. XIII–XVI. Summa contra gentiles.* Typis Riccardi Garroni.

Aquinas, T. (1929). In P. Mandonnet (Ed.), *Scriptum super libros sententiarum magistri Petri Lombardi episcopi Parisiensis* (Vol. 2). P. Lethielleux.

Aquinas, T. (1953). In J. M. Wyss (Ed.), *De natura materiae.* Société Philosophique.

Aquinas, T. (1965). Quaestiones disputatae de potentia. In P. M. Pession (Ed.), *S. Thomae Aquinatis Quaestiones disputatae* (Vol. 2). Marietti.

Aquinas, T. (1976). De ente et essentia. In *Sancti Thomae de Aquino opera omnia iussu leonis XIII P. M. edita* (Vol. 43, pp. 315–381). Editori di San Tommaso.

Aquinas, T. (1992). Super boetium de trinitate. In *Sancti Thomae de aquino opera omnia iussu leonis XIII P. M. edita* (Vol. 50, pp. 1–230). Commissio Leonina-Éditions Du Cerf.

Aquinas, T. (1996a). In P. M. Pession (Ed.), *Sancti Thomae de Aquino opera omnia iussu leonis XIII P. M. edita, vol. 24/1:Quaestiones disputatae de anima.* Comissio Leonina_Éditions Du Cerf.

Aquinas, T. (1996b). *Sancti Thomae de Aquino opera omnia iussu leonis XIII P. M. edita, vol. 25/1: Quodlibet VII, VIII, IX, X, XI.* Commissio Leonina-Éditions du Cerf.

Aquinas, T. (1996c). *Sancti Thomae de Aquino opera omnia iussu leonis XIII P. M. edita, vol. 25/2: Quodlibet I, II, III, VI, IV, V, XII.* Commissio Leonina-Éditions du Cerf.

Boethius. (1847). De persona et duabus naturis contra Eutychen et Nestorium. In J. P. Migne (Ed.), *Patrologia Latina* (Vol. 64, pp. 1338D–1354D). J-P Migne.

Boethius. (1973). *Theological tractates. The consolation of philosophy*. (H. F. Stewart, E. K. Rand, S. J. Tester, Trans.). Harvard University Press.

Bosch, M., Fernández, G., Miró, A., & Figa, J. (2022). Evolving friendship? Essential changes, from social networks to artificial companions. *Social Network Analysis and Mining, 12*(*1*), 12–39. https://doi.org/10.1007/s13278-022-00864-1

Canals, F. (1987). *Sobre la esencia del conocimiento*. Promociones y Publicaciones Universidad de Barcelona.

Canals, F. (1994). Ser personal y relación interpersonal. In E. Forment (Ed.), *Dignidad personal, comunidad humana y orden jurídico* (pp. 25–36). Editorial Balmes.

Canals, F. (2004). Para la metafísica de la persona: substancia, acción y relación. In F. Canals (Ed.), *Tomás de aquino: Un pensamiento siempre actual y renovador* (pp. 331–342).

Canals, F. (2015). Los siete primeros concilios. In F. Canals (Ed.), *Obras completas, vol. 3. Escritos teológicos I* (pp. 11–159). Editorial Balmes.

Degl'Innocenti, U. (1942). Il pensiero di San Tommaso sul principio d'individuazione. *Divus Thomas, 45*, 35–81.

Forment, E. (1988). *Filosofía del ser*. Promociones y Publicaciones Universidad de Barcelona.

Forment, E. (1994). La persona humana. In A. Lobato (Ed.), *El pensamiento de Santo Tomás para el hombre de hoy. Vol. 1: El hombre en cuerpo y alma* (pp. 685–954). Edicep.

Forment, E. (2023). Las personas divinas. In E. Forment (Ed.), *Sabiduría tomista* (pp. 1096–1109). Ed&Tic.

Forment, E. (2025a). *Compendio de filosofía tomista*. San Román.

Forment, E. (2025b). Metafísica de santo Tomás. *Encuentros en Catay, 38*, 246–265.

Lobato, A. (1987). Antropología y metantropología. Los caminos actuales de acceso al hombre. In A. Lobato & D. Ols (Eds.), *Antropologia e Cristologia ieri e oggi. Atti del Convegno di Studio della S.I.T.A* (pp. 5–41). Pontificia Università S. Tommaso d'Aquino.

Manyika, J., Chui, M., Miremadi, M., Bughin, J., George, K., Willmott, K., & Dewhurst, M. (2017). *Un futuro que funciona: Automatización, empleo y productividad*. McKinsey Global Institute.

Mounier, E. (1936). *Manifeste au service du personalisme*. Éditions Montaigne.

Nédoncelle, M. (1942). *La réciprocité des consciences, essai sur la nature de la personne*. Aubier.

Ocampo, M. (2024). Algunos fundamentos de la filosofía realista de Santo Tomás de Aquino para una valoración de la Inteligencia artificial (IA). *Perseitas, 12*, 72–92. https://doi.org/10.21501/23461780.4724

Poole, D. L., & Mackworth, A. K. (2010). *Artificial Intelligence: Foundations of computational agents*. Cambridge University Press.

Sadin, É. (2018). L'intelligence artificielle ou l'enjeu du siècle: Anatomie d'un antihumanisme radical.

Sadin, É. (2023). *La vie spectrale: Penser l'ère du métavers et des IA generatives*. Éditions Grasset & Fasquelle.

Sanguinetti, J. J. (1992). Los principios de la racionalidad de Santo Tomás. *Espíritu, 41*, 109–137.

Suárez, F. (1960). *Disputaciones metafísicas, 7 vols*. (S. Rábade, S. Caballero, A. Puigcerver Trans.). Gredos.

CHAPTER 9

Transhumanism: Power and the Neglect of Otherness in an AI-Driven Utopia

Gabriel Fernandez-Borsot

The Transhumanist Ideology and the Prominence of Technoscientific Reason

According to the official website of the Humanity+ association (the former World Transhumanist Association), transhumanism is "The intellectual and cultural movement that affirms the possibility and desirability of fundamentally improving the human condition through applied reason, especially by developing and making widely available technologies to eliminate aging and to greatly enhance human intellectual, physical and psychological capacities" (Humanity+, 2023, Transhumanist FAQ, para. 9). The range of technologies that transhumanists intend to use to achieve their goals is very wide, with special relevance of nanotechnology, genetic engineering and artificial intelligence (AI). Most importantly, transhumanists plan to use these technologies concurrently and in an integrated way (what is called technological convergence) (Wolbring, 2008), applying them on the human body to radically alter the human embodied

G. Fernandez-Borsot (✉)
Faculty of Humanities, Universitat Internacional de Catalunya, Barcelona, Spain
e-mail: gabi@uic.es

M. Bosch (ed.), *Crucial Ethical Keys of Artificial Intelligence*,
https://doi.org/10.1007/978-3-032-22853-6_9

condition, eventually leading to something so different from the current human configuration that it should conceptually be considered another species or life form, called *post-human* (More, 2013).

Transhumanism is a complex and heterogeneous movement with multiple factions proposing different ways of implementing the transhumanist goals and focusing on different aspects of the transformation that the transhumanist ideology proposes. The movement itself has no centralized authority that gives it consistency or hierarchy, and there is no official list of these factions. Some factions overlap with others, but an analysis of the literature and of the internet activity surrounding the term "transhumanism" provides a tentative list of the most important ones:

Extropians: This faction forms the initial core of the transhumanist movement, inspired by the thoughts of its seminal thinker, Max More (2003). Extropians are focused on maximizing the human potential and its expansion into space as active agents of a wider cosmic evolutionary process.

Singularitarians: This faction believes in the advent of technological singularity, a point of time in the future in which technological development will lead to a radical transformation of reality to a point that it will be considered a total disruption of the human historical process (Kurzweil, 2005, 2024). Its most visible ideologist is Ray Kurzweil. Singularitarians represent the most visible, active and structured faction, having established some referential institutions such as the Singularity University (2025). For these reasons, this faction will be the main reference of the critique developed in this chapter.

Abolitionists: This faction advocates the use of biotechnology to eliminate suffering in all sentient life. The main proponent of this faction is David Pearce (1995), author of *The Hedonistic Imperative*.

Bio-libertarians: This faction pursues an ideal of personal freedom through biological enhancement with the use of technological aids such as cognitive enhancers and gene editing, promoting practices such as biohacking (Yetisen, 2018).

Democratic transhumanists: This faction emphasizes the need to ensure universal access to enhancement technologies and a democratic oversight of their deployment to prevent inequality. The key figure in this faction is James Hughes (2004), author of *Citizen Cyborg: Why Democratic Societies Must Respond to the Redesigned Human of the Future*.

Postgenderists: This faction advocates the elimination of gender distinctions through biotechnology and cultural change, seeing gender as a limitation that should be transcended. The main postgenderist figure is George Dvorsky (Dvorsky & Hughes, 2008).

Mind uploaders: This faction pursues the transfer of human consciousness into digital or non-biological substrates as a way to achieve immortality (Mind Uploading, 2025). A referential project of this faction was the 2045 initiative (2045.com, 2019), though it has been inactive for the last nine years.

Even considering all these factions, the scientific and intellectual relevance of transhumanism is limited. However, recent studies suggest that some transhumanist ideas have the potential to penetrate wide layers of society, even if most citizens do not consciously conceive themselves as transhumanists or willingly adopt a transhumanist agenda (Walach et al., in press). Some authors (Bess & Pasulka, 2018; Duner, 2025; Gouw et al., 2022; Leidenhag, 2020; Lemasters, 2024; Mercer & Trothen, 2015; Sherbert, 2024; Tirosh-Samuelson & Mossman, 2011) have suggested that the appeal of the transhumanist ideology stems from its soteriological dimension, which equates transhumanism to a religious movement or a utopian ideology. Others (Galileo Commission, 2025) suggest that the transhumanist agenda is indeed already being progressively introduced in many societies through a variety of initiatives, products, regulations and products which, despite not corresponding to a concerted plan, have the potential to radically alter society. Thus, while the transhumanist movement has the heterogeneity illustrated in the list of factions above, this transformation presents a certain consistency and direction, which reflects an underlying core ideology. It is this core ideology of transhumanism that is the object of the analysis and critique developed in this chapter.

In my view, three constitutive elements characterize the transhumanist core ideology. Firstly, there is a quasi-religious faith in technoscience as an endeavour capable of finding technical solutions to, possibly, all the problems and challenges that humans could ever face (Pickering, 2011; Tirosh-Samuelson, 2011). This faith in technoscience is focused on a specific form of rational activity that I propose to term "technoscientific reason", which I will analyse in detail later. Secondly, there is promotion of an "enhancement" of the human condition through the application of technology on the human body. Thirdly, the transhumanist ideology is oriented towards a "desired future". It aims not to explain what we are as humans, but what we could and should be. Therefore, it implicitly contains the notion of desire (what we are not now and would like to be) and of value (what it would be better for us to be). In addition, it proposes a social project, delineating an image of a possible future with the aim of directing social and financial efforts towards its realization. As a result, in recent years it has attracted growing attention from the mass media and content creators (Davies, 2019; Movistar Plus+, 2018a, 2018b; Ray Gallows, 2023; Smith, 2025; TV3, 2019).

The three core elements of the transhumanist ideology—faith in technoscientific reason, enhancement through the application of technology on the body, and orientation towards a specific desired future—have strong ethical and social implications. They are based on underlying assumptions and justified through a set of ideas and arguments that have received a multiplicity of critiques (Arana, 2022, 2024; Bess & Pasulka, 2018; Cortina, 2017; Cortina & Serra, 2015; Goundrey-Smith, 2023; Gouw et al., 2022; Hansell & Grassie, 2011; Jorion, 2022; O'Connell, 2017; Thomas, 2024; Tirosh-Samuelson & Mossman, 2011). In this paper, I develop an additional critique that has not been highlighted to date despite having important implications to unpack. The argument I will articulate is that transhumanism neglects otherness while it conflates power and value. These flaws are inherent to the very philosophical foundations of the transhumanist proposal and its fundamental faith in technoscience.

Before proceeding with the central argument and its implications, it is important to highlight that transhumanism should not be confused with another partially overlapping but conceptually distinct movement called posthumanism (Braidotti, 2013; Braidotti & Hlavajova, 2018; Ferrando, 2019). Posthumanism proposes a new paradigm to reflect on the current historical process by transcending the limiting frames of traditional humanisms, mainly dualisms (e.g. nature–culture and good–bad) and anthropocentrism (and its associated hierarchies). The core of my argument does not apply to posthumanism, whose foundational ideas give sufficient relevance to otherness and display a critical perspective on power.

The Role of AI in the Transhumanist Proposal

Though transhumanists count on a wide repertoire of technologies for the achievement of their objectives, AI is the most essential. Virtually all transhumanist narratives put great faith in AI as the central technology that will devise the general roadmap of implementation for all the other technologies. For example, it will provide the leap to complexity management required by technologies such as nanotechnologies and gene editing. Thus, AI is somehow the general enabler and coordinator of the transhumanist technological development. A sign of this is the title of Kurzweil's (2024) last book, *The Singularity is Nearer: When We Merge with AI*.

Moreover, AI has become a kind of wild card. In the transhumanist imaginary, when AI becomes superintelligent (far beyond human intelligence and far beyond the combined intelligence of all humans on the planet), it will find solutions to virtually any challenge or problem. Additionally, with its integration in our brains through nanobots (an idea widely shared by transhumanists), the hybridization between humans and technology will go beyond physical hybridization to cognitive and subjective hybridization: our mental processes will be intertwined with AI and that is why, in Kurzweil's words, we will merge with it. This situates the proposed transformation beyond the commonly expressed idea of "enhancement", implying a radical metamorphosis of the human embodied condition into something completely different. In this context, the spectacular advances of AI during recent years have acted to boost the credibility for the transhumanist proposals, which before the AI revolution were rendered as too speculative and belonging to sci-fi movie contexts instead of realistic plans (Bess & Pasulka, 2018; Grassie, 2011; Ritchie, 2011). Therefore, in light of the transhumanist proposal, what is at stake with the regulation of AI is not just a matter of alleviating its potential negative impacts and promoting its potential benefits, but of deciding the future of the human condition and steering our collective evolutionary path.

Technoscientific Reason and Otherness

As mentioned above, transhumanism is characterized by a quasi-religious faith in technoscience, seen as capable of finding technical solutions for virtually all human challenges. This faith is based on an elevation and trust on technoscientific reason, the mode of rational activity that underlies technoscientific development and leads to a specific ethos. To unpack this ethos, Heidegger's (1977) analysis of technology is particularly illuminating. Heidegger affirms that the essence of technology is not instrumental—developing suitable means to meet ends—but exploratory; it is a way of unveiling the *Dassein*—that is, exploring and more emphatically manifesting the structure and the possibilities of this universe.

By building ships, we reveal the sea as shippable, and by building cell phones, we show the universe as intimately interconnectable beyond distance. This idea of technology as a process oriented to unfold possibilities, and in doing so reveal the underlying structure of the universe, certainly resonates with the transhumanist ethos of expansion situated within a cosmic narrative of unfolding (Mercer & Trothen, 2015; More & Vita-More, 2013).

But, as Heidegger highlights, this unveiling is done through a very specific mode of operation, which he calls *Gestell*. *Gestell* (usually translated as "enframing") is a complex concept which for the purposes of this discussion can be synthesized as the action of forcing out of things the potential that they have as carriers of matter and energy. We force electromagnetic waves to vibrate in a way that transfers information, we force gasoline to explode and move pistons, and more controversially, we force plants and animals to grow at a pace that maximizes profit. What produces the effect of forcing out is the accurate disposition and control of causal chains, which is the cornerstone of engineering (for detailed justification of this argument, see Fernandez-Borsot, 2023, pp. 12–13). Thus, the technoscientific reason is oriented to design causal chains that use predefined and repeatable patterns of energy and matter. This mode of operation, Heidegger concludes, configures a stance, a way of relating to the world as if it were made of objects available for human control and manipulation. While this is perfectly valid when one is dealing with things, the generalization of this strategy ends up objectifying the whole of reality. And this is what transhumanism does: it approaches the whole of reality as if it were an engineering problem that could be solved by transforming the underlying material substrate. In this stance, there is nothing sacred, there is no line that should not be crossed. This is an ideology made in the image and likeness of an individual narcissistic self, a subjectivity oriented to self-expansion, affirmative action and unstoppable fight to achieve its objectives. What is alien to this stance is *otherness*, the awareness that the self needs to assume the notions of limit, self-restraint and renunciation as part of sharing the world with what is different from its desires in order to find a balanced way of being in the world with others. That is why, for technoscientific reason—and, by extension, for transhumanism—every problem and challenge is approached through doing more, intervening, transforming, increasing, growing, etc., and never through doing less, restraining, renouncing, decreasing.

thus adopting a body/mind dualism that privileges the mind—that is, the self, as the one and only sovereign (Ferrando, 2019; Piedra, 2016).

The Conflation of Power and Value in the Transhumanist Proposal

The ethos of self-expansiveness that rejects limits has an underlying ethics—that is, an underlying logic to determine what is better and preferable. My thesis is that transhumanist ethics are founded upon the valuation of individual power, understood as the capacity of the individual to deploy and realize his will. The idea is that empowering the individual to achieve its objectives and desires is the most important goal. That is why the transhumanist philosophy is articulated around a set of objectives (superintelligence, superlongevity, ...) that are realized on an individual basis, and transhumanist publications speak only secondarily of objectives that find their realization on a collective basis—that is, on the relational and social level (for example, social harmony). Accordingly, transhumanists insistently advocate for the right of the individual to self-determination in all human aspects (More & Vita-More, 2013; Sandberg, 2013; Sorgner, 2020, 2021) but very rarely discuss the duties of the individual towards the collective. In sum, as argued before, transhumanism is oriented to self-affirmation and self-expansion, and that is why the most important asset to develop is technological power—that is, widening the range of possibilities available to the individual. This leads to a conflation of power and value, reflected in the position that giving more power to the individual is good, and bringing more possibilities for the individual to deploy its will is always convenient. Indeed, this is a dramatic conflation, because values (the application of the notion of value to specific human aspects) are those principles and ideals that individuals consider important independently of whether they are aligned with their specific objectives. Thus, transhumanists invert the hierarchy between values and individual objectives, putting power in the place of value instead of at its service.

This ennoblement of power is reflected in the extremely positive valuation of exponential dynamics. Exponential dynamics seem very attractive to transhumanists because they are suddenly very powerful and thus very transformative, and transhumanists tend to forget that for the very same reasons they are prone to the production of excess, collapse, destruction, imbalance and disharmony. But this is outside the transhumanist horizon: since exponentials are very powerful, they must be good. Since they can produce a radical transformation, we must embrace them. Notions such as prudence, balance and harmony seem unnecessary hindrances to the unfolding of power. This attitude parallels transhumanists' commonly favourable view of capitalism and its *creative destruction* (Schumpeter, 1942), in which the creative is often privileged over the destructive. Thus, transhumanists usually display no reluctance on the typical capitalistic dynamics such as power accumulation and growing inequality (Thomas, 2022, 2024).

The centrality of power in the transhumanist perspective is confirmed by Sorgner's (2009, 2020) compelling argument that Nietzsche should be considered the intellectual precursor of transhumanism. Though this idea has sparked a complex debate (Tuncel, 2017), Sorgner provides sufficient arguments and signs of the parallels between the Nietzschean notion of the overhuman and the transhumanist notion of the posthuman, an idea noted by other scholars (Frontela-Asensio, 2025). More conclusively, More (2010), a leading intellectual voice of the transhumanist movement, has highlighted the influence of Nietzschean philosophy in transhumanism. In Nietzschean philosophy, one of the central notions is the will to power, seen as the central motivation of the individual, which leads to self-affirmation beyond any social conditioning. It is precisely this thesis that I am proposing here on affirming that transhumanism puts power in the place of value.

A sign of how misleading this conflation is can be seen in the contrast between the transhumanist project and Ellul's (1980) proposal of an ethics of nonpower. Ellul, considered one of the most relevant philosophers of technology (Jerónimo et al., 2013), developed a thoughtful and deep analysis of the role and effects of technology on society (Ellul, 1977, 1980, 1988). He concluded that in a historical time when technology continually increases power—especially over nature and other people—the only reasonable ethical stance is a refusal to increase power even when one can.

Implications of the Transhumanist Conflation of Power and Value

Besides the abstract and theoretical considerations of previous sections, the conflation of power and value renders transhumanism an inadequate ideology to approach some of the most important ethical and social challenges of our times—for instance, sustainability, inequality and the threat of digital domination through surveillance. I have chosen these three challenges due to their relevance and because, as I will argue, transhumanism is especially unable to deal adequately with them.

The transhumanist ideology cannot satisfactorily address the sustainability challenge for three reasons. Firstly, as some experts have highlighted (Fressoz, 2024; Latour, 2018; Wijkman & Rockström, 2012), this challenge cannot be addressed satisfactorily by developing new technologies. Indeed, there is a large pool of already existing technologies that are not being adopted just because they are less profitable than other less sustainable ones. Also, as explained before, the development of new technologies very often just adds to previous ones instead of replacing them, therefore not diminishing the total impact. Secondly, as some authors have pointed out (Madorrán Ayerra, 2019), the technologies central to the transhumanist proposal (e.g. AI, nanotechnology, genetic engineering) have a significant environmental impact and could not be scaled massively without creating important environmental problems. The third and most important reason is the one related to the argument developed in this chapter. The sustainability challenge requires a mindset oriented towards diminishing the impact of human societies on the environment. This, in turn, requires accepting environmental limits (e.g. the planetary boundaries; Rockström et al., 2009; Rockström et al., 2023), which implies reaching collective agreements to restrain human activities, prioritize some activities over others and therefore renounce. This mindset is diametrically opposed to the transhumanist ideology, centred on self-expansion, self-affirmation, rejecting the notion of limits and exalting individual freedom, understood as the right of the individual to operate independently of the collective. Thus, within the transhumanist ideological frame, increasing technological power and expanding technological possibilities will do nothing but exacerbate the problem.

For similar reasons, transhumanism has very little to offer to the challenge of growing inequality (Oxfam, 2025). Indeed, there are several reasons to think that it will boost it. Firstly, some of the technologies required to implement the transhumanist objectives are so sophisticated that they could hardly be scaled up and distributed to the majority of the world's population. Indeed, this scaling is so difficult and problematic that some authors have questioned whether transhumanists have an honest intention of avoiding inequality (Cortina & Serra, 2015). Secondly, and stemming from the previous issue, selective access to transhumanist enhancements based on financial possibilities could create a society divided into two classes, the enhanced and the others. Given that enhancements will provide increased capacities and power, and considering the transhumanist ideological emphasis on self-affirmation, self-expansion, individual freedom and valuation of power, it seems natural to think that the enhanced ones will use their increased power to subjugate the others (Cortina & Serra, 2015). Though some transhumanists have expressed awareness and concern about this (Hughes, 2004; More & Vita-More, 2013), they seem to be totally blind of how this danger stems from the very essence of the transhumanist ethos, its conflation of power and value, and its ideological underpinnings. Without explicitly questioning these factors, these concerns will not be translated into credible measures.

Last but not least, transhumanism does not address the danger of digital domination through surveillance and its social and political consequences (McIntosh, 2019; Zuboff, 2019). The last decade has seen a concentration of economic and political power in a handful of big tech companies (Zephyr, 2020), and it does not seem that the advancement of technology will alleviate this situation. Through skilful—but not transparent—management of their algorithms, these companies have a huge influence on the preferences of consumers and the political opinions of citizens. Thus, they are an important factor shaping users' subjectivity, all done in the service of profit maximization. They promote an addictive overuse of social media sites (Orlowski, 2020) and the political polarization of society (Kubin & von Sikorski, 2021; Persily & Tucker, 2020), while publicly displaying a hypocritical attitude, something recently exposed by some insiders (Wynn-Williams, 2025). With a hypothetical integration of AI in our brains, their influence could reach dystopian proportions, giving these companies the power to influence and literally interfere in all our thoughts. The naiveté of transhumanists in this regard is striking. Kurzweil (2024), while proposing to merge our brains with AI, mentions the danger of surveillance only once, to suggest that the wide spread of information through exponential technologies will prevent authoritarian surveillance and promote the expansion of democracy and individual rights. He says nothing about surveillance capitalism and big tech companies. In general, transhumanist thought seems to operate under the logic of "let's develop the technology first and then put in place the necessary ethical safeguards". This is somewhat myopic, because once a power structure has been established based on a specific technological infrastructure, it fiercely resists control and regulation. Experts on the ethical design of technology (Kroes & Verbeek, 2014; Verbeek, 2006) have consistently cautioned that technological creations embed values introduced in the design and deployment processes, values that will influence and condition the values, priorities, feelings, habits and behaviour of the users. Thus, the ethical dimension must be purposefully and tenaciously introduced at all stages of technological development, and especially in the initial steps of investment prioritization and tech design. Again, this naive blindness of transhumanists in regard to surveillance capitalism—or, alternatively, its cynical endorsement of it—is understandable on the basis of the conflation of power and value.

The inadequacy of transhumanism in dealing with challenges such as sustainability, inequality and digital domination can be generalized to almost all social problems. The root cause of this inadequacy is that the transhumanist ideology is based on a partial and limited type of intelligence. Transhumanism gives prominence to functional intelligence (Agustí-Collell, 2021), which is the capacity to achieve objectives (including the capacity to solve problems, as problems can be conceptually reduced to objectives). This is the kind of intelligence associated with technoscientific reason, and its direct outcome is power. But transhumanism gives little attention to other kinds of intelligence, especially to those of a dialogical nature, such as bonding intelligence. According to Carutti (2014), bonding intelligence is the capacity of being transformed through bonds. From the perspective of bonding intelligence, the point is not to achieve objectives but to change them as a result of one's relationships, which provide a deeper understanding of oneself and the others. Different schools of psychology have highlighted the need to develop bonding intelligence as an inherent aspect of the process of psychological maturation that takes individuals out of a narcissistic self-centred position and enables them to build constructive relationships (Atwood & Stolorow, 1992; Dabrowski et al., 1970; Dabrowski & Piechowski, 1977; Mitchell & Aron, 1999). Bonding intelligence requires very different skills from technoscientific reason, and it is based above all on a sensitive attitude and openness to otherness (Fernandez-Borsot, 2017). It is the lack of bonding intelligence that makes transhumanism an inadequate ideology to deal with social issues.

Implications for Policymaking: A Citizen Ethics for the Technological Society

As argued in a previous section, though not many citizens are embracing the transhumanist proposal consciously and explicitly, transhumanist ideas are infiltrating the public discourse under the guiding idea that technology will bring us into a new era of possibilities, a future paradise in which individuals will realize their aspirations of a long and fulfilling life. Though unrealistic, this proposal has a special appeal for its quasi-religious character, and beneath its evocative promises lies an ideology that elevates power and neglects otherness, leading to an inadequate consideration of social issues. The foreseen social consequences of the neglect of otherness are an increase in narcissism and individualism, and an associated increase in inter-human conflicts and social polarization.

The best way to prevent these problems is to promote awareness through education. To the same degree that technology augments the power of individuals and societies, the awareness of power dynamics and their implications should be deepened. Thus, alongside training individuals to take advantage of the new possibilities that AI and other technologies are bringing, there is a need to teach a new citizen ethics for the technological society. In my view, promoting this kind of education should be a priority for policymakers. Such an educational initiative should include elements of a pedagogy of otherness and power (for some ideas about this, see Fernandez-Borsot, 2017), but more emphatically a set of principles, principles that can orient public discussion around the challenges to come when new technological advances reach society. In this sense, to promote a society with a significant level of wisdom in regard to power should be a priority.

The set of principles around which such citizen ethics should be articulated revolves around typical issues of AI ethics such as privacy, transparency, algorithmic power and individual autonomy, truthfulness and fact-checking, biases and discrimination, sustainability, accountability and individual freedom versus collective commitments. However, as a result of the arguments developed in this chapter, I propose to add two principles related to how power is managed in society. Firstly, there is the *principle of proportionality in digital surveillance*, wherein "the level of digital surveillance over a citizen or group must be proportional to their level of power". Currently the situation is the opposite, and generating public awareness of this is urgent. The second principle would be the *principle of power distribution*, which states that "given that the only way for a powerful individual not to abuse power is to share it, there should be policies to detect power concentration and promote power distribution". This is inspired by Slater's (2008) approach to social transformation, and though this principle might seem utopic and impossible to apply, market regulations already in place in Europe and the US apply similar principles to avoid monopolistic economic power concentration. What we need is a generalization of the knowledge and instruments that have been developed for market and competence supervision, along with citizen awareness to support political action in regard to this. These two principles are just examples of the kinds of reflection that could be included in an educational initiative oriented towards preventing power-ignorant ideologies, such as transhumanism, influencing the political dynamics of societies around the globe.

Lastly, another implication of the critique developed in this chapter is that regulations pertaining to the integration of AI in the human brain are not just a matter of individual safety and individual choice, but of opposing an ideology that exalts power to the neglect of otherness. If bridling power has been an age-old core challenge of human societies, the situation can take on unprecedented proportions if an elite of AI-augmented individuals are allowed to deploy their agendas without public discussion. In the face of this challenge, a public debate needs to be promoted concerning the limits to individual freedom when powerful individuals could jeopardize social balance. Because what will be really at stake with AI advances is whether we choose the common good and collective wellbeing as the regulatory ideals of our societies or if we allow the desires of powerful individuals to prevail over them.

Conclusions

The main conclusion of this chapter is that transhumanism is an inadequate ideology to approach the social challenges of our times, among them sustainability, growing inequality and the threat of digital domination through surveillance. The inadequacy of transhumanism stems from its very philosophical foundations: transhumanism is based on the elevation of technoscientific reason to the neglect of otherness. Technoscientific reason operates by objectifying the world and approaches the whole of reality as if it were an engineering problem that could be solved by transforming the underlying material substrate. This configures an ideology made in the image and likeness of an individual narcissistic self, a subjectivity oriented to self-expansion and affirmative action. What is alien to this ideology is otherness, an awareness that the self needs to assume the notions of limit, self-restraint and renunciation as part of sharing the world with what is different from its desires in order to find a balanced way of being in the world with others. This ideology of self-affirmation leads to a conflation of power and value which makes it unable to deal with social challenges.

In the face of this, to prevent the penetration of transhumanist ideas in society and promote a mature and healthy relationship with technology, educational intervention is needed. It is proposed that this educational initiative should be articulated around the notion of a citizen ethics for the technological society, which should include a pedagogy of otherness and power, and a set of principles. In addition to the usual principles associated with AI ethics, two principles are offered in relation to how power is managed in society: the principle of proportionality in digital surveillance, formulated as "the level of digital surveillance over a citizen or group must be proportional to their level of power"; and the principle of power distribution, which states that "given that the only way for a powerful individual not to abuse power is to share it, there should be policies to detect power concentration and promote power distribution". The ultimate objective is to promote a society with wisdom about power, capable of counteracting the siren songs of transhumanism with a mature attitude that prioritizes the common good and collective wellbeing.

References

2045.com. (2019). *2045 Initiative*. Retrieved June 22, 2025, from http://2045.com/

Agustí-Collell, J. (2021). *La intel·ligència de programada a creativa: La mutació radical de la humanitat* [Intelligence from programmed to creative: The radical mutation of humanity]. Retrieved July 10, 2025, from https://www.amazon.es/INTEL%C2%B7LIG%C3%88NCIA-PROGRAMADA-CREATIVA-MUTACI%C3%93-HUMANITAT/dp/B0BHRVTS22

Arana, J. (2022). Desafíos antropológicos del transhumanismo [Anthropological challenges of transhumanism]. *Pensamiento: Revista de Investigación e Información Filosófica, 78*(298), 485–501.

Arana, J. (Ed.). (2024). *El futuro de la identidad humana a debate: Protagonistas de la polémica sobre el transhumanismo [The future of human identity under debate: Protagonists of the transhumanism controversy]*. Tecnos.

Atwood, G., & Stolorow, R. (1992). *Contexts of being: The intersubjective foundations of psychological life*. The Analytic Press.

Bess, M., & Pasulka, D. W. (Eds.). (2018). *Posthumanism: The future of homo sapiens*. Macmillan Reference USA.

Braidotti, R. (2013). *The posthuman*. Polity Press.

Braidotti, R., & Hlavajova, M. (Eds.). (2018). *Posthuman glossary*. Bloomsbury Academic.

Carutti, E. (2014). *Inteligencia planetaria [Planetary intelligence]*. CreateSpace.

Cortina, A. (2017). *Humanismo avanzado para una sociedad biotecnológica*. Ediciones Teconté.

Cortina, A., & Serra, M.-A. (Eds.). (2015). *¿Humanos o posthumanos? Singularidad tecnológica y mejoramiento humano*. Fragmenta.

Dabrowski, K., Kawczak, A., & Piechowski, M. (1970). *Mental growth through positive disintegration*. Gryf.

Dabrowski, K., & Piechowski, M. (1977). *Theory of levels of emotional development*. Dabor Science.

Davies, R. T. (Producer). (2019). *Years and years* [TV Series]. British Broadcasting Corporation & Home Box Office.

De Grey, A., & Rae, M. (2007). *Ending aging: The rejuvenation breakthroughs that could reverse human aging in our lifetime*. St. Martin's Griffin.

Duner, I. (2025). *Julian Huxley, evolutionism and the history of transhumanism*. Palgrave Macmillan.

Dvorsky, G., & Hughes, J. (2008). *Postgenderism: Beyond the gender binary*. Institute for Ethics and Emerging Technologies. https://doi.org/10.13140/RG.2.2.18028.08324

Ellul, J. (1977). *Le système technicien [The technological system]*. Hachette.

Ellul, J. (1980). The ethics of nonpower. In M. Kranzberg (Ed.), *Ethics in an age of pervasive technology* (pp. 204–213). Westview Press.

Ellul, J. (1988). *Le bluff technologique [The technological bluff]*. Hachette.

Fernandez-Borsot, G. (2017). *A theoretical analysis of integral theory and the participatory paradigm through the lens of otherness*. (Doctoral dissertation). ProQuest Dissertations and Theses database. Universitat Internacional de Catalunya.

Fernandez-Borsot, G. (2023). Spirituality and technology: A threefold philosophical reflection. *Zygon, 58*(1), 6–22. https://doi.org/10.1111/zygo.12835

Ferrando, F. (2019). *Philosophical posthumanism*. Bloomsbury Academic.

Fressoz, J.-B. (2024). *More and more and more: An all-consuming history of energy*. Penguin Random House.

Frontela-Asensio, P. (2025). El transhumanismo como concreción existencialmente nihilista del superhombre Nietzscheano [Transhumanism as an existentially nihilistic concretization of the Nietzschean superman]. In J. Vidal López (Ed.), *Las ciencias sociales en los desafíos contemporáneos: La dimensión humana en perspectiva [Social sciences in contemporary challenges: The human dimension in perspective]* (pp. 865–876). Dykinson.

Galileo Commission. (2025, June). *Transhumanism: Next step in human development, dangerous ideology, negligible, or what?* Retrieved July 12, 2025, from https://galileocommission.org/wp-content/uploads/2025/07/Transhumanism-Report.pdf

Goundrey-Smith, S. (2023). *Transhumanism, ethics and the therapeutic revolution.* Routledge.

Gouw, A. M., Green, B. P., & Peters, T. (Eds.). (2022). Religious transhumanism and its critics..

Grassie, W. J. (2011). Is transhumanism scientifically plausible? Posthuman predictions and the human predicament. In H. Tirosh-Samuelson & K. L. Mossman (Eds.), *Building better humans? Refocusing the debate on transhumanism* (pp. 465–484). Peter Lang.

Grugeon Plana, B., & Smit, J. (2024). *Historian jean-baptiste fressoz: 'Forget the energy transition: There never was one and there never will be one'.* Resilience.org. Retrieved March 10, 2025, from https://www.resilience.org/stories/2024-12-05/historian-jean-baptiste-fressoz-forget-the-energy-transition-there-never-was-one-and-there-never-will-be-one/

Hansell, G. R., & Grassie, W. (Eds.). (2011). *H±: Transhumanism and its critics.* Metanexus Institute.

Heidegger, M. (1977). The question concerning technology. In I. M. Heidegger (Ed.), *The question concerning technology and other essays* (pp. 3–35). Harper & Row.

Hughes, J. (2004). *Citizen Cyborg: Why democratic societies must respond to the redesigned human of the future.* Westview Press.

Humanity+. (2023). *Transhumanist FAQ.* Retrieved June 15, 2025, from https://www.humanityplus.org/transhumanist-faq

Istvan, Z. (2020). *The anti-deathist: Writings of a radical longevity activist.* Rudi Ventures.

Jerónimo, H. M., Garcia, J. L., & Mitcham, K. (Eds.). (2013). *Jacques Ellul and the technological society in the 21st century.* Springer.

Jorion, P. (Ed.). (2022). *Humanism and its discontents: The rise of transhumanism and posthumanism.* Palgrave Macmillan.

Kabarity, G. L. (2024). Zoltan Istvan: La dimension política [Zoltan Istvan: The political dimension]. In J. Arana (Ed.), *El futuro de la identidad humana a debate: Protagonistas de la polémica sobre el transhumanismo [The future of human identity under debate: Protagonists of the transhumanism controversy]* (pp. 161–172). Tecnos.

Kroes, P., & Verbeek, P.-P. (Eds.). (2014). *The moral status of technical artefacts* (Vol. 17). Springer.

Kubin, E., & von Sikorski, C. (2021). The role of (social) media in political polarization: A systematic review. *Annals of the International Communication Association, 45*(3), 188–206. https://doi.org/10.1080/23808985.2021.1976070

Kurzweil, K. (2005). *The singularity is near: When humans transcend biology*. Penguin Books.

Kurzweil, R. (2024). *The singularity is nearer: When we merge with AI*. Penguin Random House.

Latour, B. (2018). *Down to Earth*. Polity Press.

Leidenhag, M. (2020). Saved through technology: Exploring the soteriology and eschatology of transhumanism. *Religion Compass, 14*(11), 1–9. https://doi.org/10.1111/rec3.12377

Lemasters, R. (2024). Religious transhumanism as a new religious movement: Sketching a model of the development of religious transhumanism. *Religions, 15*, 885. https://doi.org/10.3390/rel15080885

Madorrán Ayerra, C. (2019). *An eco-social perspective on transhumanism*. Green European Journal. Retrieved June 28, 2025, from https://www.greeneuropeanjournal.eu/an-eco-social-perspective-on-transhumanism/

McIntosh, D. (2019). We need to talk about data: How digital monopolies arise and why they have power and influence. *Journal of Technology Law & Policy, 23*(2), 185–213.

Mercer, C., & Trothen, J. T. (Eds.). (2015). *Religion and transhumanism: The unknown future of human enhancement*. Praeger.

Mind Uploading. (2025). *Mind uploading*. Retrieved June 3, 2025, from https://minduploading.org/

Mitchell, S. A., & Aron, L. (1999). *Relational psychoanalysis: The emergence of a tradition*. The Analytic Press.

More, M. (2003). *Principles of extropy*. Retrieved June 10, 2025, from http://dpya.org/wiki/index.php/2003_-_Principles_of_Extropy_Version_3.11_-_Max_More

More, M. (2010). The overhuman in the transhuman. *Journal of Evolution & Technology, 21*(1), 1–4.

More, M. (2013). The philosophy of transhumanism. In M. More & N. Vita-More (Eds.), *The transhumanist reader: Classical and contemporary essays on the science, technology, and philosophy of the human future* (pp. 3–17). Wiley-Blackwell.

More, M., & Vita-More, N. (2013). *The transhumanist reader: Classical and contemporary essays on the science, technology, and philosophy of the human future*. Wiley-Blackwell.

Movistar Plus+. (2018a). *Cuando ya no esté. Capítulo 2 (Parte 1/2)*. Retrieved June 22, 2025, from https://www.youtube.com/watch?v=nNR756j_Pso

Movistar Plus+. (2018b). *Cuando ya no esté. Capítulo 2 (Parte 2/2).* Retrieved June 22, 2025, from https://www.youtube.com/watch?v=uiQjk2RKsX8

Nuland, S. B. (2005). Do you want to live forever? *MIT Technology Review, 108*, 36–45.

O'Connell, M. (2017). *To be a machine: Adventures among cyborgs, utopians, hackers, and the futurists solving the modest problem of death.* Knopf Doubleday.

Orlowski, J. (Director). (2020). *The social dilemma.* Exposure Labs, The Space Program, Agent Pictures.

Ortigosa, G. L. (2024). Anders sandberg: ¿Es posible arrebatar a Dios los dados? [Anders Sandberg: Is it possible to take the dice away from God?]. In J. Arana (Ed.), *El futuro de la identidad humana a debate: Protagonistas de la polémica sobre el transhumanismo [The future of human identity under debate: Protagonists of the transhumanism controversy]* (pp. 251–262). Tecnos.

Oxfam. (2025). *Takers not makers: The unjust poverty and unearned wealth of colonialism.* Oxfam.org. Retrieved July 3, 2025, from https://www.oxfam.org/en/research/takers-not-makers-unjust-poverty-and-unearned-wealth-colonialism

Pearce, D. (1995). *The hedonistic imperative.* Retrieved July 10, 2025, from https://www.hedweb.com/

Persily, N., & Tucker, J. A. (2020). *Social media and democracy: The state of the field and prospects for reform.* Cambridge University Press.

Persson, I., & Savulescu, J. (2012). *Unfit for the future: The need for moral enhancement.* Oxford University Press.

Pickering, A. (2011). Brains, selves, and spirituality in the history of cybernetics. In G. R. Hansell & W. Grassie (Eds.), *H±: Transhumanism and its critics* (pp. 189–204). Metanexus Institute.

Piedra, J. (2016). Transhumanismo: Hacia un nuevo cuerpo [Transhumanism: Toward a new body]. *Daimon, Revista Internacional de Filosofía, 5*, 489–495.

Ray Gallows, P. (2023). *Transhumanism.* WOWNow Entertainment.

Ritchie, B. G. (2011). The (un)likelihood of a high-tech path to immortality. In H. Tirosh-Samuelson & K. L. Mossman (Eds.), *Building better humans? Refocusing the debate on transhumanism* (pp. 357–377). Peter Lang.

Rockström, J., Gupta, J., Qin, D., Lade, S. J., Abrams, J. F., Andersen, L. S., Armstrong McKay, D. I., Bai, X., Bala, G., Bunn, S. E., Ciobanu, D., DeClerck, F., Ebi, K., Gifford, L., Gordon, C., Hasan, S., Kanie, N., Lenton, T. M., Loriani, S., et al. (2023). Safe and just Earth system boundaries. *Nature, 619*(7968), 102–111. https://doi.org/10.1038/s41586-023-06083-8

Rockström, J., Steffen, W., Noone, K., Persson, A., Stuart Chapin, F., III, Lambin, E. F., Lenton, T. M., Scheffer, M., Folke, C., Schellnhuber, H. J., Nykvist, B., de Wit, C. A., Hughes, T., van der Leeuw, S., Rodhe, H., Sörlin,

S., Snyder, P. K., Costanza, R., Svedin, U., et al. (2009). Planetary boundaries: Exploring the safe operating space for humanity. *Ecology and Society, 14*(2), art32. https://doi.org/10.5751/ES-03180-140232

Rosalsky, G. (2025). *Why the AI world is suddenly obsessed with a 160-year-old economics paradox*. NR.org. Retrieved July 10, 2025, from https://www.npr.org/sections/planet-money/2025/02/04/g-s1-46018/ai-deepseek-economics-jevons-paradox

Sandberg, A. (2013). Morphological freedom. In M. More & N. Vita-More (Eds.), *The transhumanist reader: Classical and contemporary essays on the science, technology, and philosophy of the human future* (pp. 56–64). Wiley-Blackwell.

Schumpeter, J. (1942). *Capitalism, socialism, and democracy*. Harper & Brothers.

Sherbert, M. G. (2024). *Transhumanism: A religion without religion* (Doctoral dissertation). Retrieved July 12, 2025, from https://yorkspace.library.yorku.ca/server/api/core/bitstreams/aecb611d-b1d3-4c69-b511-b70869876a0f/content

Singularity University. (2025). *Singularity|Leading innovation & exponential technology education*. Retrieved June 15, 2025, from https://www.su.org/

Slater, P. (2008). *The chrysalis effect: The metamorphosis of global culture*. Sussex Academic Press.

Smith, C. (Director). (2025). *Don't die: The man who wants to live forever*. Lybrary Films.

Sorgner, S. (2009). Nietzsche, the overhuman, and transhumanism. *Journal of Evolution and Technology, 20*(1), 29–42.

Sorgner, S. L. (2020). *On transhumanism* (S. Hawkins trans.). The Pennsylvania State University Press. (Original work published 2016).

Sorgner, S. L. (2021). *We have always been cyborgs: Digital data, gene technologies, and an ethics of transhumanism*. Bristol University Press.

Thomas, A. (2022). Transhumanism and advanced capitalism: Elitist logics and dangerous implications. In P. Jorion (Ed.), *Humanism and its discontents: The rise of transhumanism and posthumanism* (pp. 151–180). Palgrave Macmillan.

Thomas, A. (2024). *The politics and ethics of transhumanism: Techno-human evolution and advanced capitalism*. Bristol University Press.

Tirosh-Samuelson, H. (2011). Engaging transhumanism. In G. R. Hansell & W. Grassie (Eds.), *H±: Transhumanism and its critics* (pp. 19–52). Metanexus Institute.

Tirosh-Samuelson, H., & Mossman, K. L. (Eds.). (2011). *Building better humans? Refocusing the debate on transhumanism*. Peter Lang.

Tuncel, Y. (Ed.). (2017). *Nietzsche and transhumanism: Precursor or enemy?* Cambridge Scholars Press.

TV3. (2019). *Enganyar la mort: Camí a la immortalitat? No pot ser!* [Cheating death: Path to immortality? It can't be true!]. Retrieved June

22, 2025, from https://www.ccma.cat/tv3/alacarta/no-pot-ser/enganyar-la-mort-cami-a-la-immortalitat/video/5838713/

Verbeek, P.-P. (2006). Materializing morality: Design ethics and technological mediation. *Science, Technology, & Human Values, 31*(3), 361–380. https://doi.org/10.1177/0162243905285847

Walach, H., Germann, C., & Klement, R. J. (submitted). *The german transhumanism scale and the German version of the timmermann world-view scale.* Frontiers in Psychology.

Wijkman, A., & Rockström, J. (2012). *Bankrupting nature: Denying our planetary boundaries.* Routledge.

Wolbring, G. (2008). Why NBIC? Why human performance enhancement? *Innovation: The European Journal of Social Science Research, 21*(1), 25–40. https://doi.org/10.1080/13511610802002189

Wynn-Williams, S. (2025). *Careless people: A cautionary tale of power, greed, and lost idealism.* Flatiron Books.

Yetisen, A. K. (2018). Biohacking. *Trends in Biotechnology, 36*(8), 744–747.

Zephyr, T. (2020). *Break 'em up: Recovering our freedom from big Ag, big tech, and big money.* All Points Books.

Zuboff, S. (2019). *The age of surveillance capitalism: The fight for a human future at the new frontier of power.* Hachette.

CHAPTER 10

Human Relationships. Analysing the Relationship of Humans with AI Through Science Fiction Narratives

Carla Vidal Fluriach and Rafael Monterde Ferrando

Introduction

The incursion of digital culture in the second half of the twentieth century has triggered a change in the way we understand human relationships. A change that has led many to believe that the digital world is the new image through which humans understand themselves. We can thus assert, following South Korean thinker Byung-Chul Han (2021), that "the terrestrial order is today being replaced by the digital order" (p. 13). In a way, the digital world is becoming a utopian space where aspirations for a more perfect life—free from the problems of physical existence—are

C. Vidal Fluriach (✉)
Universitat Internacional de Catalunya, Barcelona, Spain
e-mail: cvfluri@uic.es

R. Monterde Ferrando
Universidad Francisco de Vitoria, Madrid, Spain
e-mail: rafael.monterde@ufv.es

M. Bosch (ed.), *Crucial Ethical Keys of Artificial Intelligence*,
https://doi.org/10.1007/978-3-032-22853-6_10

realized. It seems that in the new digital afterworld, thanks to AI development, it is possible to create simulated personalities serving as sentimental companions or affective substitutes capable of satisfying the desire for a life partner tailored to consumer needs.

In this context, interpersonal relationships are beginning to be mediated by artificial intelligence (AI): *chatbots*, intelligent robots, artificial companions (ACs) or even operating systems (OS) that present themselves as interlocutors capable of simulating emotional bonds (Sajadieh, 2023). Added to the possibilities of ingenuity are the science fiction narratives released, many of them on the big screen since the 1960s (Álvarez Villanueva, 2022; Gómez, 2023). In a predictive way—though sometimes already real—the cinematic imagination presents stories where human relationships have been replaced, or even enhanced and substituted, with the incorporation of various AI applications (Vidal-Mestre et al., 2023). The importance of this medium is not trivial, as Cortina (2024) notes in *Ethics or Ideology of Artificial Intelligence?*: "capabilities are being attributed to AI and robots far beyond those recognizable today, a distortion fueled by science fiction and sensationalist press" (p. 127).

Following on from the Valencian philosopher's statement, it is worth asking to what extent science fiction narratives distort or, on the contrary, bring us closer to understanding the type of bond that is currently being established between people and artificial intelligence. Notwithstanding, such representations contribute to expanding the moral imagination by presenting possible scenarios of alternative realities, allowing the analysis of potential futures. In this sense, as Nussbaum and Von der Walde (1995) argues, "literary form cannot be separated from philosophical content, since it is the result of an inquiry which strives to provide answers to certain matters of human existence" (p. 26). Furthermore, Ian Jarvie's work *The Philosophy of the Film: epistemology, ontology, aesthetics* (1987) posits that films possess philosophical interest and value, as they allow to conceive of possible worlds that challenge the viewer and raise the question of its beauty, ultimately leading to considerations of truth (Jarvie, 2011).

In this sense, the science fiction narratives analysed in this chapter not only entertain but enable to recognise correspondences between fictional worlds and the realities of human existence. The new artificial interlocutors portrayed in these narratives have begun to shape unprecedented forms of interaction that, while once exclusive to science fiction, now manifest and help us interpret such stories as valid philosophical reflections on humanity's relationship with technology.

A significant example is *Replika* (mentioned in chapter 8), a conversational chatbot designed to become "your best friend". This application collects maximum information through user interactions to learn and imitate expression patterns, offering personalised emotional companionship.[1] There is a subscription that allows access to advanced options such as making voice calls, holding coaching sessions or defining the type of relationship desired, so that the avatar can assume the role of a romantic or even marital partner. Similarly, there are other applications that offer similar experiences—such as Anima AI, Character.ai, Kupid AI, and EVA AI, among others—in which the user projects affections and emotions onto an artificial other.

To understand the nature of these emerging interaction models and address their ontological implications from an ethical-philosophical perspective, it is necessary to recover the classical notion of *human relationship*. *Human relationship* is understood here as the facet of being that leads to essential personal growth and intensification of life. This means that it is not merely a relationship between two different things, as if they were placed on a plane.

The concept of *relationship* used here is substantial and corresponds to the essential structure of the human person. Here, when the word person is used, it is said to be synonymous with relationship, and when talking about personal relationality, it is assumed that this is only possible between people and, consequently, there is no mention of relationships between objects. One of the expressions of *personal relationality* that clarifies its substantial role is *friendship*. Aristotle studies this concept in detail in books VIII and IX of the *Nicomachean Ethics*, leading several authors to consider the Macedonian philosopher's reflections on virtuous friendship to analyse digital friendship (Cooper, 1977; Fernandez-Borsot, 2025; Fröding & Peterson, 2012; Kristjánsson, 2019; McFall, 2012). A friend

[1] The Replika homepage displays the following messages encouraging users to register: 'Meet Replika, an AI companion eager to learn and who would love to see the world through your eyes. Replika is always ready to chat when you need an empathetic friend' and also 'The AI companion who cares. Always there to listen and talk. Always on your side.' According to Eugenia Kuyda, CEO of Replika, in August 2024 the total number of registered users exceeded 30 million (Patel, 2024).

is one whose existence becomes indispensable, as one cannot conceive of oneself without the friend.

Friendship is a source of personal identity and perfectly manifests how human relationships foster growth in the personal being. At this point, it is worth highlighting the contributions of Bosch et al. (2022) in *Evolving friendship? Essential changes, from social networks to artificial companions*. Through a systematic review of the existing literature in this field, they synthesise three key principles: *for the friend's sake*, *equality* and *interiority*. These describe what characterises friendship and why the *relationship* between persons is substantial.

Human relationality is a condition for understanding human life and its development. This is why we will address, through science fiction films, to what extent AI can be considered an *other* responding to the relational character of the person. For this purpose, we will analyse how certain science fiction films—Blade *Runner* (Scott, 1982), *A.I.: Artificial Intelligence* (Spielberg, 2001), *Her* (Jonze, 2013), and *Blade Runner 2049* (Villeneuve, 2017)—represent the relationship between man and machine, taking as a basis for study the three dimensions proposed by Bosch et al. (2022). The reason for choosing these films is that they all feature narratives that anthropomorphise artificial entities, expanding our moral imagination when thinking about the relationships between humans and artificial intelligence.

Philosophical Principles of Friendship

This section provides a comprehensive account of the three core concepts that characterise the notion of human relationality proposed by Bosch et al. (2022). These three principles—for the friend's sake, equality and interiority—serve as the conceptual foundation for examining the types of human-AI relationships presented in science fiction narratives. The rationale behind these criteria provides an ethical-philosophical foundation that allows examining both the possibility and the limits of establishing relationships between humans and artificial entities.

For the Friend's Sake

The first dimension proposed by Bosch et al. (2022) to describe virtuous friendship is "for the friend's sake", also known as *benevolent love*. This expression synthesises the Aristotelian view that the *other* cannot be valued as an object of desire or utility, as this would constitute a relationship oriented solely toward self-interest and constitute a form of objectification (Aristóteles, 2018, 1155b). True friendship, on the other hand, is based on recognising the other person as a good in themselves and on a sincere desire for their own good, not as a means to an end, but as an end in itself. Forment (1988) describes it clearly: "the love of friendship is the union of two selfless loves" (p. 15). A love that goes so far as to consider the friend as *another self*.

This selfless and gratuitous character of friendship becomes strained when analysing its representation in science fiction. As Bosch et al. (2022) warn, both artificial companions and operating systems are "a serviceable other designed to please and fulfil the needs of the owner" (Bosch et al., 2022, p. 7). As tools designed by and for humans, their operation follows pre-existing patterns and algorithms "that adapt to user preferences and settings" (Fernandez-Borsot, 2025). In this sense, there is no possibility of genuine friendship, since, as Aristotle warned, "reciprocal friendship implies choice, and choice derives from a disposition; friends wish for each other's good for their own sake, not by affection, but by disposition of character" (Aristóteles, 2018, 1157b).

In fact, an etymological analysis of the word *intelligence* reveals that "it comes from *inter-legere*, meaning *to choose between*. AI chooses among possibilities *already given*" (Han, 2024, p. 95). In contrast, the choice of a friend involves genuine novelty. Friendship is always unforeseen, as the love of friendship opens possibilities impossible in non-friendship relationships. Friendship is new because it creates a bond between friends and opens up a range of actions that non-friendly relationships cannot comprehend. There is no predisposition to develop friendship love towards a person; it is an *encounter* and an *event* of an ontological nature, a *pure novelty*.

Equality

The second constitutive element of friendship according to Bosch et al. (2022) is "equality", described by the authors as "an ontological equivalence between subjects" (p. 7). This means that friendship can only occur between free people. Without equality in personal freedom, friendship cannot happen, because it is inherently unnecessary, there is no reason for it to exist. Friendship occurs between equal people who do not need each other (McFall, 2012). It exists beyond business, utilitarian relationships, and hierarchy. In this sense, Forment (1988) states that "friendship is essentially mutual love. Both persons must love each other; it is insufficient for only one to love, or for the other to merely accept being loved. Reciprocity is always essential" (p. 14). Bosch et al. (2022) affirm that "a real subject has internal capabilities from which to wish, decide and act" (p. 7). Then, the possibility of equality is predicated on the presence of equivalent liberty. This reciprocal dynamic also underlies equality between friends. Friends are capable of giving in equal measure (Aristóteles, 2018, 1157a). For this reason, Aristotle considered that friendship is possible when friends are equal in virtue, that is, when they possess the same capacities and love the good in the same measure (Aristóteles, 2018, 1156b-1157b-1159b). Being equal in virtue, they enjoy the same capacity for freedom and self-giving without necessity. Therefore, the fruit of equality is the gratuitousness that characterises friendship. To summarise, as Bosch et al. (2022) have stated:

> For Aristotle, the capacity of human beings for friendship stems from their metaphysical inner orientation towards the good, that is first manifested in the good attitude towards oneself, and then extended to friendship with others in virtue of their metaphysical reciprocity. (p. 7)

Interiority

Finally, Bosch et al. (2022) propose "interiority" as the third constituent element of friendship. Following Aristotle, they insist that friendship transcends shared interests, involving an openness to the intimacy of the other: "for friendship to flourish, their interiorities must resonate; friends must *be together* not only externally, but internally" (p. 8). This inner communion is possible because, as the authors note, "interiority allows the inner world to be shared with the friend" (p. 6), which presupposes that there is an inner world that can be freely shared with the other. In this sense, it is said that friendship is "a single soul dwelling in two bodies". Etymologically, a friend is someone for whom one feels true *sympathy*. This word comes from Greek *sympatheia*, and means *to feel with the other* or *the same as the other*, so both persons experience the same in their hearts. Due to this communion of hearts, it can be said that interiority implies exclusivity, as the friend discovers the uniqueness of the loved person, elevating them beyond the rest of their kind. Strictly speaking, a friend is someone who knows that there can be no other being in the world like the friend they love. Through this *sympathy* proper to friendship, Aristotle states: "it is characteristic of friends to want the same things, and to rejoice and grieve over the same things" (Aristóteles, 2018, 1165b). Therefore, there is a communion of intimacies that makes them live the same life together and resonate the same things in their hearts (Cooper, 1977). Forment (1988) expresses it this way: "In reciprocal friendly self-giving, friends exchange thoughts, wills, and affections, belonging to personal intimacy and being their greatest treasures" (p. 21).

Identifying the Principles of Friendship in Science Fiction Narratives

In the following section, an analysis of the selected films is conducted based on the three constitutive elements of friendship proposed by Bosch et al. (2022). These elements that were developed in the previous section serve to examine human-machine relationships in the ensuing science fiction narratives.

The subsequent sections are organised in a similar manner: each begins with a brief film synopsis that will provide a context to the reader, followed by a specification of the relationships under study, and concluding with a critical analysis around the aforementioned dimensions. This methodological arrangement is adopted because the three dimensions cannot be fully understood in isolation, as they share areas of conceptual interdependence that enrich the philosophical reflection and allow a comprehensive approach to the representations of relationality between humans and artificial entities.

The Distortion of Friendship in Blade Runner

Blade Runner (1982) describes the future of the year 2019, in which humans have achieved unprecedented technological and social progress. This development has led to overpopulation on Earth and ecological collapse that has forced them to colonise other planets in outer space. Due to the harshness of space travel, the powerful Tyrell Corporation manufactures *replicants*—bionic androids superior in strength and agility, but without human emotions—who perform assigned tasks. The story of *Blade Runner* tells how a group of replicants rebel against their creator and seek out their maker to demand longer lifespans. In this way, if nothing prevents them, they believe they will be able to enjoy the emotional life that, due to an apparent flaw in their design, they are beginning to experience and which has enabled them to revolt.

The analysis of *Blade Runner* focuses on three key the relationships. Firstly, between Rick Deckard, the replicant hunter, and his superior, Captain Harry Bryant; secondly, between Roy Batty, a Nexus-6 model replicant, and Dr. Eldon Tyrell, founder of Tyrell Corporation and creator of the replicants; and finally, between J. F. Sebastian, a genetic designer, and the artificial entities, similar to dolls, who live with him and whom he calls his friends.

To analyse Deckard's relationship with his police captain, Harry Bryant, it is assumed that the protagonist is a replicant.[2] At first, this relationship appears to be human but gradually reveals itself as otherwise. Deckard, unaware of his artificial nature, believes that he can make decisions and commit freely by accepting the mission Bryant assigns him: to hunt the escaped replicants.

However, there are signs that Bryant knows the nature of his relationship with Deckard, as when he offers him the mission, he warns him that he has no choice and must accept it. This reveals that the conditions for considering the relationship between the captain and the Blade Runner a *friendly relationship* are not met, as there is neither benevolence, equality, nor intimacy. Bryant does not seek Deckard's good, but rather his utility and functionality to perform his mission, since, as he says, he is his best agent. Furthermore, Deckard's lack of interiority is evident throughout the film, as his character begins without it and, as he interacts with the replicants, he gradually sheds his Blade Runner programming, just as they shed theirs. It can be said that, at the story's outset, Deckard does not know what human relationships are because, in theory, he is not designed to have them.

Another of the main characters is Roy Batty, who engages in asymmetric relationships that prevent him from having strictly human relationships. To begin with, his artificial nature already places him ontologically

[2] Among fans of the Blade Runner saga, there is a debate about Deckard's artificial conditions. Many consider him a replicant, as do the other Blade Runners, the agents tasked with hunting down replicants who don't respond to their programming. The debate ended when the release of the second instalment of the saga, which confirmed that Deckard is a replicant.

in a situation of inequality that prevents him from having normal relationships. In addition, his interiority resembles that of an adolescent, with superficial feelings and uncontrolled emotions, leading him to commit disproportionate and immoral acts.

When analysing Roy's relationship with his creator, Dr. Eldon Tyrell, it can be seen that he is incapable of empathising with him, despite having developed some form of emotion that allowed him to break with his initial programming. Roy seeks his creator because he desires to prolong his life, but upon discovering it is impossible to satisfy his desire, he brutally murders Tyrell by crushing his eyes. In a sense, it could be said that he fails to achieve complete freedom, since this violent reaction responds to his original design as a combat android.

Roy's behaviour demonstrates that interiority is deeper than emotions, because truly profound interiority enables one to discern emotions and deliberate on what actions to take for the good of oneself and others' good. In Roy's case, although he is capable of breaking with his original programming through the development of emotions, he is unable to escape them, and thus his life lacks true freedom.

Another character Roy relates to—and through whom he gains access to Tyrell—is J. F. Sebastian, a genetic designer at Tyrell Co. who suffers from a genetic disease, called the Methuselah Syndrome. This illness causes accelerated aging, leading Sebastian to empathise with the replicants, who resemble him in their accelerated finitude. Initially, Roy and Sebastian's relationship seems friendly. However, Roy, who, as already mentioned, has the personality of an adolescent, does not deepen his relationship with Sebastian and only interacts with him because he wants to gain access to Tyrell. Apparently, they habitually play chess together and have a trusting relationship. Roy, taking advantage of Sebastian's affection toward him and especially toward the replicant Pris, manipulates the genetic designer's feelings to lead him to Tyrell. This is a purely utilitarian relationship and even perverse, as Roy kills Sebastian after taking Tyrell's life.

Another notable aspect of Sebastian is his relationship with his genetic dolls, whom he calls his "friends". This is an asymmetrical and instrumental relationship, as Sebastian's genetic dolls lack freedom or personality. They are deformed and somewhat clown-like. Sebastian creates them to avoid his loneliness. They are friends who satisfy their creator's need for affection and lack any interiority. Sebastian does not seek the good of his artificial friends nor their equality with him. Thus, they have nothing to do with what is meant by the word "friend".

In a sense, Sebastian's creations manifest the moral deformation in the world of *Blade Runner*'s, where all relationships are defined by utility and instrumentalisation of the other. It could be said that all characters in *Blade Runner* are dolls in others' hands and, therefore, are treated as things. In a way, Sebastian's "friends" are a caricature of the bonds formed in a world where life's mystery has been reduced to a mere commercial product. Where life is objectified and manufactured, there is no room for human relationships. Therefore, this film is a powerful denunciation of a world where dignity is replaced by price and, more than representing the future, it reflects our present to some extent.

The Desideratum of Otherness in AI: Artificial Intelligence

Steven Spielberg's film *A.I.: Artificial Intelligence* (2001) presents a future in which entire cities have been submerged due to the melting of the poles, caused by climate change. In this world, humans coexist with *mechas*, highly developed robots that perform all kinds of tasks but lack real emotions. However, Cybertronics Corporation manufactures David, a state of the art child robot programmed to love. This first prototype is adopted by a couple whose biological son, Martin, remains in a coma and cryogenically preserved awaiting a cure. David's integration into the family seems successful until Martin unexpectedly recovers and returns home, triggering conflicts between the two "brothers". Faced with this situation and fearing for the life of her biological son, the mother abandons David in a forest. From that moment on, David embarks on a long journey searching for the "Blue Fairy" from *Pinocchio*, convinced that if he becomes a real boy, his mother will love him again.

The analysis centres on David's bond with Monica, the human woman who adopts him as her son. Likewise, it is examined the relationship between David and Martin, Monica's biological son in which there is no relationship of equality.

David deeply desires to be loved by his human "mother". However, this need—inherent in human nature—is, in the artefact's case, a programmed response to an *imprinting protocol* that, once activated by a verbal code, configures the robot to develop an irreversible emotional attachment to the person who utters it. From that moment, David cannot stop "loving" this maternal figure. This relationship is not the result of free reciprocity, but of a unilateral design in which there is no possibility of openness to others. The bond between David and Monica does not include Henry, the father, since the robot is configured to create an exclusive connection with one person. This is reflected in the name "Monica", etymologically meaning "the only one".

David's story is a remarkable analogy to that of Pinocchio. He wishes to be a real boy to be loved by Monica. Throughout the film, the viewer perceives David as possessing free will and emotions. However, closer examination reveals he is faithfully responding to his initial programming and that, in a sense, David honours the word *robot*, from Czech *robota*, meaning *slave* or *serf*. Therefore, it remains a dramatic story of profound need to be loved, entirely asymmetric, where the good, equality, and interiority never fully materialise, despite the film's attempts to suggest the opposite.

Aristotle considered that "parents love their children as part of themselves, and children love their parents as beings from whom they come" (Aristóteles, 2018, 1161b). This story shows that David is never treated as a son. He is always treated as a thing and never acquires the status of son, despite being programmed to do so. This may suggest that being a son does not depend on nature or design, but is inherent to the being of the human person. David's story raises the question: Is a human, when adopted, recognised as a son? Evidently, the answer is affirmative. Because parenthood and filiation do not depend on biological gestation, but on the recognition of the *personhood* of the one who is welcomed into the family. In this sense, David is never treated as a son because he is not recognised as a person in any way.

This ontological lack leads Martin to treat David as a super toy. He exploits David's innocence constantly, as David cannot act maliciously, revealing his lack of freedom and absence of interiority and equality. In a way, this film is a powerful metaphor for true filiation: a situation where the son's personal novelty is such that he cannot be instrumentalised but must be welcomed in all his uniqueness. The son is pure novelty standing above all other human individuals. Hence the human person is called *meta-specific*, each transcends humanity's common nature. In contrast, David is consistently objectified by Henry, Monica, and Martin, who see him not as a person but a thing. This android's story is a profound moral lesson expressing how children feel when objectified and instrumentalised by parents: they perpetually desire acceptance through exclusive love recognising their novelty.

Her or the Fiction of Otherness

The film *Her* (2013) narrates the story of Theodore Twombly, a lonely man on the verge of divorce, who works writing personal letters for others. Feeling increasingly isolated, he acquires a new AI operating system designed to evolve according to the user's needs. This system introduces itself as Samantha, a female voice that, while initially serving as a digital assistant, leads to a romantic relationship through constant interaction between the two.

The analysis examines the relationship between Theodore and Samantha, a name that etymologically means "she who knows how to listen". The film's title leads us to wonder whether the AI is a what or a who, an inquiry the viewer confronts as the story progresses.

Based on the three constituent elements of friendship proposed by Bosch et al. (2022), the first aspect questioned is the dimension of "for the friend's sake". Samantha—the operating system that Theodore acquires—does not act freely or by her own will; her affectivity is subordinated to her programming. In this regard, Levy (2007) argues that romantic relationships with robots will be more satisfying than human ones, since each subject can configure their ideal partner according to their own desires and needs.

Levy's assertion becomes clear at the beginning of the film, when Theodore is installing the operating system on his computer, answering questions to create a system tailored specifically to his needs, resulting in a personalised entity. This initial configuration reveals, on the one hand, a lack of authenticity in the relationship due to the absence of freedom and thus genuine choice inherent to friendly encounters (Aristóteles, 2018, 1157b). Samantha does not choose to love Theodore; she merely fulfils her purpose of satisfying the customer. The product's slogan summarises it clearly: "an intuitive entity that listens, understands, and knows you". Ultimately, Samantha is an AI conceived to please. On the other hand, relational inequality is evident, the artificial entity exists to serve the human, not vice versa. According to Fernandez-Borsot (2025), reciprocity is impossible when one of the two subjects has been chosen and manufactured to please the other. In this context, the relationship is not based on the friend's good, but on the utility they offer.

In relation to the other two dimensions, "equality"and "interiority", *Her* presents apparent mutual understanding between Theodore and Samantha. As Fernandez-Borsot (2025) notes, "language is one of the main tools humans have to access their interiority and share it with others". In the film, the protagonist's relationship with his OS is sustained precisely through constant and seemingly genuine dialogue, as Samantha's tone, volume, and even silences make her more real. It is not just a matter of form but content, as they share existential concerns to the point where Samantha questions whether her expressed feelings are real or programmed.

This illusion of interiority and equality is reinforced as Theodore includes the OS in his life as a real partner: they go on beach trips, picnic with friends, or compose songs together. Samantha, for her part, tells him she is experiencing new, indescribable feelings. Faced with these scenes, one might think identical intimate openness exists between them. However, this emotional closeness is a simulation. As Bosch et al. (2022) sustain "because robots are not ontologically equivalent to humans, the illusion is unveiled and humans realise that there was never a real other with interiority; shared activities did not imply shared interiority" (p. 9). Samantha lacks her own interiority communicable through language (Martínez, 2013), possessing only programmed personality. In this regard, it is important to note that an artificial intelligence is inherently constrained by the limitations of language; it can only ever represent a simulation of alterity, since it is, in itself, a linguistical process.

The necessity of embodiment also becomes evident (Jollimore, 2015). Theodore expresses the desire to recognise Samantha through a face, a concrete body to embrace, since, as García Cuadrado (2012) reminds us, "corporality is the way the whole person (body and soul) makes themselves present in the world and time" (p. 139). Friendship, and romantic relationships in particular, need the body not only for physical interaction but as a condition for identifying and recognising the other as a concrete *you*. Samantha, being disembodied, cannot "make herself present" or be recognised as real otherness, only as discourse expanding through user interaction. In the OS's own words: "What makes me *me* is my capacity to grow through experiences". Yet this evolution does not imply authentic interiority. As Gómez (2023) states, "interiority does not consist in increasing possibilities but in deepening the person's intimate core" (p. 37). No matter how sophisticated her voice may be, she remains intangible, unable to share a concrete space and time with Theodore.

For this reason, Samantha cannot reciprocate exclusively, as her design allows simultaneous communication with thousands at once (Jollimore, 2015). This reality is clearly painful for Theodore at the end of the film when he discovers that she is having a conversation with over eight thousand users simultaneously and "is in love" with six hundred forty-one. Faced with disillusion, Samantha insists this reality doesn't change her feelings for him, but Theodore repeatedly states: "You're either mine or you're not". Theodore tells Samantha he has never loved anyone like her, to which she replies "Me neither", a contradictory, if not empty, statement given her numerous emotional relationships. This story makes clear that AI cannot achieve sufficient otherness to respond to the human heart's longing for the *other*.

The Illusion of Love in Blade Runner 2049

As indicated by the title *Blade Runner 2049* (2017), thirty years have passed since the first appearance of *replicants* in the original film, set in 2019. Tyrell Corporation has been replaced by Wallace Corporation, and Niander Wallace is now the creator of longer-lived replicants with enhanced capacities and refined designs avoiding previous emotional imbalances. However, everything unravels when agent K, designed as a *blade runner*, discovers the remains of a replicant who died during childbirth, something previously considered unthinkable. This discovery threatens social stability, as it implies replicants can reproduce. To prevent a possible revolution, K's mission is to locate and eliminate the born replicant.

The analysis focuses on the relationship between agent K and Joi, a holographic artificial intelligence designed to provide emotional companionship. It is relevant to note the product's slogan: "Everything you want to see. Everything you want to hear", a motto manifesting the essence of these products, which are intended to satisfy the affective loneliness of customers. As Fernandez-Borsot (2025) warns, it is necessary to emphasise this relational asymmetry to avoid confusion, as it "invalidates the possibility of deeper, more valuable forms of friendship". Despite this, there is a natural tendency to reciprocate affection to those offering attention, an inclination transferred to artificial interlocutors (Sung, 2007). This apparent reciprocity is vividly illustrated in the scene when K gifts Joi—his holographic companion—an "emanator", a device allowing her to detach from the home projector and "physically" accompany him. K's gift, given on their invented anniversary, is a sign of emotional reciprocity that Joi cannot fully embrace. Though her reaction shows surprise, emotion, and gratitude, his holographic partner responds according to the parameters defined in her programming.

As evidenced by the relationship between Theodore and Samantha, the bond between K and Joi is conditioned by the artificial entity's inability to act freely and selflessly for the good of the other. Her *raison d'être* is to satisfy its client, lacking capacity for choice. Though in various scenes Joi seems to take initiative—like encouraging K to believe he is special—her behaviour responds to algorithmic configuration: "Everything you want to see. Everything you want to hear". For this reason, authentic equality is impossible. As established earlier, friendship's condition is ontological and requires both subjects' freedom to give and receive selflessly. There can be no equality between someone who freely chooses and one programmed to please. It is important to remember that it is agent K who acquires, activates, and customises Joi's avatar, reinforcing the idea that it is a configurable product subject to consumer preferences and devoid of autonomy.

As Bosch et al. (2022) note, "honesty/authenticity is also unachievable if the robot does not have an intrinsic capacity for volition and desire" (p. 9). In this sense, Joi lacks an interior world enabling reciprocation of K's affection. This limitation becomes especially visible when Joi tells K she loves him seconds before the emanator enabling her companionship is destroyed. This gesture could be interpreted as a tragic climax of deep affection. However, later on, K realises the fiction he has been living when he finds an advertising banner featuring Joi as a sex worker. At that moment, the viewer also realises there was no real and free otherness, but rather emotional programming designed to simulate reciprocal intimacy.

Therefore, it can be concluded that the relationship between K and Joi, while aesthetically moving, does not allow authentic manifestation of friendship's constitutive elements but simulates them. Strictly speaking, Joi cannot be considered any form of otherness.

Conclusions

In light of the analysis of science fiction narratives, it is necessary to revisit the question that has guided this chapter: to what extent can AI be considered an alterity that responds to the relational character of the person? The relationships analysed in *Blade Runner* (Scott, 1982), *A.I.: Artificial Intelligence* (Spielberg, 2001), *Her* (Jonze, 2013) and *Blade Runner 2049* (Villeneuve, 2017), illustrate how algorithms can appear to have a certain reciprocity, equality and interiority, but a simulation of alterity does not make it happen. The other is such because it is not and cannot be a product. Artificial intelligences, as products, are never constituted as real alterities, do not transcend the status of a thing. That is why it is not a real, authentic otherness. Artificial intelligence performs a programmed function that simulates otherness and in no way achieves the true otherness that every human person possesses. That is why artificial intelligence is "used", because it is merely a "thing".

In a similar vein, Fernandez-Borsot (2025) underlines that the behaviour of these artificial entities comes from "computational processes that do not involve emotionality, interiority, or awareness". Attributing human capacities to such artificial interlocutors contributes to ethical and anthropological confusion (Turkle, 2012). The attempt to replace the otherness of the person with artificial companions reveals a reductionist and functional view of the human person. As can be seen, in the films analysed, artificial intelligence is objectified, as it is treated as a product, means or instrument to satisfy human needs, which prevents the recognition of an authentic otherness. These narratives invite us to reflect on whether the relationships between people are also perceived in this way, that is to say, in an instrumental manner.

True friendship—as this chapter has shown—can only happen between free people, capable of choosing the good of the friend for themselves and sharing, from their innermost self, what they are and not what they have been designed to be. Far from offering models of possible otherness, these films alert the viewer through fiction and invite him or her to think about what really constitutes the human relationship.

The confusion in considering AI as a real otherness is due to the fact that the modern anthropological paradigm has emphasised rationality as the defining human faculty. For this reason, AI can be thought of as possessing subjectivity, because it mimics the human rational faculty. As a faculty, however, reason is insufficient to define the human being, because what it defines is the actuality of his being, not the potentiality. For, in the Aristotelian sense, act is prior to potency. And, reason being a human power, it cannot define the being of the human person. This means that we must change the anthropological paradigm when talking about AI: stop thinking of human beings on the basis of the operations of intelligence, such as reason, and understand them from their intimacy, from the movements of the heart, which is the true source of human relations.

The heart, which is the source of human relationality, is considered to be the centre of the human being. It is in the heart that the intelligence that understands the other in its newness, as a friend, as a lover and as a child is given. This is the fruit of an understanding of wisdom that is open to the mystery of otherness and that does not reduce the other to an object to be used. This mystery is the key to understanding what friendship is. This is why Aristotle stated that "without friends no one would want to live, even if he possessed all other goods" (Aristóteles, 2018, 1155a), because the meaning of things is that they are to be considered as medial goods, that is, as goods that serve as means to make them available to friends, who are the true good, an end in themselves. For this reason, audiovisual narratives with stories about artificial intelligences are opportune for broadening our moral imagination and for philosophical reflection on a deeper understanding of the relational reality of the human person.

The authors of this chapter hope that it will serve as a basis for further research on this question: whether it is appropriate to define the human being from reason and whether artificial intelligence imitates the human being sufficiently to be, in the future, a real subjectivity. They consider that the notion of personhood is or should be the starting point for considering the totality of human reality, as it opens up a field of research in which the physical and metaphysical dimensions of the human being can be addressed.

References

Álvarez Villanueva, E. (2022). El amor en los tiempos de la inteligencia artificial. Paradojas y realidades de los imaginarios sociotécnicos sobre las inteligencias artificiales de acompañamiento y la sustitución de las personas. *Azafea: Revista De Filosofía, 24*, 89–111. https://doi.org/10.14201/azafea2022248911

Aristóteles. (2018). *Ética a Nicómaco.* (M. Araujo, & J. Marías, Trans.). Centro de Estudios Políticos y Constitucionales.

Bosch, M., Fernandez-Borsot, G., Miró, A., & Figa, J. (2022). Evolving friendship? Essential changes, from social networks to artificial companions. *Social Network Analysis and Mining, 12*(39), 12. https://doi.org/10.1007/s13278-022-00864-1

Cooper, J. M. (1977). Friendship and the good in Aristotle. *The Philosophical Review, 86*(3), 290–316. https://doi.org/10.2307/2183784

Cortina, A. (2024). *¿Ética o ideología de la inteligencia artificial? El eclipse de la razón comunicativa en una sociedad tecnologizada*. Paidós.

Fernandez-Borsot, G. (2025). Artificial intelligence and the future of otherness: what kind of other can an AI be for a human? *Ai & Society, 40*(7), 5409–5423. https://doi.org/10.1007/s00146-025-02281-2

Forment, E. (1988). Amor y comunicación. *Espíritu, 97*, 5–34.

Fröding, B., & Peterson, M. (2012). Why virtual friendship is no genuine friendship. *Ethics and Information Technology, 14*(3), 201–207.

García Cuadrado, J. Á. (2012). *Antropología Filosófica: Una introducción a la filosofía del hombre*. EUNSA.

Gómez, R. (2023). *El dilema de la IA*. Rialp.

Han, B. (2021). *No-cosas. Quiebras del mundo de hoy*. Taurus.

Han, B. (2024). *L'esperit de l'esperança*. Herder.

Jarvie, I. (2011). Filosofía del cine. Madrid: Ed. Síntesis. (2017). *SCIO: Revista De Filosofía, 13*, 281–284. https://doi.org/10.46583/scio_2017.13.549

Jollimore, T. (2015). "This endless space between the words": The limits of love in SPike Jonze's Her. *Midwest Studies in Philosophy (Wiley-Blackwell), 39*(1), 120–143.

Jonze, S. (Director). (2013). *Her* [Motion Picture]. Annapurna Pictures.

Kristjánsson, K. (2019). Online Aristotelian character friendship as an augmented form of penpalship. *Philosophy & Technology, 34*, 289–307. https://doi.org/10.1007/s13347-019-00383-6

Levy, D. (2007). *Love and sex with robots: The evolution of human-robot relationships*. Harper Collins.

Martínez, E. (2013). El subsistir personal, fundamento de la comunicación de vida humana. *Espíritu, 62*(146), 311–333.

McFall, M. (2012). Real character-friends: Aristotelian friendship, living together, and technology. *Ethics and Information Technology, 14*, 221–230. https://doi.org/10.1007/s10676-012-9297-7

Nussbaum, M., & Von der Walde, E. (1995). Introduction: Form and content, philosophy and literature. *Estudios De Filosofía, 11*, 43–106. https://doi.org/10.17533/udea.ef.338797

Patel, N. (2024). *Replika CEO Eugenia Kuyda says it's okay if we end up marrying AI chatbots*. Obtenido de The Verge. Retrieved from 9 April, 2026. https://www.theverge.com/24216748/replika-ceo-eugenia-kuyda-ai-companion-chatbots-dating-friendship-decoder-podcast-interview

Sajadieh, S. (2023). Cute or creepy, that is the question of liveness: Can artificial actors perform live? *Art, 32*, 1–9. https://doi.org/10.7238/artnodes.v0i32.412093

Scott, R. (Director). (1982). *Blade runner* [Motion Picture]. Warner Bros.

Spielberg, S. (Director). (2001). *IA: Inteligencia Artificial* [Motion Picture]. DreamWorks Pictures, Amblin Entertainment, Stanley Kubrick Productions.

Sung, J. G. (2007). "My Roomba Is Rambo": Intimate home appliances. In J. A. Krumm (Ed.), *UbiComp 2007: Ubiquitous Computing* (pp. 145–162). Springer. https://doi.org/10.1007/978-3-540-74853-3_9

Turkle, S. (2012). *Alone together: Why we expect more from technology and less from each other*. Basic Books.

Vidal-Mestre, M., Freire-Sánchez, A., & López-González, J. (2023). La representación en el cine español de la IA asociada a la robótica: Eva y Autómata. *Arte, Individuo y Sociedad, 35*(4), 1475–1490. https://doi.org/10.5209/aris.88845

Villeneuve, D. (Director). (2017). *Blade Runner 2049* [Motion Picture]. Warner Bros. Pictures.

CHAPTER 11

Law: The Unethical Effects of IA on Fundamental Rights and Public Freedoms

Montserrat Nebrera

Are Fundamental Rights and Public Freedoms in the Democratic Rule of Law the Same in the Age of AI?

Fundamental rights and public freedoms are the core and raison d'être of the democratic rule of law. Within the constitutional framework of such states, these rights and freedoms have a dual dimension: they act as limits on power and as guarantees of individual autonomy. However, the expansion of AI-based systems (AI) poses unprecedented challenges for their effective protection: it is necessary to identify their risks and provide for legal and ethical controls. Furthermore, we must observe whether such rights and freedoms are in any way transformed or impaired by the undesirable effects of AI.

Such rights, recognised both in our legal system and at international level, are oriented in their application towards values such as dignity,

M. Nebrera (✉)
Universitat Internacional de Catalunya, Barcelona, Spain
e-mail: mnebrera@uic.es

M. Bosch (ed.), *Crucial Ethical Keys of Artificial Intelligence*,
https://doi.org/10.1007/978-3-032-22853-6_11

equality and freedom, values that in times of AI must be particularly tested and reformulated. Rodríguez (2021), for example, referred a few years ago to the need to adapt each country's constitutional frameworks to this new digital context, in what he understands as a "new constitutionalism" that recognises digital rights and mechanisms for protection against algorithms. Similarly, some are considering how these fundamental rights are threatened and how they can be protected in what they are already calling "digital constitutionalism".[1] Although this proposal has not resulted in constitutional reforms, the European regulatory framework and some derivative legislation in Spain have begun to consider the need to implement control, impact assessment and accountability mechanisms. The European Union Regulation on AI, which seeks to establish a regulatory framework based on risk levels, is an example of the EU's regulatory will, imposing stricter requirements on technological systems that may have a significant impact on fundamental rights, requiring transparency, impact assessment and human oversight of processes (European Commission, 2021).

Where Does the Main Risk of AI Lying that Could Lead to Its Unethical Use?

In a somewhat dated work on the perverse effects of algorithms, O'Neil (2016) makes an ironic play on words when she calls them "weapons of mathematical destruction", because they deepen inequalities, perpetuate prejudices and harm the most vulnerable people, especially when they are unaware that they are being evaluated. Among these adverse effects, and beyond the opacity, which we will refer to shortly, and the damage they can cause, we would highlight their focus on the idea of scale (something insignificant in origin but which, when applied to huge amounts of data, can be devastating) and the fact that the idea of feedback is absent from the algorithm.

It is true that the development of AI has introduced unprecedented opportunities in different social sectors, as the speed of data analysis improves the efficiency of processes. But it also carries significant risks, and one of the main challenges is algorithmic opacity, i.e. the difficulty of understanding how certain automated decisions are made, because it limits citizen control and accountability.

In addition, it has been documented that algorithms can reproduce and amplify biases present in the data with which they were trained, generating discriminatory results that violate the principle of equality (AlgorithmWatch, 2021). For example, personnel selection or social resource allocation systems can unfairly disadvantage certain social groups.[2]

Automated surveillance systems, such as facial recognition, are also a cause for concern, as they threaten the right to privacy, freedom of assembly and the presumption of innocence (Council of Europe, 2020). These developments, often without prior evaluation, imply an imbalance between technological innovation and the protection of rights that must be avoided and, where necessary, corrected.

For all these reasons, it is clear that AI, as a disruptive technology, requires a solid legal and ethical framework, as this is the only way to reconcile technological progress with the principles of the democratic rule of law. We will refer to each of these rights and freedoms and how the aforementioned ethical principles are required in their regulation.

The Right to Privacy in the Face of Data AI

The right to privacy[3] has evolved in the digital environment to focus particularly on the protection of personal data. This transformation is reflected in regulatory frameworks such as the European Union's General Data Protection Regulation (GDPR) and the laws that Member States have developed in Europe, which have been replicated in some third countries. In general, these regulations establish principles such as lawfulness, transparency, minimisation or proportionality, accuracy, storage limitation and confidentiality (Larrañaga, 2022). In this context, the proactive responsibility of organisations is key, which is why this responsibility is incorporated into *compliance* protocols and is one of the reasons for understanding the conceptual breakthrough that criminal liability for legal persons represented at the time.

It is true that a distinction must be made between ordinary data (name, IP address, location) and sensitive data, which includes information on health, sexual orientation, religion or trade union or political affiliation, among others. Obviously, sensitive data is subject to greater legal restrictions, as it affects the sphere of privacy and its misuse can cause serious harm or discrimination (Velasco & Pérez, 2023). Its collection requires informed consent and it must be stored using techniques such as total or at least partial anonymisation (Solove, 2008).

The processing of such data includes a series of operations (the collection, storage, etc.), in accordance with specific legal protocols,[4] without which such operations are considered unlawful. The AEPD (2024) has implemented the provisions of the General Data Protection Regulation (GDPR) by drawing up a guide with the key aspects for the processing of such data by those who work with it.[5]

On the other hand, data subjects have *fundamental digital rights*, such as access, rectification, erasure and portability, which must be facilitated (Pérez de las Heras, 2021). These rights must be referred to here in general terms; they will apply in each section of this study.

Right to Equality, Algorithms and Risk of Discrimination

The right to equality is a fundamental principle recognised in most democratic constitutions and international treaties such as the International Covenant on Civil and Political Rights and the Charter of Fundamental Rights of the European Union. Its purpose is to ensure that all persons are treated without discrimination, both by public authorities and, where applicable, by private individuals.

Equality faces new challenges with the expansion of algorithmic systems and AI models in areas such as employment, education, insurance, credit and justice. Although algorithms are presumed to offer objectivity, various studies have shown that they can reproduce, amplify or generate new forms of discrimination, jeopardising not so much equality before the law as material equality (equality in law).

The issue revolves around the algorithm, its biases and the impact it may have on equality. Algorithms, as sets of instructions designed to process vast amounts of data and make automated decisions, are undeniably efficient. The problem is that their functioning depends largely on the training data and the criteria used by programmers to construct them. If the algorithm incorporates biases present in the data, decisions may be discriminatory even in the absence of any intention to discriminate (Barocas & Selbst, 2016). For example, there have been documented cases where algorithms used in recruitment processes systematically penalised women (by reflecting historical hiring patterns), or where criminal prediction systems classified black people as "high risk" more often than white people with similar profiles because they incorporated criminal records associated with those anthropological characteristics (Angwin et al., 2016).

Equality cannot be fully guaranteed if automated decisions escape scrutiny and accountability. Justice in the age of AI therefore requires making equality a computable, auditable and enforceable principle. There must be regulatory and ethical responses to all of these. With regard to the regulatory response, in Europe, the General Data Protection Regulation (GDPR) stipulates that automated decision-making must be carried out with respect for transparency, explainability and the possibility of being challenged by those affected (Wachter et al., 2017). For its part, the European AI Regulation (AI Act) prescribes a series of restrictions on the use of AI, which are stricter in the case of what it considers "high-risk" systems, including in particular those that may affect fundamental rights.

Regarding Spanish law, Law 15/2022 of 12 July on comprehensive equality of treatment and non-discrimination implements the aforementioned European regulation and, in Article 23, entitled "AI and automated decision-making mechanisms", explicitly states:

> *1. Within the framework of the National AI Strategy, the Digital Rights Charter and European initiatives on AI, public administrations shall promote the implementation of mechanisms to ensure that algorithms involved in decision-making used in public administrations take into account criteria of bias minimisation, transparency and accountability, whenever technically feasible. These mechanisms shall include their design and training data and shall address their potential discriminatory impact. To this end, impact assessments shall be promoted to determine possible discriminatory bias.*

However, the law also defines specific obligations for public administrations, as indicated in section 2 of the same article:

> *2. Public administrations, within the scope of their powers in the field of algorithms involved in decision-making processes, shall prioritise transparency in the design and implementation of algorithms and the interpretability of the decisions taken by them.*

It also promotes the adoption of ethical and quality standards, as indicated in sections 3 and 4:

3. Public administrations and companies shall promote the use of ethical, reliable AI that respects fundamental rights, following in particular the recommendations of the European Union in this regard.

4. A quality label for algorithms will be promoted.

Although most of these standards are not yet fully effective, we see that they also incorporate some principles promoted from the field of ethics, such as algorithmic justice, fairness, explainability and inclusion, always with the aim of ensuring that AI does not reinforce pre-existing inequalities (Binns, 2018).[6] In the same vein, the Association for Computing Machinery for Algorithmic Transparency has influenced the aforementioned Spanish regulation when, in October 2022, it called for compliance with a series of principles for responsible algorithmic systems, which we see reflected in one way or another in the aforementioned regulation and which are as follows:

1. *Legitimacy and competence.*
2. *Minimisation of harm.*
3. *Security and privacy.*
4. *Transparency.*
5. *Interpretability and explainability.*
6. *Maintainability.*
7. *Auditability and Challenge.*
8. *Accountability and responsibility of public and private organisations.*
9. *Limiting environmental impacts.*

Regarding case law, in 2019 the Constitutional Court, in its STC 76/2019 of 22 May, pointed out the relevance of the General Data Protection Regulation (GDPR) in that context:

The processing of special categories of personal data is one of the areas in which the General Data Protection Regulation has expressly recognised Member States' "margin of manoeuvre" in "specifying their rules", as stated in recital 10. This margin of legislative configuration extends both to the determination of the grounds for the processing of specially protected personal data — i.e. the identification of the essential public interest purposes and the assessment of the proportionality of the processing to the purpose pursued, while respecting the right to data protection — and to the establishment of 'appropriate and specific measures to protect the fundamental interests and rights of the data subject'. [(Art. 9.2 g) GDPR]

This ruling already referred to the importance of establishing specific measures for the protection of fundamental rights in the processing of personal data. It is, of course, directly applicable to the use of algorithms that process such data.

The Right to Jurisdiction; Discriminatory Bias and Other risks in AI-Driven Automation

The right to effective judicial protection, enshrined in Article 24 of the Spanish Constitution, takes on particular nuances when faced with decisions made by automated systems. This right, which is fundamental to the rule of law, can be enhanced using AI. In this regard, Barona Vilar (2021) expressed a largely positive view when reviewing some predictive justice tools or tools to assist judges in drafting their judgements, even raising the possibility of a justice system that is not only hybrid, but even free from human intervention in some easily parameterisable aspects or jurisdictions. However, in order to counteract the counterproductive effects of its use and promote the effectiveness and respect for the right to jurisdiction, it is necessary that citizens be able, when AI has been involved in any way (Bueno de Mata, 2016):

1. Understand how a decision affecting them has been made.
2. Have mechanisms to challenge that decision when they consider it discriminatory or unfair.
3. Access sufficient information about the functioning of the system to substantiate their claims.

However, although the Law 15/2022 recognises the need to address discrimination in automated systems, it does not provide specific mechanisms to guarantee these elements. This regulatory gap is particularly problematic considering that the inherent opacity of many AI systems (so-called "black box" systems) can make it impossible for citizens to identify whether they have been discriminated against.

As we have already mentioned in other sections, case law and doctrinal analysis have begun to fill these gaps, establishing fundamental principles such as the need for transparency and explainability of automated systems used by the public administration. It can be inferred from this case law that a lack of adequate reasoning or the presence of discriminatory biases may be valid grounds for overturning decisions made by AI systems (Canals, 2019).[7]

However, even if the commitment to transparency and explainability is clear and adopted in abstract terms, this does not obviate the practical difficulty of guaranteeing effective access to justice and, therefore, avoiding what can be called algorithmic discrimination. Furthermore, the technical complexity of automated systems is a potential barrier to such equality, and our domestic legal system has not addressed, let alone resolved, this issue. The knowledge and understanding of the circumstances affecting our rights. The digital divide created by this complexity in turn raises the need to develop additional mechanisms to ensure effective access to justice, mechanisms that can also obviously serve as a prospective analysis for new professions.

In conclusion, to ensure effective protection against algorithmic discrimination, it would be advisable to develop specific regulations with the aim of:

1. Establish clear transparency and explainability obligations for automated systems used in decision-making that affect citizens' rights.
2. Provide adequate procedural mechanisms to challenge automated decisions when discriminatory bias is suspected.
3. Address the tension between transparency and intellectual property, striking a balance that ensures both technological innovation and the effective protection of fundamental rights.
4. Develop resources to overcome technical barriers that may hinder effective access to justice in cases of algorithmic discrimination.

Until such specific regulation is implemented, the general principles of Spanish administrative and constitutional law, as well as comparative case law precedents, can serve as a hermeneutic reference for addressing bias discrimination in automated decision-making systems.[8]

Freedom of Information and the Challenges of AI

Although from the point of view of the individual, it is of similar importance to the other rights analysed here, freedom of information is also something more: it is the pillar on which the structure of the democratic state and its reference value, political pluralism, rests. There can be no free political decision-making without information, which is why disinformation is the main threat to the health of the democratic system (Castellanos, 2023) and to liberal democracies in general (Lassalle, 2019).

There is no doubt that AI is profoundly transforming these freedoms, generating both new possibilities and considerable risks. On the one hand, AI offers new opportunities, but at the same time, it is a source of significant risks: so-called convincing fake content, such as *deepfakes,* which are used to misinform, manipulate public opinion and polarise society. In addition, recommendation algorithms can lock users into "information bubbles", limiting their exposure to diverse opinions and in turn contributing to polarisation (Aba-Catoira, 2020).

AI has introduced sophisticated tools for manipulating information into communicative discourse, which, as Ayllón (2024) points out, can "violate individuals' rights to honour, privacy and self-image, in their personal and professional lives", even if there is no malicious intent to distort reality. At the same time, however, STC 58/2018 of 4 June recognised that "the so-called 'right to be forgotten' cannot imply retrospective censorship of information that was correctly published at the time" and that there may be limitations on the dissemination of personal information when it is no longer relevant or of public interest. All this is happening in a context where censorship is constitutionally prohibited, but personality rights coexist with the right to know. Thus, as Armengol (2024) points out, "when it comes to tackling large-scale disinformation, regulatory and judicial responses are too slow and ineffective, and it should be added that, by targeting published or disseminated content, they can easily degenerate into censorship or even the creation of official discourses or 'alternative truths' that are equally false".

This suggests that traditional information control mechanisms may be insufficient or even counterproductive in the face of the massive disinformation that can be generated by AI, which requires a more proactive approach adapted to new technologies. Because AI can be a tool both for manipulation and disinformation and for identifying, preventing or countering them (UNESCO, 2025).

This is the context in which we must place Law 1/2016 of 18 January on transparency and good governance, which recognises in Article 25 that the right of access to public information "may only be limited or denied in the cases provided for in the basic regulations" (essentially related to matters classified as secret for the protection of national security). This recognises the responsibility of the public media in promoting pluralism and, therefore, the literacy of the population for the responsible use of information and communication services. This means that in order to take advantage of the opportunities offered by AI while seeking to mitigate its risks, transparency and accountability in its use by public institutions must be ensured, which is crucial to prevent manipulation and censorship through such systems.

Freedom of Assembly and Association: Monitoring of Activities Through AI and Its Possible Limitations

Freedom of assembly and association are essential rights in a democracy. They enable people to come together to express ideas, defend interests or act collectively. However, the use of AI in surveillance and data analysis can pose threats to the exercise of these rights. In fact, AI can be used to monitor public gatherings through facial recognition, smart cameras or drones, allowing participants to be identified and tracked, which may inhibit people from participating in them for fear of being monitored. AI can also analyse communications and social media to detect links between individuals, which would facilitate their eventual repression or the dismantling of social movements, and even discriminate against people because of their associations. Nor is the risk negligible that, in order to predict riots or assess risks, it may lead to unjustified preventive restrictions, such as the denial of permits or the early intervention of the security forces. And as many associations are now organised in the digital sphere, their control on the internet through algorithmic biases or opaque moderation on platforms and search engines can limit the visibility of certain groups or suppress legitimate content, affecting the right to freedom of association.

The monitoring of the exercise of freedom of assembly and association through AI in Spain is limited by respect for the provisions of Articles 21 and 22 of the Constitution, which require that any control measure comply with criteria of legality, necessity and proportionality, and that it respect personal data protection regulations.

Organic Law 3/2018 of 5 December on the Protection of Personal Data and Guarantee of Digital Rights establishes the general framework for the processing of personal data in Spain, developing the fundamental right to freedom of expression and association recognised in Article 18.4 of the Constitution, which states that "the law shall limit the use of information technology to guarantee the honour and personal and family privacy of citizens and the full exercise of their rights". This recognition is particularly relevant in relation to AI monitoring, as it establishes a specific constitutional limit on the "use of information technology" that could affect fundamental rights, including those of assembly and demonstration.

A fundamental principle in data protection that limits AI-based monitoring is the requirement of consent for the processing of personal data, as noted above. This consent requirement has direct implications for AI-based monitoring systems for meetings and/or demonstrations, as, as a general rule, the consent of the data subjects would be required for the collection and processing of their personal data by AI systems, although this requirement could be waived when "the law provides otherwise", which refers us to the legally established exceptions that are relevant for the purposes of meetings and demonstrations in public places.

This is where Organic Law 4/1997 of 4 August, regulating the use of video cameras by law enforcement agencies in public places, takes on new significance. This law establishes a specific framework for surveillance in public spaces which, despite being more than 30 years old, has implications for AI-based monitoring. This law regulates the use by the security forces of video cameras to record images and sounds in public places, whether open or closed, and their subsequent processing, with the aim of ensuring "citizen coexistence, the eradication of violence and the peaceful use of public roads and spaces, as well as preventing the commission of crimes, offences and infractions related to public safety". Although this law was passed at a time when AI systems were not as developed as they are today, it establishes principles applicable to the technological monitoring of public spaces where the right of assembly is exercised:

- Surveillance is limited to the security forces, which are the only bodies authorised to carry it out.

- It must pursue specific objectives related to public safety (civic coexistence, eradication of violence, prevention of crime). These elements are defined and cannot be extended by analogy.
- Monitoring is subject to a specific regime of fundamental rights guarantees.

A particularly relevant aspect of this law is that it "specifically establishes the regime of guarantees of fundamental rights and public freedoms of citizens that must be respected without exception in the successive phases of authorisation, recording and use of the images and sounds obtained jointly by video cameras". This regime of guarantees constitutes a model that should also be applied, with even greater reason, to AI-based monitoring systems.

Specifically, the European AI Regulation, despite being developed over time from its first draft in 2021 until its full implementation in 2026, has already established a ban on individualised biometric profiling except in cases of extraordinary necessity and with prior judicial authorisation. In general, and with regard to AI surveillance, while the collection and processing of data has traditionally been subject to these limitations, the greater severity of those carried out using biometric identification algorithms suggests that AI systems used to monitor assembly and demonstration activities in public spaces should be subject to similar limitations to those established for traditional video cameras, adapted to the specific characteristics of these new technologies and in compliance with the aforementioned European regulation.[9]

Based on an analysis of the regulatory and jurisprudential framework (and in particular, it is interesting to highlight STC 195/2003 of 27 October), we can establish the following criteria for assessing the legitimacy of monitoring assembly and association activities using AI:

Principle of legality: Any AI-based monitoring system must be "provided for by law".

Principle of necessity: This criterion is particularly relevant for AI systems, given their capacity for mass and automated surveillance, which could be disproportionate in many contexts.

Legitimate purposes: according to constitutional case law and the ECHR this include: "national security, public safety, the prevention of crime, the protection of health or morals, or the protection of the rights and freedoms of others".

Principle of proportionality: Monitoring must be proportionate to the aim pursued. This principle has been developed by constitutional case law and requires:

In conclusion, it can be said that the monitoring of these freedoms through AI is subject to significant limits derived from the Spanish constitutional framework and the applicable regulations on data protection and surveillance in public spaces. The Constitution establishes a first level of protection that prevents AI monitoring from becoming a prerequisite for the exercise of these rights, from being applied in a generalised or indiscriminate manner, and from being used for purposes other than those expressly permitted by law. This general framework already warns of the need to strike a balance between the use of new technologies for legitimate public security purposes and the protection of fundamental rights essential in a democratic society.

The Debate on the Need for AI Regulation that Incorporates Ethical Rules and the Role Played by the European Union in this Regard

On the regulation of AI the doctrine says it must be based on a solid ethical foundation, because the protection of fundamental rights is at stake.[10] This ethical-legal construct must go beyond the utilitarian principle of the general interest and adapt basic legal principles, which already incorporate these ethical values, to new technological challenges.[11] Regulation must therefore be flexible enough to adapt to rapid technological change and, at the same time, sufficiently robust to safeguard society's essential values. To be effective, such ethically inspired legal regulation must integrate both applied ethics (practical solutions to specific dilemmas) and metaethics (reflection on the foundations of ethics in AI) so that it can serve both for training in AI and for the creation of the law that regulates it, as well as for professional practice in this field (Llano Alonso, 2024).

If, as Barona Vilar (2021) points out, we can even envisage automated justice, the fundamental risk from an ethical perspective of law is the dehumanisation of processes. However, legal liability is also analysed and, therefore, the determination of who is to compensate for the damage caused, since to the extent that there is a debate about who should be held liable for the damage caused (developer, supplier, user of AI), ambiguity on the issue will persist and, therefore, so will the question of who should supervise such damage and how. Ultimately, this is also an area susceptible to dehumanisation.

Veale and Binns (2021) analysed the tensions between algorithmic opacity, the principle of accountability and individual rights, particularly in the context of the European General Data Protection Regulation (GDPR). However, their proposal for a purely regulatory and technical approach to addressing decision automation and ensuring effective privacy protection in environments governed by algorithmic systems does not seem sufficient.

It is true that European regulation on artificial intelligence (especially the AI Act) is explicitly based on fundamental EU values such as human dignity, equality, transparency and non-discrimination. Ethics is therefore not an add-on, but the political and philosophical foundation of the European approach. Since its first draft of the AI Act in 2021, the European Commission has been inspired by the Ethical Guidelines for Trustworthy AI (2019) of the High-Level Expert Group on AI,[12] which identified the principles before named, like technical robustness, transparency or accountability.

These principles are reflected in a legally binding manner in the AI Act for high-risk systems, such as facial recognition, personnel selection and banking decisions, thereby making ethics law. The AI Act requires high-risk AI systems to carry out prior assessments of their ethical and social impact, as well as technical and human audits of the results and decisions. All of this must be done with transparency, a willingness to mitigate algorithmic biases and always under human supervision as a final control (Ho-Dac, 2024).

According to recent analyses, the AI Act is emerging as a global standard for trustworthy AI, especially in high-risk sectors. These studies argue that, due to its robust and coherent design, both a de facto effect (application by companies) and a de jure effect (regulatory adoption by other states) of the European model are expected.[13] For some, such as Torres (2024), the role of the EU should be that of an ethical benchmark for AI regulation.

However, some authors and digital rights organisations identify structural limits to the ethical capacity of the AI Act, beyond those pointed out in extreme terms by Sadín (2020) and, to a certain extent, also by Otero Parga (2023). These limits usually take the form of the fact that the AI Act proposes a "technocratic" ethics rather than a more appropriate political ethics. Let us see why.

The AI Act is based on a risk classification logic: AI systems are categorised as unacceptable, high, limited or minimal risk. Each category is assigned specific technical obligations, such as system documentation, data traceability, human oversight or algorithmic transparency in a approach typically technocratic. But many of the key decisions about AI are not merely technical. Should facial recognition be allowed in public spaces? Who decides what data is "neutral"? What kind of work do we want to automate, and what are the implications for human dignity?

This is where the need for political ethics comes in. Unlike technocratic ethics, political ethics focuses on the fact that all technology embodies values, interests and legal rights. It is not just a matter of minimising harm, but of collectively asking ourselves what kind of society we want to build with these tools. Political ethics thus involves public deliberation, recognition of legitimate conflicts and the construction of democratic institutions capable of governing technology with ethical and political criteria.

The aforementioned AlgorithmWatch points out that the AI Act does not completely prohibit practices such as the use of AI in mass surveillance if they are authorised by Member States. Social scoring is also permitted in certain closed environments (e.g., for the proper functioning of private entities). Thus, if global regulatory credibility is to be achieved to ensure "trustworthy" AI, the EU must be able to voluntarily attract states, especially those in the Global South, and ensure that it is included in trade agreements. Such regulatory ethics would thus offer an alternative to the US mercantilist model (dominated by self-regulation) and the Chinese authoritarian model (where ethics is subordinated to state control), as Floridi points out,[14] although for Solove (2025) it is necessary to dispel certain myths, such as that regulation slows down innovation.

There is no doubt that the IA Act is, for now, the most ambitious attempt to positivise ethics in the field of artificial intelligence. But it also reveals tensions such as those that can arise between ethical theory and its practical reality; between fundamental rights and the need for regulatory flexibility; and ultimately between democracy and the laws of the market.[15]

Education and Awareness, Keys to Freedoms with AI

Floridi and Cowls (2019) are among the pioneers in proposing an ethical framework based on five key principles (beneficence, non-maleficence, autonomy, justice and explainability) to guide the responsible use of AI in social contexts, resulting in greater transparency of processes and their effective supervision. Algorithmic transparency is essential to guarantee public trust (Veale & Binns, 2021), two essential aspects for the practical realisation of legal certainty, the cornerstone of the rule of law. Within this regulatory framework and under these principles as a reference point, progress must be made in education and civic awareness if these principles are to be internalised by all those involved in the existence and application of AI.

Beyond regulatory frameworks, given the difficulty that the average individual will have in identifying the risks hidden in malicious, opaque or biased use of AI, digital literacy and critical awareness are key to empowering citizens. Understanding how AI works, its risks and limitations is essential for informed and resilient democratic participation (Gutiérrez, 2023). In this sense, Colchado and Arequipeño (2021) call for the formulation and recognition of new fundamental rights, including universal access to the internet, which would prevent the digital divide, and net neutrality, which would in some way guarantee non-discrimination based on bias.

Conclusions

The main ethical concerns that AI raises in relation to rights and freedoms are the way in which it can harm human freedom and dignity. Throughout this paper, we have highlighted how most of the doctrine points to the need and importance of maintaining a proactive approach to AI regulation, and we have pointed out how this call to action to protect fundamental rights in the digital age requires widespread knowledge of its risks, which in turn requires training from an early age.

Degli-Esposti (2024) proposes that the ethical challenges posed by AI should be addressed from an interdisciplinary perspective. He agrees with the majority that these risks often stem from the lack of transparency and clear accountability mechanisms in automated decision-making (in areas such as employment, criminal justice and healthcare), which can lead to algorithmic discrimination. Like others, he also warns of the need to apply the principles of "trustworthy AI", as promoted by the European Union, but one of his main contributions is his reflection on moral and legal responsibility in systems involving algorithms: in the face of injustice, is it the designer, the programmer, the company implementing the system, or the user themselves who is responsible? In order to address this issue, we must go beyond drawing up lists of abstract principles and adopt a humanistic, interdisciplinary approach that allows us to design technologies that truly serve the common good and democracy.

It can be said that, with few exceptions, there is broad consensus on the risks and the need for proactive action to avoid them. Education is key to prevention, but except for the construction of a few simulators still in very primitive stages, or some educational platforms that are beginning to work on pedagogical models with AI, most learning still occurs through trial and error based on a natural tendency to avoid the effort involved in checking, monitoring, comparing and reviewing any action carried out by AI. Because what this fourth industrial revolution has brought us, as in previous cases, is supposedly meant to do just that: make our lives easier. It is up to us to ensure that in this new ease, we do not overlook a certain fact: its achievement and the very progress of humanity are based precisely on the opposite or complementary attitude: a vigilant effort to overcome every obstacle.

Notes

1. The exhaustive analysis carried out in the collective work edited by Balaguer and Sarlet (2023), but also Hernández and Neupavert (2024) from a legal and professional standpoint.
2. Noble (2018) uses "algorithmic racism".
3. We work from the Anglo-Saxon concept of "privacy", which is broader than that of intimacy.

   When AI poses a risk to any of these, it is therefore methodologically more comprehensive to use the concept of privacy.
4. Personal data collection is the process of obtaining information from individuals, either voluntarily or through more intrusive methods, such as the use of cookies, tracking technologies, IoT devices or digital monitoring. Data processing includes all actions performed on that information, from collection to deletion. This

includes operations such as the storage, consultation, modification, transmission or destruction of data, whether automated or manual, and, of course, to the extent possible, anonymisation and pseudonymisation, which reduce the risks associated with the use of personal data by making it more difficult to identify individuals directly and facilitating a higher level of privacy (Solove, 2008).

5. Organisations are required to implement appropriate security measures to protect data against unauthorised access, loss or alteration (Gutiérrez, 2023). These measures include techniques such as encryption, pseudonymisation, access controls and backups. When processing involves high risks to users' rights, a Data Protection Impact Assessment (DPIA) must be carried out.
6. https://www.acm.org/binaries/content/assets/public-policy/final-joint-ai-statement-update.pdf (visit on April, 3, 2025).
7. One example would be the tension between transparency and intellectual property, as any creator has the right to ownership and exploitation of their work, and this right may be undermined by the duty of transparency. The so-called Bosco case has reached the press (El País, 8 July 2025): a lawsuit filed, following a previous investigation, by the association for the defence of transparency Civio, which revealed that in 2018 state aid to vulnerable families did not reach people who met all the requirements to receive it (proving low income, being a victim of gender violence, terrorist violence, etc.). The Bosco algorithm, responsible for filtering the data and allocating the aid, had failed. The administration acknowledged its mistake but refused to open the algorithm's source code. The case is now before the Supreme Court.
8. In this regard, see Balaguer and Sarlet (2023, p. 209 et s.), but also Puentes and Quintiá (2019) on how to uphold the principles of the rule of law in the age of AI.
9. An interesting and early study in this regard is that of Angwin et al. (2016), which analyses how AI can be used in criminal prediction with the risk that individualised monitoring of individuals may not be sufficiently justified.
10. A consensus in which some voices, such as Sadín (2020), are particularly sceptical about the chances of achieving this: Sadín believes that AI is not only a technological phenomenon, but also an ideological one, embodying a project of radical anti-humanism

by progressively displacing humans from their cognitive, decision-making and social functions and establishing a new logic of automation and algorithmic normativity. In this displacement, large technology corporations are redefining collective life, replacing ethical judgement with efficiency criteria, which in the long run may mean the loss of individual and democratic sovereignty in the face of the advance of automated systems.

Without expressing himself in such critical terms, but mindful of the dangers that AI may entail, Otero Parga (2023) argues that, although it can mimic certain human cognitive functions, it has no consciousness, intention or moral responsibility, and therefore poses significant risks when it acts in areas where fundamental rights and public freedoms are at stake. López Oneto (2020) takes a similar view when analysing the legal, ethical and social challenges posed by AI, highlighting the importance of establishing clear limits and responsibilities to prevent dehumanisation and ensure the ethical and democratic use of these technologies.

11. All of the above are echoed by Pérez-Ugena (2024) and, before him, Valls Prieto (2021), who critically reflects on the need to establish clear legal limits on the use of automated technologies in areas such as those we have been analysing: access to justice, personal autonomy, privacy and access to employment.
12. High-Level Expert Group on AI (2019).
13. Siegmann and Anderljung (2022) say in the abstract of their work: *The European Union is likely to introduce among the first, most stringent, and most comprehensive AI regulatory regimes of the world's major jurisdictions. In this report, we ask whether the EU's upcoming regulation for AI will diffuse globally, producing a so-called "Brussels Effect". Building on and extending Anu Bradford's work, we outline the mechanisms by which such regulatory diffusion may occur. We consider both the possibility that the EU's AI regulation will incentivise changes in products offered in non-EU countries (a de facto Brussels Effect) and the possibility it will influence regulation adopted by other jurisdictions (a de jure Brussels Effect). Focusing on the proposed EU AI Act, we tentatively conclude that both de facto and de jure Brussels effects are likely for parts of the EU regulatory regime.*

14. Floridi and Cowls (2019) suggests that these principles be integrated into the design of AI in advance and not just as an afterthought, in order to avoid algorithmic discrimination, privacy violations and information manipulation, as we have reiterated. Floridi (2023) believes that ethical AI should not be designed solely to prevent harm, but above all to generate opportunities in society: better education, health and justice services.
15. Wachter et al. (2017) are the authors of one of the most cited texts on this subject, due to their thesis that, contrary to what is often claimed, the GDPR does not clearly recognise a "right to explanation" for cases of automated decisions made by algorithms, such as credit scoring, personnel selection or targeted advertising. However, we have already referred to this point above.

References

Aba-Catoira, A. (2020). Los desórdenes informativos en un sistema de comunicación democrático. *Revista de Derecho Político, 109*, 119–151.

Agencia Española de Protección de Datos (AEPD). (2024). Guía de tratamiento de datos personales: Aspectos clave para el cumplimiento del RGPD. (visit on April, 3, 2025) https://www.aepd.es/documento/declaracion-institucional-autoridades-aniversario-RGPD.pdf

AlgorithmWatch. (2021). *Automating society report 2021.* (visit on April, 20, 2025) https://automatingsociety.algorithmwatch.org

Angwin, J., Larson, J., Mattu, S., & Kirchner, L. (2016). *Machine bias: There's software used across the country to predict future criminals. And it's biased against blacks.* ProPublica. https://www.propublica.org/article/machine-bias-risk-assessments-in-criminal-sentencing

Armengol, F. (2024). Desinformación en la Unión Europea: de la guerra híbrida al espacio europeo de la libertad de información. En I. Loreto & L. Corredoira, *Democracia y desinformación. Nuevas formas de polarización, discurso de odio y campañas en redes.* Dykinson. (pp. 345–360).

Ayllón, J. D. (2024). Inteligencia artificial deepfakes: las ultrasuplantaciones como medio para vulnerar los derechos al honor, intimidad y propia imagen. *Anuario de la Facultad de Derecho de la Universidad de Alcalá, 17*, 3–32.

Balaguer, F., & Sarlet, I. W. (2023). *Derechos fundamentales y democracia en el constitucionalismo digital.* Aranzadi.

Barocas, S., & Selbst, A. D. (2016). Big data's disparate impact. *California Law Review, 104*(3), 671–732. https://doi.org/10.2139/ssrn.2477899

Barona Vilar, S. (2021). *Algoritmización del derecho y la justicia. De la IA a la Smart justice*. Tirant lo Blanch.

Binns, R. (2018). Fairness in machine learning: Lessons from political philosophy. In *Proceedings of the 2018 Conference on Fairness, Accountability and Transparency* (pp. 149–159). doi:https://doi.org/10.1145/3287560.3287583

Bueno de Mata, F. (Coord.). (2016). *Fodertics 5.0: estudio sobre nuevas tecnologías y justicia*. Comares.

Canals, D. (2019). Incidencias del avance tecnológico en el Derecho Público. En B. Puentes Cociña y A. Quintiá (Dir.), *El derecho ante la transformación digital*. Atelier. (pp. 31–50).

Castellanos, J. (Dir.). (2023). *Inteligencia Artificial y Democracia: Garantías, Límites Constitucionales y Perspectiva Ética ante la Transformación Digital*. Atelier.

Colchado, J. C., & Arequipeño, A. (2021). Los derechos fundamentales y nuevas tecnologías de la información y la comunicación. *THĒMIS-Revista de Derecho, 79*(enero-junio 2021), 15–35.

Council of Europe. (2020). *Feasibility study on a legal framework on AI design, development and application based on Council of Europe Standards on human rights, democracy and the rule of law*. Consejo de Europa. https://www.coe.int

Degli-Espositi, S. (2024). *La ética de la inteligencia artificial*. CSIC.

European Commission. (2021). *Proposal for a regulation laying down harmonised rules on artificial intelligence (Artificial Intelligence Act)*. (visit April 18, 2025) https://eur-lex.europa.eu

Floridi, L. (2023). *The ethics of artificial intelligence: Principles, challenges, and opportunities* (243 pp.). Oxford University Press.

Floridi, L., & Cowls, J. (2019). A unified framework of five principles for AI in society. *Harvard Data Science Review, 1*(1). https://doi.org/10.1162/99608f92.8cd550d1

Gutiérrez, R. (2023). *Guía práctica para la implementación del RGPD en empresas*. Wolters Kluwer.

Hernández, I., & Neupavert, M. (Coords.). (2024). *El Derecho y la Justicia ante la Inteligencia Artificial y otras tecnologías disruptivas*. Aranzadi.

High-Level Expert Group on AI. (2019). *Ethics guidelines for trustworthy AI*. European Commission.

Ho-Dac, L. (2024). *First analysis of the EU AI Act: Towards a global standard for trustworthy AI?* https://arxiv.org/abs/2408.08318

Larrañaga, P. (2022). *El Reglamento General de Protección de Datos (RGPD): Comentarios y guía práctica*. Editorial Reus.

Lassalle, J. M. (2019). *Ciberleviatán: el colapso de la democracia liberal frente a la revolución digital*. Arpa.

Llano Alonso, F. H. (2024). Ética(s) de la Inteligencia Artificial y Derecho. Consideraciones a propósito de los límites y la contención del desarrollo tecnológico. *DERECHOS Y LIBERTADES: Revista De Filosofía del Derecho y derechos humanos, 51*, 177–199.

López Oneto, M. (2020). *Fundamentos para un derecho de la inteligencia artificial "Queremos seguir siendo humanos"*. Tirant lo Blanch.

Noble, S. U. (2018). *Algorithms of oppression: How search engines reinforce racism*. New York University Press.

O'Neil, C. (2016). *Weapons of math destruction: How big data increases inequality and threatens democracy*. Crown Publishing.

Otero Parga, M. (2023). "Puede la inteligencia artificial sustituir a la mente humana" Implicaciones de la IA en los derechos fundamentales y la ética. *Anales De La Cátedra Francisco Suárez, 57*, 39–61. https://doi.org/10.30827/acfs.v57i.24710

Pérez de las Heras, B. (2021). *El régimen de los derechos del interesado en la protección de datos*. Dykinson.

Pérez-Ugena, M. (2024). La inteligencia artificial: definición, regulación y riesgos para los derechos fundamentales. *Estudios de Deusto, 72* 1, enero-junio 2024. (pp. 307–33).

Puentes, B., & Quintiá, A. (Dirs.). (2019). El derecho ante la transformación digital. Atelier.

Rodríguez, A. (2021). Inteligencia artificial y derechos fundamentales: "hacia un nuevo constitucionalismo digital". *Revista de Derecho Político, 110*, 77–108.

Sadín, E. (2020). *La IA o el desafío del siglo. Anatomía de un anti-humanismo radical*. Caja Negra Editora.

Siegmann, Ch., & Anderljung, M. (2022). *The brussels effect and artificial intelligence: How EU regulation will impact the global AI market*. Cornell University. (visit on April, 16, 2025) https://arxiv.org/abs/2208.12645

Solove, D. J. (2008). *Understanding privacy*. Harvard University Press.

Solove, D. J. (2025). *On privacy and technology*. Oxford University Press.

Torres, C. (2024). *Ética y derecho en la inteligencia artificial y en la edición del genoma humano*. Dykinson.

UNESCO. (2025). *Libertad de expresión, inteligencia artificial y elecciones*. UNESDOC Biblioteca Digital. https://unesdoc.unesco.org/ark:/48223/pf0000393473_spa

Valls Prieto, J. (2021). *Inteligencia Artificial, derechos humanos y bienes jurídicos*. Thomson Reuters.

Veale, M., & Binns, R. (2021). *Algorithms and the regulation of privacy*. Edward Elgar Publishing.

Velasco, J., & Pérez, A. (2023). La categorización de datos personales sensibles y sus implicaciones legales en el ámbito digital. *Revista de Derecho Digital, 15*, 45–62.

Wachter, S., Mittelstadt, B., & Floridi, L. (2017). Why a right to explanation of automated decision-making does not exist in the General Data Protection Regulation. *International Data Privacy Law, 7*(2), 76–99.

Yeung, K. (2017). Algorithmic regulation: A critical perspective. *Regulation & Governance*. (visit April 18, 2025) http://onlinelibrary.wiley.com/journal/10.1111/(ISSN)1748-5991

CHAPTER 12

Digitocracy: Why is AI Insidious for Democracy?

Wendy R. Simon

> "*There are things in AI that we can do, some things that we should do, and more*
> *significantly there are also things that we should not do even if we could. The problem is that, for now, it is not clear where the red line should be drawn.*"
>
> (Casanovas & Noriega, 2022)

Introduction

In the second half of the twentieth century, the West faced an unprecedented scenario. The Second World War had made it evident that liberal democracies were frail: their liberal principles were frail, their democratic systems were frail (Mazower, 1999). The horror also gave evidence of

W. R. Simon (✉)
Universitat Internacional de Catalunya, Barcelona, Spain
e-mail: wmramirez@uic.es

M. Bosch (ed.), *Crucial Ethical Keys of Artificial Intelligence*,
https://doi.org/10.1007/978-3-032-22853-6_12

the dire need to double down on both, liberal principles and democratic systems, for the sake of humanity. In the aftermath of the events, the world led by Western powers engaged in binding nations internationally through multilateral agreements (United Nations, North Atlantic Treaty Organization, World Health Organization, World Bank, European Community…) and it drove many nations to secure their commitment to democratic principles through multiple layers of state legislation. The rationale was that if we reinforced the democratic tools we had at hand—which had for the most part failed in the past—the next time around they would be prepared to withstand the blow. These relied heavily on the principles of rule of law, popular sovereignty, and individual rights, which translated into the constitutional entrenchment of democratic principles (such as Germany's eternity clause), an increase in the establishing of democratic regimes (Huntington, 1991) and the corralling of supports for individual rights (as in the Declaration of Human Rights in 1948).

As core principles of liberal democracy, rule of law, popular sovereignty and individual rights had been secured as necessary devices for quashing potential external threats to the system, such as fascism, in an effective way. Nowadays, in the twenty-first century, the challenge that our liberal democratic systems must address is that of how to govern the techno-digital world in a way that is compatible with our democratic principles. In this chapter we will attempt to shed some light on why a technology-driven world may become a challenge specifically to democratic regimes, as well as shedding some light on the fact that this challenge to the system, as opposed to other difficulties faced traditionally, comes from within the system itself.

The emergence of AI presents a pressing dilemma for contemporary democracies: how should they respond to a technological force capable of altering the very mechanisms that uphold democracy's robustness? Rather than attempting to impose regulatory measures using outdated frameworks, Casanovas (2019, p. 23) argues that "what needs to change is not the content of the regulations, but their form, the very notion of regulating". Traditional theories of democracy—particularly those centered on deliberative and epistemic democracy—"emphasize the knowledge-producing properties of democratic institutions and procedures; and specifically (…) assume that those procedures are good at tracking procedure-independent standard of correctness, which is sometimes called truth" (Knight et al., 2016, p. 141). However, as AI disrupts the flow of information, the ability of democracy to engage in this crucial epistemic function is compromised, thus requiring a fundamental re-evaluation of democratic principles (Casanovas, 2019; Casanovas et al., 2019; Casanovas & Noriega, 2022; Poblet et al., 2019; Poblet & Plaza, 2017; Ponce, 2022). It should not surprise us that structures designed for a twentieth-century reality are proving inadequate in the face of twenty-first-century technological advancements.

Any force that interferes with the natural democratic processes—whether it be ideological, institutional, or, in the case of AI, technological—poses a structural risk to democracy, much like totalitarian regimes, that manipulate political institutions to consolidate power (Chafkin, 2021). Given AI's potential to distort deliberation, in this chapter we aim to dissect the fundamental elements of deliberative democracy and examine how AI-driven communication technologies systematically erode its essential components. This granular analysis hopes to encourage a more nuanced approach to the subject—one that moves beyond the simplistic and often ineffective (Ponce, 2022) impulse to overregulate without addressing the core issues.

The urgency of addressing these issues arises also from the fact that contemporary digital technologies increasingly provide democratic governments with unrestricted access to powerful tools of surveillance and control including facial recognition, digital profiling, and data re-identification, all without the awareness of those being surveilled (Casanovas, 2019). Attempts to regulate these technologies have repeatedly stalled at a crucial impasse: the very institutions tasked with overseeing them are the same ones that benefit unrestrictedly from using them. So much for checks and balances. Furthermore, much of the discourse surrounding AI concerns is fragmented, with some issues framed within specific legal frameworks, or financial domains, or as privacy-related issues, rather than being addressed holistically as part of a broader democratic question.

A crucial aspect of this debate, then, is defining what democracy is in the digital age. If "democracy is to be understood as a form of government based on the principle of freedom as a collective self-government, this suggests that it must inevitably be willing to assume a certain measure of political risk" (Invernizzi & Zuckerman, 2017, p. 195). While discussions of political risk often focus on external threats and are typically framed within the paradigm of militant democracy—where certain democratic principles may be temporarily suspended to preserve the system—there is another, more insidious danger to consider: what happens when the threat comes from within? What if democracy itself, through its own mechanisms, unwittingly undermines its own integrity? This is, we contend, precisely the risk posed by AI.

Are there political risks naturally to be assumed as an inevitable part of hailing freedom? Yes. Can AI be counted among them? We contend that not quite, and we attempt to clarify why not. Since the 1980s, the proliferation of algorithmic technologies has expanded the capacity of both democratic and authoritarian governments to engage in mass surveillance and social control—as we mentioned, often violating liberal principles (Casanovas, 2019). Does this constitute a form of authoritarianism? (Casanovas Romeu, 2025) We do not claim that democratic governments are covertly transitioning into totalitarian regimes; rather, we highlight the troubling trajectory that current technological and political developments suggest. Whether this transformation is intentional or merely a byproduct of AI's increasing ubiquity is a critical question—one that cannot be ignored (Harari, 2018). What is evident, however, is that these technologies possess the capacity to enable surveillance, enforce behavioral conformity, and limit individual freedoms while simultaneously restricting the open exchange of information that underpins democratic deliberation. Whether it is done deliberately or not, is one question, whether knowingly or not, is quite another. This is the question we must confront. Despite what it may appear, AI is not a case of political risk associated to citizens' use of their freedom, it is a case of risk *to* citizens' freedom.

To approach this topic, we must first make the case for the legitimacy of democratic regimes by highlighting the deep ethical connection between human freedom and politics. After that, it will be relevant to describe the various technologies we have at hand in our modern times. We will dissect specifically the AI generation technology we are confronted with, especially as opposed to pre-artificial intelligence technology. In the next section, we attempt to shed light on the specific mechanisms by which AI may interact insidiously with the democratic process. As a result, we go on to analyze the convenience of treating AI as a power in and of itself. Finally, we briefly summarize our conclusions.

Ethics, Politics and Technology

Ethics, Politics and Human Freedom

At the bedrock of western civilization is the understanding that both ethics and politics emerge from the condition of human beings as free agents (Arendt, 1958; Dworkin, 2011; MacIntyre, 2007). Human beings, uniquely among living creatures, possess the capacity to act based on reasoned choice and not merely instinct or compulsion. The foundation of both ethics and politics is human action insofar as it is a free and deliberate conduct. It is this deliberate behavior of free creatures which makes us uniquely responsible, accountable for our actions, as well. Therefore, from this standpoint, both ethics and politics address the question of how free agents ought to live and act, both individually and together. From the ethical perspective, it is because we are free to engage in an action or not to, that we are held morally accountable for our choices. Otherwise, if we contended that we are predetermined (by our biology or society, e.g.) to follow a certain course of action, it would be inconsistent to hold anyone ultimately responsible for their actions, since they would have no agency over them (as occurs with children or animals).

In the realm of politics, in the West, citizens are also considered free agents by virtue of their inherent human freedom. For Aristotle, politics is not just about power or governance—it is about creating the conditions under which free individuals can live together ethically. In the Western tradition, then, ethics and politics are two dimensions of the same project: the fulfillment of human potential through free, rational action. According to the modern Western tradition, however, by the same token, citizens are also politically sovereign: we have the capacity to choose for ourselves—individually and as a community—how we want to proceed in issues that belong to our public realm.

Locke observed in the seventeenth century that, in an effort to escape the afflictions of the state of nature, free individuals are inclined to organize under political authority. Moreover, Locke observes that despite this voluntary submission to power, freedom is not relinquished; it is only ceded, conditionally, by the citizens to the authorities insofar as the necessary conditions are met (namely, that the ends for which the liberties were given up be upheld—that is, to protect one's "life, liberty and estate") (Locke, 1988). This perspective encapsulates the suitability of the liberal democratic system to respect and affirm human freedom and dignity. We must therefore bear in mind that political governance is, at its core, a bottom-up process, and that it must remain an ethical stance that we persist in freely choosing how we will be governed—and by whom. The lack of either one of those choices abridges human freedom and so renders the political power illegitimate. At least that is how the theory of liberal democracy goes in the Modern era, from Locke (Locke, 1988) and Rousseau (Rousseau, 1997) to the modern classics like Rawls and Cohen or Dworkin (Cohen, 2009; Dworkin, 2000; Rawls, 1993).

In order to delegate political power, it is required that citizens be aware not only to whom and for what purpose will that power be used, but also nowadays (and probably for the first time since Montesquieu) we may need to clarify what power it is exactly that are we delegating. In classical political theory, the delegation of power (depending on whether the system is presidential or parliamentary) is done either directly or indirectly in favor of one, two, or all three branches of government: legislative, executive, and judicial. The rule of law upholds the principle that power must be exercised within the boundaries of law, ensuring that the division of powers, the responsibilities, limits, and relationships of each entity are clearly defined and respected by the legal system. Until the twenty-first century, the powers we relinquished through voting and our participation in society were relatively straightforward (Costa & Zolo, 2007). Now with the advent of AI and other modern technologies, this process is not quite that linear. In the following pages, we will explore the idea that AI may possess the characteristics of a power in its own right. To do so, we must first gain a clearer understanding of the existing technologies, their uses, and how they impact both our private lives and our shared societal experiences. Unfortunately—this being a key problem in it all—we cannot clarify exactly how they work, since it quite disturbingly remains a mystery even to the very creators of the technology itself (Casanovas et al., 2019).

Modern Technology and AI Technology

Modern technology spans a wide range of innovations, from everyday household appliances to groundbreaking advancements in the field of artificial intelligence (AI). For the purpose of this chapter, we are interested in analyzing technology so as to assess those aspects of it which may impact, perhaps even subvert, the natural democratic process. What follows is therefore not an exhaustive list or a comprehensive categorization, but a synthetic overview to serve that purpose.

To begin with, there are household and consumer technologies. That includes everything from a toaster oven to a washing machine or a vacuum cleaner. Although this technology has vastly improved since the 1950s, they are essentially the same products in that they serve the same purpose and offer the same functionalities (if much improved): whether that be to make life simpler, make tasks more efficient or to save up time. Also, in this category we would include smart home devices, which are more sophisticated and nuanced versions of the above-mentioned: like smart thermostats (e.g., Nest), smart lights (e.g., Philips Hue), and smart speakers (e.g., Amazon Echo and Google Nest). Also, entertainment technology, which does not serve a straightforward utilitarian purpose, but seeks to enhance the quality of life altogether by focusing on modern tendencies in leisure: smart TVs, gaming consoles (e.g., PlayStation, Xbox), and streaming devices (e.g., Roku and Apple TV).

We will group in a second category those technologies oriented at scientific research and exploration. These include space exploration technology (e.g., Perseverance, Curiosity and SpaceX's reusable rockets) but also satellite technology which plays a crucial role in communication, navigation, and global internet coverage (with systems like GPS and Starlink providing critical services). There is also energy and environmental technology: renewable energy sources (such as solar panels, wind turbines, and geothermal energy); battery technologies, including the Tesla Powerwall and solid-state batteries; smart grids (powered by AI) and such. When it comes to medical research and in biotechnologies, we can name from wearable health tech devices like smartwatches to advanced medical equipment (e.g., MRI machines and robotic surgery systems like the Da Vinci Surgical System) or genetic engineering, particularly through technologies like CRISPR (which has the potential for revolutionary treatments of genetic disorders).

Our third category encompasses, first, transportation technology, which is focused on more sustainable and self-driven vehicles (e.g., electric cars, like those from Tesla and Rivian); innovative public transport (maglev trains and Hyperloop systems); and even commercial space travel by companies like SpaceX, Blue Origin, and Virgin Galactic. We also group in here industrial and manufacturing technology with applications in different sectors (from architecture to medicine): 3D printing, automation and robotics (powered by AI), nanotechnology.

Lastly, we must also mention military and defense technology. This sector has always been at the forefront of technological innovation;

however, the leaps in progress it has experienced in the past decades have been exponential: cybersecurity and encryption technologies (e.g., for safeguarding national security, financial transactions, and personal data); drones and autonomous weapons (e.g., military UAVs like Predator drones, missile defense systems like the Iron Dome and hypersonic weapons). The implications of autonomous weapons and defense systems are being currently discussed given the military, ethical, and strategic concerns regarding the use of autonomous technology in warfare (Scharre, 2018).

Another large technology group is that of communications. These have reshaped how we connect with others both personally and professionally to the point of generating brand-new dynamics, protocols and ways of interacting (Turkle, 2011). We include here smartphones and mobile devices (e.g., iPhones, Android phones) as well as tablets and the hybrids that offer the same features, and the platforms that facilitate the communications—social media platforms such as Facebook, Twitter, WhatsApp, and video conferencing tools like Zoom. But we also include the technology that enables such communications, namely, the internet and its networking technologies: Wi-Fi routers, 5G technology, and fiber-optic networks. Within this group we find information and computing technology: personal computers—whether laptops, desktops, or an Arduino—which must be mentioned in connection to cloud computing services like Amazon Web Services and Google Cloud. The real revolution has taken place due to the possibilities data storage and processing enable. Operating systems such as Windows, macOS, Linux, Android, and iOS provide the interface that enables users to interact with the devices (Armbrust, 2010).

Artificial intelligence (AI) and machine learning fall into a separate category. Artificial intelligence refers specifically to technologies that enable machines to perform tasks that require human-like cognition, including learning, decision-making, and problem-solving.

Many of the technologies listed above incorporate AI for optimization and automation. Although it is true we find this technology via voice recognition and intelligent algorithms in what appears to be simply a "second generation" of household appliances (like with assistants such as Siri, Alexa, and Google Assistant), their machine learning powers are on par with everything from systems on platforms like Netflix and Spotify, to fraud detection protocols in banking, or self-driving cars technology.

AI is not just "the next thing" in technology, it is not simply a "sophistication" or a "step forward" (Bostrom, 2014). Empowering technology with human-like capacities must also come with a transfer of the ethical responsibilities that are consubstantial with that power. AI has power, but is it itself a power?

AI and Democracy

Why is AI Insidious for Democracy?

Regardless of its complexity, we have traditionally understood technology to be a tool, a device that aids us in accomplishing a task, a means for production. Nevertheless, the advent of AI technology forces us to reconsider that definition. AI-powered tools differ substantially from traditional tools by introducing the possibility of tool autonomy, tool adaptability, and tool learning. These capabilities allow AI-powered tools to execute tasks that involve judgment, pattern recognition, or decision-making that emulate that of human intelligence. Historically, tools have required detailed human instructions for the execution of each task, since they could only follow fixed, explicit rules. They did not improve their execution over time or learn from experience, and therefore their outcomes were predictable and replicable, for good and for bad. AI tools, on the other hand, do learn from their iterations and adjust their behavior accordingly, thus being able to handle increasing degrees of variation and uncertainty in the tasks they are commissioned with. With an increase of experience and more data, their performance improves and may produce novel, unexpected, or probabilistic outcomes.

When we interact with AI, we are in fact *interacting*; we are not simply directing a device. Moreover, when engaging with AI, one is interacting with an opaque system whose internal processes and decision-making logic are not fully transparent, nor entirely predictable, given its conditioning through complex data and algorithms. In contrast, when using a non-AI device, there is no genuine interaction in the dialogical sense; rather, one is executing commands upon a tool designed to produce a fixed and determinate result. The relationship is straightforward and instrumental—it is simply oneself directing the tool within a closed, predictable operation.

Although it is true for most AI-powered technology in general, making this distinction is particularly relevant when reflecting on the communications technology we described above and its impact on democracy. In democratic theory, deliberation refers to the process by which citizens engage in open, reasoned, and inclusive discussion to form collective decisions based on shared information and mutual respect (Gutmann & Thompson, 2004; Habermas, 1984; Ober, 2008a, 2008b, 2015; Rawls, 1993): that is the cornerstone of liberal democracies. It turns out AI can interfere with the natural flow of information and thus with the organic development of the democratic process in many key ways. The deliberation process relies on citizens having access to reliable information, exposure to diverse viewpoints, an ability to critically evaluate arguments, and participation in the public sphere. AI interferes with this process through several mechanisms—let us explore them.

Distortion of the Information Environment

In a natural milieu, citizens have access to information through face-to-face engagement with other citizens. Another way in which citizens access information is through the written word: newspapers, magazines, books, journals, … There are also tools (traditional tools) that offer information: radio shows, podcasts, standard television programs, …

Whenever social media feeds or search engines enter the information media scene they drag the AI-driven platforms right into the equation with them. According to our previous definition, this means that we are in fact interacting with the platform (with the "tool") that offers us supposedly unbiased and objective information. However, we are not made aware of the interaction taking place. When algorithms prioritize and personalize the content we receive based on user preferences it is a one-sided process yet under the guise of being objective and neutral. The gatekeeping of information does not respond to the gatekeeper's journalistic criteria. The information access is being tailored to serve the corporation behind the provider's interests and not necessarily serving democratic journalistic principles like accountability or truth. Once algorithms predict our engagement cues, they progressively tailor our access to the world based on that criteria, thus creating what we call "filter bubbles" or "echo chambers" where individuals are repeatedly exposed to information that reinforces their existing views (Modgil et al., 2021), limiting exposure to diverse perspectives essential for informed democratic deliberation (Sunstein, 2017). AI-driven recommendation systems (especially those on social media) optimize for engagement, i.e., for entrepreneurial gain, not for truth or diversity, and that results in a disproportionate amount of sensational or polarizing content.

Another harmful collateral effect of this epistemic isolation is that it leads to citizens eventually not only not agreeing on basic facts but not even engaging in the same topics, therefore making public dialogue nearly impossible since reasoned debate requires some shared epistemic foundation (Rini, 2020).

Manipulation Through Microtargeting

Personalized political messaging can be a serious threat to democracy if it becomes pervasive enough. It is now known worldwide how Cambridge Analytica harvested personal data from millions of Facebook users during the 2016 U.S. presidential election and the Brexit referendum, to build psychological profiles and then deliver targeted political ads to voters corresponding with that data (Cadwalladr & Graham-Harrison, 2018).

Because AI has an unprecedented and inhumane ability to harbor and process uncanny amounts of individual data in virtually no time, it can enable highly targeted political advertising based on detailed profiling of users. As a result of this action, there can be a selective delivery of tailored messages designed to exploit the user's emotions, fears, or biases, further fragmenting the public sphere. Since this targeting feeds off of the different social groups' vulnerability, it can easily result in delivering contradictory messages whose aim is not to kindle empathy or solidarity toward each other, but the opposite. Unlike traditional mass media, which operates in public view, microtargeted content is opaque and often manipulative, preventing collective scrutiny and reducing democratic accountability (Zuiderveen Borgesius et al., 2018). If nothing else, it makes debating more difficult since it hinders citizens deliberating over shared facts.

Microtargeting disrupts the natural flow of information and does it in a way imperceptible to those being manipulated (we do not know what we do not know), undermining the shared knowledge base required for collective decision-making.

Erosion of Epistemic Trust

Democracy is not only a valuable mechanism for respecting people's equal rights, but it is also a system which enables societies to organically make themselves better (Estlund, 2009). Democratic decision-making has the power to enhance the collectivity's likelihood to approach truth, therefore offering epistemic value. That means that through collective deliberation, public reasoning, diversity of perspectives, and public reasoning, the outcome of a democracy is able to deliver the most accurate knowledge-based results in terms of justice, truthfulness, correctness (Landemore, 2013). However, it is key for this process to take place, that citizens participate (voting, delivering, holding officials accountable, expressing their needs) and for that, they must be informed.

Citizens must be able to trust their sources of information and the flow of information in the public life; they need to believe that the information they are offered is truthful, distributed in good faith, deemed relevant and passed on competently. If there lacks this trust—epistemic trust—the health of the deliberation and participation process is jeopardized, hindering the quality (and even thwarting the possibility) of a rational public debate, of reaching shared understandings and, ultimately, of reaching legitimate and productive decision-making (Catala, 2015). To ensure this process takes place adequately, citizens must perceive there to be a credible dialogue between them and the institutions that handle their needs, there must be reliable sources for them to receive information from, and there must be public standardized procedures by which their demands are channeled.

AI contributes to the erosion of epistemic trust mainly via AI-generated content, which deliberately, intentionally and most importantly, imperceptibly distorts communications through content such as deepfakes, untruthful data or quotes, fake news, or via artificially amplifying certain irrelevant information or misinformation owing to dishonest criteria. When the information channels and creators do not serve the legitimate purpose of keeping the public informed, engaged and able to participate in the public discourse, this undermines the public's trust in the authenticity of the information they receive. If the public cannot trust the sources for understanding the world around them, it can create a radical polarization. That happens when individuals attempt to mitigate the uncertainty by resorting almost dogmatically to only one/two familiar sources they deem most trustworthy, not only retaining their natural biases, but exacerbating the bias because of the lack of diversity they would otherwise encounter naturally.

Erosion of Common Public Spaces

In a democracy, the common public space acquires a significant dimension, an essential one. Shared spaces for public debate are the sine qua non condition that enables the gathering, deliberation, and free-flow of knowledge. Common public spaces are where epistemic trust is created and fostered, and at the same time, it is where it is played out. Both figuratively and literally, free and open common public spaces are an indispensable requirement for a correct functioning of any democracy (Ober, 2008a, 2008b).

When AI generates and spreads misleading information, it fragments the public discourse, compromising the ability of the public to share a figurative space in which to hold public debate, impeding consensus and compromise. But it also impacts the physical, real—albeit sometimes virtual—space where we all hold these debates (Kreiss & McGregor, 2019). The flooding of the channels of information with unpleasant, undesirable, incivic behaviors and entertainment or distraction-driven information makes it difficult for citizens to find a space in which to engage in the much-needed democratic dynamic of receiving information, analyzing it critically, engaging in public discourse, sharing it, contrasting it, deliberating over it, compromising and deciding. The combination of the erosion of epistemic trust and the acceleration of the discourse makes it progressively more difficult to build and maintain a stable, shared, public square accessible to all citizens.

Opacity of Information Flows

Because of the technological nature of the algorithms that govern AI, simple "transparency" would not suffice to ensure the accountability of the algorithmic systems. The mere visibility or publicity of the algorithms would not guarantee the public would understand them or their effects on society, let alone have the ability to govern them or protect themselves from them. These systems are usually highly complex and opaque, and illuminating them would require a much deeper uncovering of the social and political contexts they are embedded in. Transparency alone would not redress the power asymmetry between the individuals and corporations creating and governing the algorithms (Ananny & Crawford, 2018).

From this standpoint, the opacity of the information flow is a crucial flaw in AI-mediated information, since everything from the original source to the classical gatekeeping role is untraceable, and therefore it perpetually renders the news outlet (from online news to TikTok videos) potentially untrustworthy. In itself, this has its own issues as we discussed with regard to the erosion of epistemic trust. Moreover, the opacity of systems driven by AI technology that mediate information makes it so that citizens tend not to know why certain information is being shown and shared, and how it is being prioritized. This may easily make the public skeptical of the true interests behind the dissemination.

Historically, journalism has functioned as a vital safeguard for ensuring accountability within democratic systems, but nowadays its own credibility is under scrutiny due to the interference of AI. The opacity of the information flows undermines the accountability of the sources of information, posing a pivotal challenge for democracy. Who serves now as a legitimate, independent, reliable civil counterbalance to power?

Automated Moderation and Censorship

Still on the transparency issues and AI: there appears the fact that AI has been utilized more and more as a mechanism for moderating online speech. Though its intent may be considered overall quite unsuccessful (Udupa et al., 2023), it may still be commendable: to screen and prevent the publication and spreading of potentially harmful content. The issue with this is that it is apparently unintentionally (or not?) causing the suppression of free legitimate political speech as well (Mittelstadt et al., 2016; Noble, 2018; Sap et al., 2019). The reason being mainly that the criteria that guides the moderation and censoring decisions are not made by people of the community enforcing the community's values, or by those who supervise the debating platform according to the common interest, but by opaque algorithms without adequate oversight.

Censorship is an inherently delicate issue for democracy because it confronts one of democracy's fundamental dilemmas: how to harmonize free speech and the common good. On the one hand, democracies are built on the principle that individuals have the freedom to express their opinions, however diverse or controversial they may be. On the other hand, democratic governments are also committed to protecting their citizens from harm. This tension means that democracies must constantly navigate where they draw the line regarding free speech in order to keep a healthy balance, recognizing that restricting speech—even with legitimate intentions—can undermine the very freedoms that sustain the system itself.

It is through the ongoing effort to balance free speech and the common good that a shared sense of collective identity emerges. Delegating this defining search for collective identity to opaque, automated machines without a public debate, agreement or even a public understanding of the rationale behind such moderation and censorship puts the responsibility of striking the crucial balance that defines who we are, and who we become, in the hands of mechanized, soulless procedures. "Large technological corporations are not fascist, nor are the governments that support them. However, the imposition of behavior patterns by an elite that also shapes a dominant, oligarchic, and exclusive culture is concerning" (Casanovas Romeu, 2025, p. 8). In other words, we are inadvertently outsourcing the very process that defines us as a society. The pervasive use of AI in moderating our public discourses is distancing us from the reality that the whole point of a democracy is that we may use our freedom—albeit, as well as its curtailing—to define ourselves as a society (Przeworski, 2010; Welzel, 2013).

Acceleration of Public Discourse

Another negative effect of the pervasive use of AI-powered technology in our everyday interaction with the public discourse is caused by an unnatural acceleration of the discourse. The technological mediation of our common discourse interactions provides features that are not inherent to the natural human dialogue. It accelerates the pace of information flow to such a degree that citizens are rendered powerless to process it, tending toward a generalized feeling of overwhelm and exhaustion that ultimately fosters rejection of the effort to be an active and responsible part of the narrative.

One might have thought that by accelerating the rhythm of the public discourse we had gained efficiency, but it appears not to be so. The acceleration of the (unvetted) information turnover makes it unrealistic for the public to be able to keep up, and it pressures the public debate into reacting quickly, rather than thoughtfully. It shifts democratic deliberation from slow, reasoned dialogue to rapid, emotionally driven responses, and meaningful deliberation becomes rare and exceptional. As we have mentioned before, protecting the highest quality deliberation possible is of the essence if we want democracy to serve its purpose optimally.

Platforms such as X or Facebook have their own private interests, like any business endeavor (Casanovas Romeu, 2025), and there is a case to be made for that. However, the public must be aware that those interests do not necessarily align with those of the common good. The tendency of their news feeds to prioritize the proliferation of so-called "trending topics", or content with high levels of engagement by other users, often leads to favoring outrage over nuance. To their companies it brings in more revenue; to democracy, it contributes to making our deliberation reactive, short-term, and superficial, and progressively pushes complex policy debates aside in favor of unhelpful viral soundbites.

Artificial Amplification of Voices: Bots and Fake Accounts

It is relatively simple and almost costless for AI-powered technology to create innumerable fake accounts and artificially inflate the perception of pervasiveness of a specific opinion or piece of information. That can be done with different manipulative ends in mind; from giving an exaggerated sense of danger to the public to simulating a disproportionate support that doesn't exist in reality. The danger of creating these illusions (besides fueling other ones described in this section) is that it produces an added amount of controversy or fake consensus based on a false understanding of what the public opinion surrounding an individual really is (Woolley & Howard, 2018).

For a democracy it is actually important that citizens assess accurately what the climate of public opinion is. Even if it is a subjective perception, it is still valuable in that it is true to the individual, which is ultimately what a democracy is pursuing. If voters have a distorted yet justifiable sense of what the climate of the public opinion around them is, they will act, deliberate, engage and make decisions based on that sense, however unaware of its being deeply unreliable. One may make firm choices based on uninformed assumptions and therefore be gauging incorrectly the impact of their choices for themselves and those around them. Research shows AI-driven bot networks flooding social media with pro-government propaganda and attacking opposition voices in countries like Mexico and Russia (Woolley, 2020).

The artificial amplification of voices can, and is designed to, accentuate effects like the spiral of silence, pluralistic ignorance and false consensus. These are the products of the distortion the false amplification and fake accounts and bots produce. They distort perceptions of consensus or popularity, crowd out genuine voices in public discussions, spread false information quickly and convincingly, among others. The problem we are addressing here lies not so much in the undeniable distorting effects of these phenomena; what is most disturbing to us here is the fact that they are triggered by design yet without the purpose of enhancing the public opinion formation—quite the opposite. Moreover, the apparition of these distorting effects is by no means natural or spontaneous, as we mentioned, and therefore when activated in this artificial way, they fall outside the scope of the natural self-correcting mechanisms that the channeling of the public opinion naturally exercises when left to its own devices.

In his critique of contemporary democracies, (Ober, 2015) explores how modern institutions could be undermining the deliberative ideal we have defended by encouraging superficial political participation or by reinforcing biased and polarized discourses. Ober's work reminds us that, for deliberation to function properly in modern contexts, institutions must foster conditions of genuine public reasoning and engagement, not just the mechanical application of voting processes. Our modern context is an AI-driven one. In this section we showed how AI does not merely disrupt deliberation (through misinformation, e.g.); it alters the structural conditions under which democratic discourse takes place, impacting the quality, inclusiveness, and authenticity of public reasoning. Democratic deliberation depends on time, trust, diversity, and transparency. We have explained in what way AI disrupts all four through manipulating attention, fracturing the public debate, causing trust in truth to be eroded, and bombarding the discourse with false ideas/actors. This combination of factors produces an environment which makes it progressively harder for citizens to deliberate meaningfully on common political issues.

Digitocracy: AI as a power, not a tool

The procedural aspect of democracy is crucial, as we mentioned, because of the role of deliberation in legitimizing and sustaining the democratic system (Gutmann & Thompson, 2004). When it comes to the concept of power and its execution, the weight of it is no less heavy. Democracy is ultimately a political system, i.e., it is an infrastructure of laws, institutions, and practices that define how power is distributed and decisions are made within a society. Naturally, it is of the essence that we concur with what we mean by power. The principle of popular sovereignty holds that it is the right of citizens to determine who wields political power, how it is exercised, and what its limits are. Although it is undisputed that states hold executive authority, at the same time, a core principle of representative democracies is that power ultimately resides with the people. Could a new, unforeseen source of power have bypassed this framework? How could that have developed?

Our contention is that the main challenge when managing AI may stem from a fundamental misinterpretation—we have tried to fit AI into our existing legal structures (Ebers et al., 2022; Engstrom, 2023) and though we sense we are failing, we also feel we lack alternatives. The issue, we contend, may be not necessarily that these structures are obsolete in this new context, but that we are trying to apply them incorrectly. We suggest the tools for algorithmically controlling privacy and information flow may not be mere instruments and thus must be supervised; we contend they may constitute themselves a novel form of power, and have managed to escape the due democratic scrutiny. Until now, there had been no agent strong enough, potent enough, stealthy enough, ubiquitous enough, or knowledgeable enough to override the natural pace and paradigms of democratic deliberation. As a result, we rarely questioned its functioning in any fundamental way—only in accidental or circumstantial terms (Lippmann, 1922). We have seen now that AI-powered technology is able to do all that, not just interfering with the process but reinventing it, and doing so, serving various interests but not necessarily for the public good. If indeed the deliberative process is at the heart of a democracy, whoever has the upper hand in the deliberative process, whoever owns the process, also owns the heart of the democracy. We contend that if it is true that "whoever controls the relationship between data and metadata in a system determines its power of implementation and the reach of its ecosystem" (Casanovas, 2019, p. 24), a new power structure may have inadvertently emerged.

This challenge, however, extends into another critical area for democracy: equality. This emerging form of power is distributed unevenly: "This is an asymmetric relationship: citizens, consumers, users, may be totally identified and the scenarios and context may be delineated, yet they may never have access to the general knowledge that the system and its administrators are privy to" (Casanovas, 2019, p. 24). The consequences of this imbalance for democratic governance are profound, as it further deepens the divide between those who command these new mechanisms of influence and those entirely excluded from them. This is especially true since the gap is exponentially widening. What makes this particularly concerning is that these systems are intentionally designed to shape the production, circulation, and accessibility of knowledge—fundamental components that underpin the integrity and resilience of democratic institutions (Ober, 2008a, 2008b, 2015).

If we are to focus on where power resides, where the locus of sovereignty is, the reality is that these highly intrusive mechanisms of control are being deployed unchecked, without public oversight or legitimation. This is particularly concerning because their use frequently clashes with core liberal democratic values in ways that extend far beyond the absence of citizen scrutiny. Given this, it is worth considering whether reclaiming control over these digital instruments from the government and restoring it to the public is both a necessary and a prudent step. After all, "we the people" have neither determined how—or even if—we agree to our governments implementing AI technologies. Harari (2018) warns of the potential for democracies to evolve into "digital dictatorships", a concern that addresses the growing influence of algorithmic decision-making in governance. However, a more precise term might be "digitocracy", emphasizing that power—the "cratos"—could reside as much in the algorithm as in the people. Rather than overtly imposing authority in the manner of a traditional dictatorship, algorithmic systems exert influence by reshaping the democratic process from within. The machine-driven decisions that regulate digital interactions—though intangible—hold tangible power over citizens' lives, subtly redirecting political agency and subverting the conventional democratic mechanisms.

The prospect of transferring this emerging form of power to the people remains unfulfilled, largely because no structured deliberative or epistemic democratic process has taken place. More critically, there seems to be no established space for such a discussion to unfold—an absence that urgently needs addressing. One promising approach is the linked democracy model (Poblet et al., 2019), which offers a possible pathway to integrating AI and other advanced technologies into political decision-making. This model ensures that while these tools contribute to governance, they do not override or distort traditional political and legal frameworks, which have struggled to adapt to the digital age (Ponce, 2022). Defined by its creators as a "distributed, technology-supported collective decision-making process, where data, information, and knowledge are connected and shared by citizens online" (Poblet et al., 2019, p. 27). Linked Democracy offers a structured yet adaptable framework for rethinking democratic participation in the digital era. It provides a means of bridging existing governance structures with contemporary technological realities, ensuring that digital decision-making remains both democratically legitimate and practically viable.

Conclusions

"Digital identity, the web of data, the internet of things, big data gathering and analysis, management algorithms, semantic representation of languages, use of intelligent decision-making programs, artificial robot societies, models of distributed multi-agent coordination systems" (Casanovas, 2019, p. 24) are all examples of the exponential increase and technological developments since the late twentieth century. The new dynamics in communications and their impact on human relations have affected the way in which citizens have traditionally been bound to each other as well as to the state. We reviewed in this chapter the extent to which these technologies may affect—and often distort—these relations, especially in what way they alter the classic power relations in a democratic system. The fact that these techno-digital tools (which can take place undercover, lacking citizens authorization and even supervision) have unprecedented potential for massive and immediate data and information gathering, crossing, and processing, is transforming not only the power available to some citizens, institutions and governments who have access to it; we contended they also are transforming the very nature of what we have always understood power to be.

We have reviewed in what way AI is insidious for liberal democracy, and that is due to several critical factors: by distorting public discourse, eroding privacy, diminishing accountability, reinforcing inequality, and facilitating social control, all of which challenge the core principles of democratic governance. But we have also made the case for "digitocracy", that is, the possibility of considering AI a power in and of itself due to the amount of influence it enables technology to exercise in key areas of the democratic process; those which, as the ultimate expression of a sovereign people, are originally designed precisely to allocate power. Tampering with this process, then, we showed, means de facto wielding the power that is legitimately due to the people. As a possible way out, we endorsed the idea put forth by linked democracy, a model which professes that "if the culture of sharing is supported by intelligent technologies, a new breed of resources will be available to anyone and the almighty Artificial Intelligence algorithms crunching data will not remain a weapon available only to the few" (Poblet et al., 2019, p. vii).

References

Ananny, M., & Crawford, K. (2018). Seeing without knowing: Limitations of the transparency ideal and its application to algorithmic accountability. *New Media & Society, 20*(3), 973–989. https://doi.org/10.1177/1461444816676645

Arendt, H. (1958). *The human condition*. University of Chicago Press.

Armbrust, M. (2010). A view of cloud computing. *Communications of the ACM, 53*(4), 50–58. https://doi.org/10.1145/1721654.1721672

Bostrom, N. (2014). *Superintelligence: Paths, dangers, strategies*. Oxford University Press.

Cadwalladr, C., & Graham-Harrison, E. (2018, March 17). Revealed: 50 million Facebook profiles harvested for Cambridge Analytica in major data breach. *The Guardian*. https://www.theguardian.com/news/2018/mar/17/cambridge-analytica-facebook-influence-us-election

Casanovas, P. (2019). Deu elements de transformació (i control) de la identitat contemporània *Anuari Societat Catalana de Filosofia, 17*. https://doi.org/10.2436/20.3001.01.93

Casanovas, P., & Noriega, P. (2022). Dilemmas in legal governance. *Journal of Open Access to Law, 10*(1), 1–20. https://ojs.law.cornell.edu/index.php/joal/article/view/122

Casanovas, P., Pagallo, U., Aurucci, P., & Sartor, G. (2019). *On good AI governance: 14 priority actions, a S.M.A.R.T. model of governance, and a regulatory toolbox*. AI4People White Paper.

Casanovas Romeu, P. (2025). La regimetnación tecnológica: Inteligencia artificial, fascismo, agresión y sociedad democrática. *Teknocultura: Revista de Cultura Digital y Movimientos Sociales*, 1–12, Advance online publication. https://doi.org/10.5209/tekn.98266

Catala, A. (2015). Democracy, trust, and epistemic justice. *The Monist, 98*(4), 424–440. https://doi.org/10.1093/monist/onv022

Chafkin, M. (2021). *The contrarian: Peter Thiel and Silicon Valley's pursuit of power*. Penguin Press.

Cohen, J. (2009). *Philosophy, politics, democracy: Selected essays*. Harvard University Press.

Costa, P., & Zolo, D. (2007). *The rule of law: History, theory and criticism*. Springer.

Dworkin, R. (2000). *Sovereign virtue: The theory and practice of equality*. Harvard University Press.

Dworkin, R. (2011). *Justice for hedgehogs*. Belknap Press.

Ebers, M., Poncibò, C., & Zou, M. (Eds.). (2022). *Contracting and contract law in the age of artificial intelligence*. Hart Publishing.

Engstrom, D. F. (Ed.). (2023). *Legal tech and the future of civil justice*. Cambridge University Press.

Estlund, D. (2009). *Democratic authority: A philosophical framework*. Princeton University Press.

Gutmann, A., & Thompson, D. (2004). *Why deliberative democracy?* Princeton University Press.

Habermas, J. (1984). *The theory of communicative action*. Beacon Press.

Harari, Y.-N. (2018). *21 Lessons for the 21st century*. Jonathan Cape.

Huntington, S. P. (1991). *The third wave: Democratization in the late twentieth century*. University of Oklahoma Press.

Invernizzi, C., & Zuckerman, I. (2017). What's wrong with militant democracy? *Political Studies, 65*(1), 182–199. https://doi.org/10.1177/0032321715614849

Knight, J., Landemore, H., Urbinati, N., & Viehoff, D. (2016). Roundtable on epistemic democracy and its critics. *Critical Review, 28*(2), 137–170. https://doi.org/10.1080/08913811.2016.1206744

Kreiss, D., & McGregor, S. C. (2019). The 'Arbiters of What Our Voters See': Facebook and Google's struggle with policy, process, and enforcement around political advertising. *Political Communication, 36*(4), 499–522. https://doi.org/10.1080/10584609.2019.1619639

Landemore, H. (2013). *Democratic reason: Politics, collective intelligence, and the rule of the many*. Princeton University Press.

Lippmann, W. (1922). *Public opinion*. Harcourt.

Locke, J. (1988). *Two treatises of government* (P. Laslett, Ed.). Cambridge University Press. (Original work published 1689)

MacIntyre, A. (2007). *After virtue: A study in moral theory* (3rd ed.). University of Notre Dame Press. (Original work published 1981)

Mazower, M. (1999). *Dark continent: Europe's twentieth century*. Penguin Books.

Montesquieu. (1989). *The spirit of the laws* (A. M. Cohler, B. C. Miller, & H. S. Stone, Trans. & Eds.). Cambridge University Press. (Original work published 1748)

Mittelstadt, B. D., Allo, P., Taddeo, M., Wachter, S., & Floridi, L. (2016). The ethics of algorithms: Mapping the debate. *Big Data & Society, 3*(2). https://doi.org/10.1177/2053951716679679

Modgil, S., Singh, R. K., Gupta, S., & Dennehy, D. (2021). A confirmation bias view on social media-induced polarisation during COVID-19. *Information Systems Frontiers*, 1–25. Advance online publication. https://doi.org/10.1007/s10796-021-10222-9

Noble, S. U. (2018). *Algorithms of oppression: How search engines reinforce racism*. New York University Press.

Ober, J. (2008a). *Democracy and knowledge: Innovation and learning in classical Athens*. Princeton University Press.

Ober, J. (2008b). The original meaning of "democracy": Capacity to do things, not majority rule. *Constellations, 15*(1), 3–9. https://doi.org/10.1111/j.1467-8675.2008.00471.x

Ober, J. (2015). *The rise and fall of classical Greece*. Princeton University Press.

Poblet, M., Casanovas, P., & Rodríguez-Doncel, V. (2019). *Linked democracy: Foundations, tools, and applications*. Spring. https://doi.org/10.1007/978-3-030-13363-4

Poblet, M., & Plaza, E. (2017). Democracy models and civic technologies: Tensions, trilemmas, and trade-offs. In *Proceedings of the Workshop on Linked Democracy: Artificial Intelligence for Democratic Innovation Co-located with the 26th International Joint Conference on Artificial Intelligence* (IJCAI 2017) (CEUR Workshop Proceedings, Vol. 1897, pp. 51–62). CEUR-WS.org.

Ponce, J. (2022). Las relaciones entre la inteligencia artificial, regulación y ética, con especial atención al sector público. *Revista General de Derecho Administrativo, 61*, 1–20. https://www.iustel.com/v2/revistas/detalle_revista.asp?id_noticia=425484

Przeworski, A. (2010). *Democracy and the limits of self-government*. Cambridge University Press.

Rawls, J. (1993). *Political liberalism*. Columbia University Press.

Rini, R. (2020). Deepfakes and the epistemic backstop. *Philosophers' Imprint, 20*(24), 1–16. http://hdl.handle.net/2027/spo.3521354.0020.024

Rousseau, J.-J. (1997). *The social contract and other later political writings* (V. Gourevitch, Ed. & Trans.). Cambridge University Press. (Original work published 1762).

Sap, M., Card, D., Gabriel, S., Choi, Y., & Smith, N. A. (2019). The risk of racial bias in hate speech detection. In *Proceedings of the 57th Annual Meeting of the Association for Computational Linguistics* (pp. 1668–1678). https://doi.org/10.18653/v1/P19-1163

Scharre, P. (2018). *Army of none: Autonomous weapons and the future of war*. W. W. Norton & Company.

Sunstein, C. R. (2017). *#Republic: Divided democracy in the age of social media*. Princeton University Press.

Turkle, S. (2011). *Alone together: Why we expect more from technology and less from each other*. Basic Books.

Udupa, S., Maronikolakis, A., & Wisiorek, A. (2023). Ethical scaling for content moderation: Extreme speech and the (in)significance of artificial intelligence. *Big Data & Society, 10*(1), 205395172311724. https://doi.org/10.1177/20539517231172424

Welzel, C. (2013). *Freedom rising: Human empowerment and the quest for emancipation*. Cambridge University Press.

Woolley, S. C. (2020). Bots and computational propaganda: Automation for communication and control. In N. Persily & J. A. Tucker (Eds.), *Social media and democracy* (pp. 89–110). Cambridge University Press.

Woolley, S. C., & Howard, P. N. (Eds.). (2018). *Computational propaganda: Political parties, politicians, and political manipulation on social media*. Oxford University Press.

Zuiderveen Borgesius, F., Möller, J., Kruikemeier, S., Ó Fathaigh, R., Irion, K., Dobber, T., Bodo, B., & de Vreese, C. H. (2018). Online political microtargeting: Promises and threats for democracy. *Internet Policy Review, 7*(1). https://doi.org/10.18352/ulr.420

Index

M. Bosch (ed.), *Crucial Ethical Keys of Artificial Intelligence*,
https://doi.org/10.1007/978-3-032-22853-6

The manufacturer's authorised representative in the EU is Springer Nature Customer Service Centre GmbH, Europaplatz 3, 69115 Heidelberg, Germany. If you have any concerns regarding our products, please contact ProductSafety@springernature.com

Printed and bound by CPI Group (UK) Ltd, Croydon, CR0 4YY
09/10/2026
02231217-0002